Praise for "Reel Heroes & Villains"

"A daring model of heroism and villainy. Allison and Smith's analysis forever changes the way we view movie characters."

Dr. Robert Giacalone
Professor of Business Ethics, University of Denver

"A must-read for all fans of heroes and villains in the movies."

Dr. James Beggan
Professor of Sociology, University of Louisville

"Those mad geniuses, Allison and Smith, are back. Here are the secrets of the villains you love to hate, by the writers you love to read. Cinema's worst villains are no match for Allison and Smith."

Rick Hutchins, Author of *The RH Factor*

"A dive into the minds of those you love to hate. Allison and Smith examine the shadowy reflection of heroism."

Jesse Schultz, Author of *Alfheim*

"A revolutionary way of understanding heroes and villains in the movies. This book is Allison and Smith's tour de force."

Dr. James Beggan
University of Louisville

Contents

Acknowledgements xiii
Introduction xv

I. Reel Heroes Taxonomy   1

1. Why Study Movies?   3

2. Our Original Model   5
2.1. Upgrade 1: Protagonist and Antagonist 6
2.2. Upgrade 2: Refined Transformations 6
2.3. Upgrade 3: Refinement of the Lone Hero or Villain 7
2.4. Upgrade 4: Romantics and Henchmen in Duos 7
2.5. Upgrade 5: Heroic and Villainous Systems 7
2.6. Upgrade 6: Attributes 8

3. Our New Model of Heroism and Villainy   9

4. Dimension 1: Character Type   11
4.1. The Hero 12
4.2. The Villain 12
4.3. The Anti-Hero 13
4.4. The Anti-Villain 14

5. Dimension 2: Transformation   15
5.1. Transitions 16
Negative to Positive Transformation 17
Negative to More Negative Transformation 17
Negative to Negative—A Non-Transformation 18
Negative to Positive to Negative Transformation 18
Positive to Negative Transformation 19

Positive to More Positive Transformation 19
Positive to Positive—A Non-Transformation 20
Positive to Negative to Positive Transformation 20
5.2. Types of Transformation 21
Moral Transformation 21
Mental Transformation 22
Emotional Transformation 22
Physical Transformation 23
Spiritual Transformation 23

6. **Dimension 3: Quantity**   **25**
6.1. Single 25
Lone 25
Self 26
The Face of Ensemble or System 26
The Mastermind 27
The Henchman 27
6.2. Duo 28
Buddy Duos 28
Romantic Duos 29
Hero and Sidekick 29
Mastermind and Henchman 30
Divergent Duos 30
6.3. Ensemble 31
Family 31
Fraternity/Sorority 32
Police/Military 32
Team 33
6.4. System 33
Government 33
Organization/Corporation 34
Institution 34
Nature 34

7. **Attributes**   **37**
7.1. Competent 37
7.2. Misunderstood/Deceptive 38
7.3. Mysterious 38

7.4. Simple/Mindless/Pure (Evil or Good) 39
7.5. Catalytic or Mentor 39
7.6. Episodic 39

8. Pulling It All Together   **41**
8.1. Louis Zamperini in *Unbroken* 41
    Character Type: Protagonist 41
    Transformation Arc: Positive to More Positive 41
    Transformation Type: Emotional 42
    Quantity: Single 42
    Attributes: Competent 42
8.2. Walter Keane in *Big Eyes* 42
    Character Type: Antagonist 42
    Transformation Arc: Negative to More Negative 43
    Transformation Type: Moral 43
    Quantity: Single 43
    Attributes: Deceptive 43

9. Summary   **45**
9.1. Types of Hero Journeys 46
9.2. Types of Villain Journeys 46
9.3. Differences Between Heroes and Villains 47
9.4. Conclusions 48

II. Reel Heroes Movie Reviews 2014   **49**
    22 Jump Street 51
    3 Days to Kill 56
    The Amazing Spider-Man 2 61
    American Sniper 66
    Big Eyes 72
    Birdman 77
    Boyhood 83
    Captain America: The Winter Soldier 88
    Dawn of the Planet of the Apes 94
    Deliver Us From Evil 100
    Divergent 105
    Draft Day 111

Dumb and Dumber To 116
Earth to Echo 120
Edge of Tomorrow 124
The Equalizer 129
The Fault In Our Stars 134
Get On Up 139
The Giver 144
Godzilla 149
Gone Girl 154
The Grand Budapest Hotel 159
Guardians of the Galaxy 164
Heaven Is For Real 169
The Hobbit: The Battle of the Five Armies 174
The Hundred Foot Journey 179
The Hunger Games: The Mockingjay - Part 1 184
The Identical 189
The Imitation Game 194
Interstellar 199
Jack Ryan: Shadow Recruit 205
Jersey Boys 210
The Judge 214
Labor Day 219
Lucy 224
Maleficent 229
Million Dollar Arm 234
The Monuments Men 238
Neighbors 243
Nightcrawler 248
No Good Deed 254
Non-Stop 258
The Other Woman 263
Ride Along 268
RoboCop 272
Selma 277
St. Vincent 283
The Theory of Everything 288
Transcendence 292
Transformers: Age of Extinction 297

Unbroken 303
Whiplash 308
X-Men: Days of Future Past 314

III. Best Heroes and Villains of 2014   319

Best Movies of 2014 321
Best Heroes of 2014 328
Best Villains of 2014 335

IV. Appendix   343

Reel Heroes Indexes 345
Reels Index 346
Heroes Index 348
Villains Index 350
About the Authors 352
Other Books by Scott Allison and Greg Smith 353

Acknowledgements

This book would not have been possible without the generous help and support of so many extraordinary people. We are indebted to the ideas and inspiration of several great thinkers who have illuminated our understanding of heroes. These heroic luminaries include Joseph Campbell, Chris Vogler, Carl Jung, and Phil Zimbardo. Their work continues to inspire us and shape our thinking.

We are also deeply grateful for all the assistance and sacrifices made by our family and friends. In particular, we thank Connie Allison, Heather Allison, Sara Allison, Robert Allison, Claire Lawrence Bergvall, Victor Smith, Amber Smith, Heather Smith, and Denise Woods. The unfailing love and support of these individuals has been invaluable. We also thank all our colleagues and friends at Agile Writers and at the University of Richmond, who have all provided us with much-needed wisdom, guidance, and moral support.

We also acknowledge the valuable contributions of our editing team, especially April Michelle Davis, Jamie Blair, and Karyn Kuhn. Our graphic artist, Bonnie Watson, as usual did an excellent job with the design of our book cover and we thank her for sharing her talent and efforts. We are also grateful to Regal Westchester Theater where we see the majority of the movies that we've reviewed in this book. Finally, we extend our thanks to Sedona Taphouse, where after each movie ingest delicious snacks and drinks while we argue about the Reel Heroes and Villains who are the subject of this book.

Introduction

(Dr. Scott Allison, Professor of Psychology, University of Richmond)

It's been four years since Greg Smith and I began watching movies together with the goal of gaining a better understanding of movie heroes and hero stories in general. Two years later, we began blogging our reviews and analyses of movie heroes at ReelHeroes.net. Our reviews of movie heroes then led to the publication of our first book, *Reel Heroes: Volume 1: Two Hero Experts Critique The Movies*, which was released in 2014.

Before we discuss how this book goes beyond our first Reel Heroes book, let's introduce ourselves. My name is Scott Allison and I've been a Professor of Psychology at the University of Richmond for the past 28 years. Over the past decade, I've been researching the psychology of heroism. In my research, I pose the following questions: How do people perceive heroes? Why do people need heroes? What factors distinguish a hero from other people? I find heroism to be fascinating subject to study and I've published numerous books and articles on the subject.

(Greg Smith, Founder of Agile Writers of Richmond, VA)

And I'm Greg Smith, founder of the Agile Writer Workshop in Richmond Virginia and the creator of the Agile Writer Method for writing a first-draft novel in 6 months. Since 2011 the Agile Writer Workshop has created over 30 first-draft novels and published 5 of them. We are guided by Joseph Campbell's "Hero's Journey" as laid out in his seminal work *The Hero with a Thousand Faces*. We also borrow from screenwriting techniques as described in books by screenwriters Christopher Vogler and Michael Hauge.

Scott and I met in 2005 when we were both members of an improvisational comedy troupe. We didn't know of our mutual interest in heroes at the time. But after we both had left comedy to pursue other interests, Scott published his first book on heroism: *Heroes: What They Do and Why We Need Them*. That's when we realized we had a common interest in heroes and the movies. Since then we've been going to movies on Sunday afternoons and comparing notes on heroes in the movies.

 I'm glad you mentioned our old improv comedy troupe, Greg. Performing there was an experience that piqued my interest in good characters and good storytelling. During our training and experience with that group, the importance of characterization was drilled into us. But we never were told the details of crafting a good story, nor were we informed of how the hero's journey could be an instrumental part of good storytelling. We developed those ideas later and they are made clear on our website and in our first book.

Our approach to understanding heroes is based largely on Joseph Campbell's groundbreaking book, *The Hero With A Thousand Faces*, in which Campbell proposes that all great myths and legends throughout the ages have basically told the same hero story. In the classic hero journey, the hero is summoned on an adventure to an unfamiliar world fraught with danger. The hero is missing some important inner quality that is needed to achieve his or her mission. During the journey, the hero receives help from friends and mentors, and resistance from obstacles and villains. The hero discovers the missing quality which enables him or her to accomplish the mission. Once transformed, the hero then transforms the original world from which he or she came.

In our first book, *Reel Heroes: Volume 1* published in 2014, we wanted to understand and create a taxonomy of heroism. We reviewed over 75 first-run movies released in 2013 and came up with a hierarchy of heroes. With this book *Reel Heroes & Villains* we undertake the challenge of what makes a great villain. We are still looking at what makes a hero, but a great hero needs a great villain.

And I think we've succeeded. We have expanded and generalized our understanding of the hero to encompass the villain. What we've found is that the villain looks a lot like a hero, with some missing components. In this book we'll expose a clear hierarchy of heroes and villains and explain that it is the transformation that a character undergoes that determines if they are a hero or a villain.

 Exactly, Greg. We think you'll be pleased with this new comprehensive classification scheme designed to better understand both heroism and villainy. As you point out, the most striking aspect of our new updated model is that it highlights the many ways that good hero characters and good villain characters are similar to each other. In my first book on heroism, I discuss how there exists a fine line between heroes and villains. In fact, my research has found that four of the eight characteristics of heroes can also be used to describe villains. These four common characteristics are *strength, intelligence, charisma,* and *resilience.*

Of course, villains differ from heroes in important ways and our new taxonomy takes these differences into account. We believe that our model can serve as a useful instructional tool for budding authors and for students of film and storytelling. Good heroes and good villains follow particular patterns and exhibit common structural traits that should be considered with great care when developing characters for a story.

In constructing a model of villainy, we were first led by the classic tripartite division in literature that identifies three primary conflicts that people confront: (1) Man vs. Man, (2) Man vs. Self, and (3) Man vs. Nature. We decided to integrate this tripartite model into our new model, such that "Man", "Self", and "Nature" are now incorporated into our groupings of individuals, duos, ensembles, and systems.

Our current findings indicate there are three dimensions or components to heroes in the movies. They are: *Character Type* (Protagonist, Antagonist), *Transformation* (Moral, Mental, Spiritual, Emotional, Physical), and *Quantity* (Single, Duo, Ensemble, or System). In the next sections we'll expand on these components and cite movies from 2014 that exhibit these components.

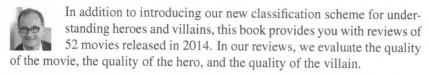 In addition to introducing our new classification scheme for under-standing heroes and villains, this book provides you with reviews of 52 movies released in 2014. In our reviews, we evaluate the quality of the movie, the quality of the hero, and the quality of the villain.

First, we rate each movie on a scale from 1 to 5 Reels. Our evaluation of a movie is based on the following criteria: How entertaining was the movie? How good was the story? How memorable were the characters? How well was it filmed? Below are the specific criteria we use:

One Reel = The movie is atrociously bad and a total embarrassment. Don't see it no matter what.

Two Reels = The movie is pretty bad. You may want to see it after it leaves the theaters if you like the actor(s) or the movie genre.

Three Reels = The movie is average, maybe even somewhat enjoy-able. Flip a coin to determine whether you want to pay $$ to see it in the theater.

Four Reels = The movie is good. It's worth the price of admission to see it on the Big Screen.

Five Reels = The movie is excellent. Run, don't walk, to your nearest theater to see it.

Our evaluation of the hero is based on our expertise on heroes and hero journeys. Both of us are experienced teachers and authors of hero stories, and our analyses are based on Joseph Campbell's groundbreaking book on the mythic structure of hero tales around the globe. For each movie that we review, we rate the primary hero on a 1 to 5 Heroes scale.

One Hero = The main hero is a disaster as a character. The hero's journey in the movie is ineptly delineated and doesn't fit the classic pattern at all.

Two Heroes = The main hero is a poorly developed character. There are some elements of the hero journey present but they aren't portrayed well at all.

Three Heroes = The main hero is a fairly average hero. Elements of the hero journey are there, and have their moments, but overall the hero isn't particularly noteworthy.

Four Heroes = The hero is well-crafted and inspiring. We see the hero's journey in full form and we are moved by it.

Five Heroes = The hero is an extraordinarily riveting and memorable character. The hero's journey is portrayed in exemplary fashion and the actor playing this hero is likely to be nominated for an Oscar.

We look for certain qualities in a villain. A good villain should be a challenging, memorable foe for the hero. For each movie that we review, we rate the primary villain on a 1 to 5 Villains scale.

One Villain = The villain is weak. Either there is very little backstory about the villain, or the villain's character is very poorly developed, or the villain offers no challenge to the hero.

Two Villains = The villain is below average. We don't learn much about the villain or the villain is a peripheral part of the hero's journey.

Three Villains = An average villain who has a somewhat compelling personality but doesn't live up to his or her full potential as a character.

Four Villains = The villain is above average. He or she is charismatic and memorable, has an interesting backstory, and offers a formidable challenge to the hero.

Five Villains = The villain is a tour-de-force character who almost steals the show. The villain's journey is told in vivid, compelling detail, and the actor playing the villain is likely to receive an Oscar nomination.

It's been a great year for movies. I've enjoyed looking at these heroes and their corresponding villains. It looks like the villains have a lot more texture than I at first thought. I'm going to enjoy shining a bright light on what makes a great villain.

Let's do that now. The next section of the book describes our new classification scheme for heroes and villains in detail. Just sit back and enjoy the ride.

Part I.

Reel Heroes Taxonomy

1. Why Study Movies?

Over the past decade, the two authors of this book have devoted much time and thought to answering two interrelated questions: (1) What makes a good movie? and (2) What makes a good movie hero? Scott Allison has been interested in the psychological process underlying good hero characters and captivating hero stories. Greg Smith has been interested in understanding hero patterns in stories and using these patterns to create new, effective works of fiction. By understanding what people see in fictional heroes, we can better understand what we look for in heroes in the real world.

Movies provide an ideal platform for understanding heroes and hero journeys. Let's face it. Movies move us. They combine sights, sounds, and storylines that, when woven together well, can transport us into another world and ignite our souls. Good movies leave us feeling exhilarated and inspired. They can also impart universal truths about ourselves, other people, and the world.

Much of the authors' thinking about heroes and villains has been guided by the works of Joseph Campbell, a comparative mythologist who discovered that all hero stories throughout the ages followed the same general pattern. The fact that all human societies from all time periods in history resonate to the same story speaks volumes about the psychological and emotional power of good hero tales. Here is a synopsis of the universal pattern that Campbell detected [1]:

1. The hero starts out in a safe, familiar world.

2. The hero is summoned, either willingly or unwillingly, into a new, dangerous, unfamiliar world.

3. The hero is charged with some goal or mission.

---

[1] Campbell, J. 1949. *The Hero with a Thousand Faces*. New York: New World Library.

4. The hero encounters other people who fill important social roles—friends, mentors, lovers, sidekicks, and father figures are common.

5. The hero then acquires some missing internal quality to attain the goal.

6. The hero is transformed significantly and returns to the familiar world.

7. The hero then delivers the meaning of the journey to others.

When movie makers acknowledge this universal pattern, we usually get a satisfying movie-going experience. But when they ignore this ancient, time-honored paradigm, the story generally falls flat.

Understanding villainy in good stories is also important. Yet strangely, very little attention has been paid to villains. What role do villains play in crafting a good story? How and why do villains become villains? What forms do villainous characters assume in the movies? A good hero must have a compelling villain, or the story falls flat.

In this book, we offer a rare glimpse into the world of the villain. We will still focus on heroes, but now we provide an analysis of villainy, too. We propose a comprehensive model of types of heroes and villains, which shows the ways that heroes and villains share similar characteristics and highlights interesting points of departure. We'll also compare and contrast the hero's journey with the villain's journey.

This book also provides reviews of the heroes and villains in 52 movies released in 2014. You'll note that some of our reviews may seem to contradict our conclusions noted above. We ask the reader to remember that we reviewed these movies first, when they came out. Later, in early 2015, we composed this synthesis of what we had seen. So you'll see firsthand how our thoughts about movie heroes and villains evolved.

To illustrate the evolution of our thinking, consider our review of 2013's *Pain & Gain*, which we included in our 2014 book *Reel Heroes: Volume 1*. In this review, we claimed that the movie was a villain story because the lead characters had no redeeming qualities. However, our current view is that *Pain & Gain*'s protagonists are, indeed, anti-heroes because they are immoral characters occupying the lead role of the film. Furthermore, we consider them tragic anti-heroes because they undergo a change from immoral to more immoral during the course of the film. We'll discuss this idea in more detail shortly.

2. Our Original Model

Our first book, *Reel Heroes: Volume 1* (2014), represented our first effort to develop a classification scheme of heroes in the movies. We based our taxonomy on our analysis of 75 movies that we reviewed in 2013. From our analysis, we identified three major categories of heroism based on the quantity of heroic characters in the story. These hero categories were (1) lone heroes, (2) duo heroes, and (3) group ensemble heroes. In addition, we made differentiations within each of these categories. Below is an outline of our 2014 model:

1. Lone Heroes

    a) Transformed Individuals

    b) Non-Transformed Individuals

2. Duo Heroes

    a) Buddy Heroes

    b) Divergent Heroes

    c) Hero and Sidekick

3. Group Ensemble Heroes

    a) Family Hero Ensembles

    b) Fraternity Hero Ensembles

    c) Police/Military Hero Ensembles

One strength of our 2014 model was its differentiation among lead characters of different quantities. To the best of our knowledge, our model was the first to highlight the social structure of heroism, demonstrating that heroes operate as lone individuals, as duos, or as group entities. This hierarchical structure of heroism is consistent with the way that social scientists divide the social world into size units.

When we expanded our view to include villainy, we found that there were holes in our model. For example, we hadn't taken into account that the main character in the story isn't always a heroic figure. Sometimes, it's an evil character who is the lead. This and other deficiencies caused us to refine and extend our new model. Let's take a look at how our new model improves upon our 2014 model.

2.1. Upgrade 1: Protagonist and Antagonist

One thing we've learned from the movies (and from other sources) is that heroes and villains sometimes look a lot alike. There can be considerable overlap in the characteristics and story arcs of both heroes and villains. This realization has led us to propose that any taxonomy that describes heroes should also be used to describe villains.

2.2. Upgrade 2: Refined Transformations

Our 2014 model was also useful in establishing that some heroes in the movies undergo a personal transformation whereas others do not. A limitation of this model was that it only distinguished between transformed and non-transformed heroes at the level of the single individual hero. Our new model allows for transformations for heroic and villainous entities of all sizes, including duos and group ensembles. Moreover, our new classification scheme describes specific types of character transformations: moral, mental, emotional, physical, and spiritual.

2.3. Upgrade 3: Refinement of the Lone Hero or Villain

Our new updated classification scheme also makes more differentiations among the various kinds of lone heroes and lone villains. Lone heroes or villains can be (1) the leader, or mastermind, of a large organization; (2) the "face" of a large organization; (3) an individual occupying a middle-management position or who is a minor cog within a large organizational machine; or (4) a "henchman" who answers to a mastermind character above him or her in the organizational chain.

2.4. Upgrade 4: Romantics and Henchmen in Duos

We can also see that the 2014 scheme identified three types of duo heroes: buddies, divergents, and heroes/sidekicks. We've retained these three types of duos in our updated model.

Our new hero model now also includes two additional duo entities. The first is called a *romantic duo*. Romantic duos are similar to buddy duos in that they refer to two individuals who often start out disliking each other but soon develop a mutual friendship. The difference is, of course, that romantic duos become lovers.

The second duo that we've added to our new model is the *mastermind and henchman* duo. This duo refers to a boss–subordinate power relationship between two individuals. One person reports to, and takes orders from, another more powerful person.

2.5. Upgrade 5: Heroic and Villainous Systems

Our new scheme also recognizes large *systems* of entities that include organizations, governments, institutions, and forces of nature. Protagonist systems are non-existent because audiences need a human being with which to identify. A lone hero can be the face of a system (e.g., James Bond representing the British Secret Service), but the system is peripheral to the story. Villainous systems are quite common. They often appear as the nameless, faceless opposition to the hero. Lone villains can be the face of a system (e.g., Darth Vader representing the Galactic Empire).

One type of system is an *organization*, which can include organized crime, corporations, armies, police forces, and governmental agencies, among others. This type of system is extremely common in the movies. Another system, which we call an *institution*, refers to an established set of codes or norms that can exert a powerful effect on movie protagonists (such as institutional racism and sexism). Systems also include *forces of nature* which are large and powerful natural phenomena including death, disease, weather, and even gravity and time itself.

2.6. Upgrade 6: Attributes

Our 2014 scheme did not address the importance of character *attributes* that are independent of the quantity of heroic or villainous entities. We now propose that heroic and villainous characters can assume one or more attributes that meaningfully describe the characters. Common attributes can include whether the hero or villain is competent, misunderstood, deceptive, mysterious, simple/mindless/pure (evil or good), catalytic or mentor, episodic.

3. Our New Model of Heroism and Villainy

Our new updated model of heroism and villainy now recognizes three independent dimensions of heroism: character type (protagonist, antagonist), transformation (moral, mental, emotional, physical, spiritual), and quantity (single, duo, ensemble, system). We also now acknowledge the importance of various protagonist and antagonist attributes that play a pivotal role in defining the lead characters in stories.

Here is our new model in outline form:

1. Character Type

    a) Protagonist (hero or anti-hero)

    b) Antagonist (anti-villain or villain)

2. Transformation of the Protagonist(s) or Antagonist(s)

    a) Moral Transformation

    b) Mental Transformation

    c) Emotional Transformation

    d) Physical Transformation

    e) Spiritual Transformation

3. Quantity of Protagonist(s) or Antagonist(s)

    a) Single

        i. Lone

        ii. Self

          iii. The Face of Ensemble or System

          iv. The Mastermind

          v. The Henchman

    b) Duo

          i. Buddy Duo

          ii. Romantic Duo

          iii. Hero and Sidekick

          iv. Mastermind and Henchman

          v. Divergent Duo

    c) Ensemble

          i. Family

          ii. Fraternity/Sorority

          iii. Police/Military

          iv. Team

    d) System

          i. Government

          ii. Organization/Corporation

          iii. Institution

          iv. Nature

4. Attributes

    a) Competent

    b) Misunderstood

    c) Deceptive

    d) Mysterious

    e) Simple/Mindless/Pure (Evil or Good)

    f) Catalytic or Mentor

    g) Episodic

Let's now dive into the details of our new model of heroism and villainy.

4. Dimension 1: Character Type

In keeping with the terminology of classic literary drama, we divide the main characters of a story into two types: the protagonist and the antagonist. The protagonist is the main or lead character who is charged with a mission. The antagonist is the character who exists to prevent the protagonist from achieving the mission.

Over the last year, we've found that the protagonist of the story isn't always heroic in the traditional sense. Sometimes the protagonist is evil (as in the case of Louis Bloom in *Nightcrawler*). So, to call this person a "hero" seems counterintuitive. Likewise, the oppositional character is not always evil (witness Madame Mallory in *The Hundred Foot Journey*). So calling this person a "villain" seems unfair.

Our new model's focus on character type allows us to call every lead character a protagonist, allowing us to distinguish between protagonists who are moral or competent (heroes) and protagonists who are immoral or inept (antiheroes). Most protagonists are heroes, but every once in a while Hollywood turns the table and gives us a movie featuring an anti-hero protagonist.

According to our model, any character who opposes the protagonist is called an antagonist. Antagonists can also be either moral or competent (antivillains) or immoral or inept (villains). When the protagonist is a hero, the antagonist is always a villain. The hero–villain set up is by far the most common protagonist–antagonist combination in storytelling. In the rare cases when the protagonist is an anti-hero, the antagonist must be an anti-villain. For example, because Louis Bloom is the anti-hero of *Nightcrawler*, the police officers who oppose him are the anti-villains.

The following table may help to clarify the differences between the four types of characters in a movie:

A Character who	ends up Positive	ends up Negative
is the Protagonist	Hero	Anti-Hero
is the Antagonist	Anti-Villain	Villain

Table 4.1.: The Hero Matrix

4.1. The Hero

Our definition of a movie hero is based on the type of person he or she is at the end of the film. If the lead character, or protagonist, is a moral or competent person at the end of the film, then we would call that person the hero of the story. To be the hero, the character doesn't have to be perfect. Nor does the character have to start out virtuous. He or she only needs to have earned our admiration for either remaining or evolving into a moral or competent person in some way.

Not all hero characters follow the classic hero's journey as described by Joseph Campbell. Comic book superheroes, for example, are protagonists who are just as super-moral and competent at the beginning of the story as they are at the end. In our opinion, the superhero movie genre is the one genre in which the hero transformation seems to be unnecessary for the movie to be considered high quality. In general, the most endearing and memorable movie heroes are ones who grow or evolve in meaningful ways during the course of the film.

If we define a hero as a protagonist who becomes a moral or competent character at the end of the movie, then we propose that there are four ways that this pattern can unfold: (1) the hero can start out as a good person and remain that way throughout the film; (2) the hero can start out as a wretch and transform into a good person; (3) the hero can start out slightly good and evolve into someone even better; (4) the hero can start out good, become bad, and then redeem him- or herself at the end.

4.2. The Villain

Classically, the villain is considered to be an antagonist character who attempts to thwart the goals of the hero. We find this definition to be problematic as sometimes the antagonist is not necessarily evil or bad. So we focus instead on what type of individual the antagonist is at the end of the movie. If the antagonist is a negative character at the film's conclusion, then we consider him or her a villain. But if the antagonist is a positive character, we give this person a new name; we call this person the *anti-villain* (more about that below).

As we'll see in the next section, there are five types of transformations. One type is a moral transformation. If the antagonist starts out as a moral character and evolves into an immoral character, we consider him or her a villain. A good example of this is Dr. Will Carter (Johnny Depp) from the movie *Transcendence*. He starts out as a good and moral scientist. But when his mind is emptied into a computer system, he becomes a villain bent on world domination.

But antagonists don't have to be evil. If you look at the movie *Heaven is for Real*, you'll find that Pastor Burpo's board of directors confronts him and demands that he either stop preaching his message or leave the church. They fear the media attention they're getting and want to fire Burpo. They aren't evil. But they have transformed from a positive emotional state of geniality to a negative state of paranoia. So by our definition, they are the villains in the story.

Only when the antagonists end up in a negative state do we call them the villains. Now let's look at what happens when the protagonist ends up in a negative state.

4.3. The Anti-Hero

The anti-hero is any lead character, or protagonist, who is an immoral individual at the end of the movie. There are four ways that characters can assume anti-hero status: (1) They can start out negative and remain that way throughout the film; (2) they can start out slightly negative and then grow into an extremely negative character; (3) they can start out negative, evolve and grow into someone good, but then take a moral nosedive at the end; and (4) they can start out as a virtuous person and then fall from grace by becoming a negative character.

Consider our earlier example of 2013's *Pain & Gain*. The three lead characters start out as somewhat positive people. But through a series of transgressions they become more and more corrupt as they try to kill a Quiznos owner.

Because they are the protagonists and end up in a negative state, we consider them anti-heroes.

4.4. The Anti-Villain

An anti-villain is an antagonist who turns out to be the virtuous opposition to an evil protagonist. Anti-villains often appear in movies that focus on the life story of criminals. There is a long cinematic history of such movies; they include *Scarface*, *Bonnie and Clyde*, *Butch Cassidy and the Sundance Kid*, *Natural Born Killers*, *A Clockwork Orange*, and *Nightcrawler*. The anti-villain in these movies is usually a cop or perhaps even an entire police force.

5. Dimension 2: Transformation

Joseph Campbell argued that all great classic hero stories from ancient myth and legend featured a meaningful metamorphosis on the part of the hero. The transformation can only occur if protagonists are able to discover, or recover, a quality that they lack, but need, to successfully achieve their mission. From our analysis of movies, we propose that the transformation of the protagonist can be moral, mental, emotional, physical, or spiritual. Or, in the case of a weak movie or an ineffective story, the transformation can be minimal or absent. In some movies, the antagonist undergoes a transformation as well.

Generally speaking, the transformation takes one of eight forms. We propose that the direction of the transformation can range from positive to negative or vice versa. Keep in mind that positive usually means moral or competent and negative means immoral or incompetent. The transformation can also be characterized by its type (moral, mental, emotional, physical, or spiritual). Here are the eight types of transformation that we've observed, along with a label to describe a character who undergoes such a transformation.

1. **Negative to Positive:** the enlightened good

2. **Negative to More Negative:** the irredeemable bad

3. **Negative to Negative:** the untransformed bad

4. **Negative to Positive to Negative:** the regressed bad

5. **Positive to Negative:** the fallen bad

6. **Positive to More Positive:** the classic good

7. **Positive to Positive:** the untransformed good

8. **Positive to Negative to Positive:** the redeemed good

Keep in mind that the type of hero that a character becomes is not determined by the hero's initial role in the film (protagonist or antagonist) but where the character ends up when all the transformational dust has settled. Characters that end up in a positive state are heroes or anti-villains, and characters that end up in a negative state are anti-heroes or villains. For example, a protagonist who transforms from negative to positive is an *enlightened hero*, whereas an antagonist who transforms from negative to positive is an *enlightened anti-villain*.

To clarify the meaning of the eight transformations, let's consider the transformation of Ellis in the 2013 movie *Mud*. Ellis is a young boy who starts out lovably naïve about the world and grows in his sophistication. This is a positive to more positive transformation. Because he is the protagonist, we call him the hero of the film, and more specifically, he becomes a classic hero.

In another example, 2014's *Nightcrawler*, Louis Bloom starts out as a petty thief (a negative character) and grows to be a corrupt and manipulative murderer (an even more negative character). As the protagonist, he is an anti-hero, and his moral transformation from negative to more negative renders him an irredeemable anti-hero.

From these examples (and more listed below), it should be clear that a character's role as a protagonist is not enough for us to consider him or her a hero. We need to know what transformation the character undergoes and what the character is like at the end of the movie. Characters who end up in a positive state are heroes or anti-villains, and those who end up in a negative state are villains or anti-heroes.

5.1. Transitions

The most effective and memorable heroes and villains undergo a significant personal transformation—or they bring about a transformation in others. As you saw in section 4.0, there are eight types of transformations. We'll now itemize each and give examples.

Negative to Positive Transformation

A common hero pattern is for the protagonist to start out as a negative character and through mentoring and trial becomes positive in the end. In *Labor Day*, Josh Brolin plays an escaped convict named Frank. Frank starts out as a desperate man who abducts a woman and her son to elude the police. He ends up befriending the boy and falling in love with the woman who in turn falls in love with him. In the end, he turns himself into the police so that the woman doesn't get charged with aiding a fugitive.

Frank undergoes an emotional transformation from uncaring to caring. His good nature is uncovered, and he ultimately values his newfound "family" over his own need to escape. Because he becomes positive, we consider him a hero, even though he started out as an immoral villain. We see the same pattern in Bill Murray's role as Vincent in the 2014 film, *St. Vincent*.

Occasionally, the antagonist undergoes a transformation from negative to positive. This is often a character who starts out as a villain character, but sees the error of her ways. We see this transformation in 2014's *The Hundred Foot Journey*. In it, Madam Mallory owns a classic French restaurant. When an Indian family moves in across the street, she uses all manner of treachery to undermine the newcomers. But after the young Indian chef gets injured in a fire started by one of her employees, Madam Mallory realizes that she had followed a dark path that is not in her true nature. She takes the young chef under her wing and mentors him to become a world-class chef. This transition from an immoral to a moral character makes her an enlightened anti-villain.

Negative to More Negative Transformation

Some protagonists are negative at the very start of the movie, and the entire film is devoted to showing how these characters spiral even further downward. In 2014, the film *Nightcrawler* depicts Louis Bloom as a loser and petty thief with great ambition to acquire money and influence. Like a cancer, his bad nature grows and grows in size and power. Bloom transforms from routine scummery to a grotesque level of evil. His murderous ways make him an irredeemable anti-hero.

Sometimes the antagonist in a film is a character whose evil grows in magnitude throughout the movie. In 2014, *The Amazing Spider-Man 2* shows an example of a character, Harry Osborn, who is at first merely a slight irritant to the hero, Spider-Man. Soon Harry develops an intense hatred for Spider-Man and assumes the role of a super villain called the Green Goblin. We learn an important lesson about villains: they either fail to transform or they undergo a perverse transformation toward heightened self-aggrandizement and narcissistic empire-building.

Negative to Negative—A Non-Transformation

Although it is a rare occurrence, a movie's protagonist may be an anti-hero who remains unchanged, and therefore untransformed, throughout the entire movie. This type of anti-hero is rare because a steady, unwavering display of evil throughout a film runs the risk of boring viewers. When we do encounter untransformed anti-heroes in the movies, they had better be charismatic and entertaining or the movie will have no chance of succeeding. This type of charismatic appeal describes the classic movie, *The Sting*, which features two non-transformed buddy anti-heroes.

A far more common "bad guy" in the movies is the non-transformed antagonist who plays the role of the protagonist's nemesis. An example of this type of antagonist is the pair of Russian villains in 2014's *Jack Ryan: Shadow Recruit*. These villains are evil from start to finish, making them somewhat uninteresting. Some untransformed villains are not disappointing at all; consider the monsters in horror films. When done well, these types of villains can be exhilarating to watch and fun to root against.

Negative to Positive to Negative Transformation

There are rare instances in which a protagonist or antagonist undergoes two transformations during the same movie. One type of dual-transformation occurs when a character starts out as a negative character, then grows more positive, but then takes a nosedive and ends up a negative character again.

An example of a protagonist who undergoes these two transformations is Charlie Gordon in the 1968 movie *Charly*. Charly is mentally challenged but becomes a genius after undergoing an intelligence-enhancing experiment. Unfortunately, the effects of the experiment are short-lived and Charly returns to his original impaired mental state at the end.

An example of an antagonist who undergoes this kind of dual transformation is the enigmatic Magneto character from the *X-Men* franchise. Magneto violently opposes humans and wants mutants to become the dominant species on earth. However, Magneto joins forces with Dr. Xavier in *X-Men: Days of Future Past* and fights heroically with them and for them. His alliance with the X-Men was short-lived and eventually Magneto returned to his villainous ways.

Positive to Negative Transformation

Occasionally we meet a main character who starts out as a benevolent person, but transitions to evil over the course of the film. Examples of such protagonists include Michael Corleone in *The Godfather*, Teddy Daniels in *Shutter Island*, and Harvey Dent in *The Dark Knight*. We call this type of character a "fallen anti-hero."

It's rare for the antagonist in a film to show this same transition from good to evil. One possible example is the character of Nina, the news director in *Nightcrawler*. She isn't a bad person until Louis Bloom shows up and challenges her to air his controversial news videos. Nina succumbs to temptation and becomes a fallen villain, demonstrating that anti-heroes can have a corrupting influence on the antagonists they encounter.

Positive to More Positive Transformation

The classic hero story starts with a protagonist who is relatively good at first. This type of character is generally liked by the audience and gains immediate empathy. The hero then undergoes a difficult trial and emerges even more virtuous in the end.

In *Heaven is for Real,* we meet Pastor Todd Burpo. As a preacher, he starts out as a moral man. When his son has a near-death experience and reports to his father that he's visited Jesus in heaven, Burpo preaches the revelation to his congregation. The word gets out, which brings unwanted celebrity to the church, and the church elders decide to evict Burpo. Ultimately, Pastor Burpo delivers an impassioned sermon, which convinces them that all is right with the world. Burpo attains a stronger belief in God and heaven through his struggles. Because he grows in his understanding of the world and of God, we consider him a classic hero.

At times a character is both the antagonist and a good person. We usually see this character in anti-hero stories. In the anti-hero story, the lead character (who is immoral) is impeded by some force of good (like a police officer). We call this type of antagonist the *anti-villain*. It can happen that the anti-villain grows and becomes a better person thanks to the actions of the anti-hero. For instance, in the 2002 movie, *Catch Me If You Can*, the anti-hero, Frank, is a clever fraud who eludes FBI agent Carl (the anti-villain), who must grow in his professional abilities to catch Frank.

Positive to Positive—A Non-Transformation

As we noted earlier, heroes don't always grow or evolve during the course of a movie. We see this non-transformative pattern in the superhero movie genre and in many Tom Cruise movies, such as *Oblivion* and *Mission Impossible*. In these movies, the protagonist is a paragon of virtue from the moment the film begins until the moment it ends. These films have the potential to be dull, as audiences usually resonate to stories in which the protagonist undergoes a significant change of some type. Superhero movies seem to be able to get away with a non-transformation. We apparently love our superheroes despite the fact that (or even perhaps because) they are unwavering in their super-virtue.

More commonly, we see this pattern of uniform positivity in antagonists who try to stop anti-heroes from wreaking havoc on the world. When Louis Bloom is causing people to die in *Nightcrawler*, the police are on his trail. The cops never change in their level of "goodness." Law enforcement often plays a minor role in movies about bad guys, and we expect cops to remain steadfast in their attempt to stop the anti-hero throughout the movie.

Positive to Negative to Positive Transformation

Some lead characters start out positive but somehow fall into negative behavior. Then they suffer through trials and tribulations and must find their way back to being positive. This type of hero comes full circle, forever changed by his or her experience. We call this protagonist a *redeemed hero*.

A notable example of a redeemed hero in 2014 is found in the film *Maleficent*. In this movie, Maleficent is a benevolent fairy who is brutally betrayed and disfigured by a young man named Stefan. This incident causes Maleficent to become a bitter witch who casts evil spells on the innocent. But when Maleficent grows to love a young girl named Aurora, we see this love soften her heart and help return her to her original state of goodness. Maleficent may have fallen, but she is able to redeem herself. King Thorin in *The Hobbit: The Battle of the Five Armies* is another example of a hero who plunges downward but is able to right himself at the end.

Antagonists can also undergo this same redemption process. Darth Vader in the *Star Wars* franchise is a prominent example, although his two transformations do not occur within the same movie. Originally a Jedi Knight on the side of good, Darth Vader falls to the dark side and opposes the hero Luke Skywalker. Later, Vader redeems himself by saving Skywalker's life.

5.2. Types of Transformation

As we've mentioned, the transformations that characters can undergo include moral, mental, emotional, physical, or spiritual transformations. There is some overlap among these transformations. A moral transformation, for example, can be partly emotional and partly spiritual. Let's examine each type below.

Moral Transformation

The classic moral transformation portrayed in countless movies is the protagonist's evolution from an immoral character to a moral character. One of our favorite examples is found in Bill Murray's character, Phil Connors, in the 1993 film, Groundhog Day. While there are shades of gray in morality, most stories attempt to make the moral transformation clear for the sake of the moviegoer.]The classic moral transformation portrayed in countless movies is the protagonist's evolution from an immoral character to a moral character. One of our favorite examples is found in Bill Murray's character, Phil Connors, in the 1993 film, *Groundhog Day*. While there are shades of gray in morality, most stories attempt to make the moral transformation clear for the sake of the moviegoer.

At times, we witness moral transformations in supporting characters. Friends and allies of the hero or the villain can change allegiances, for example. In 2008's *The Dark Knight*, the character of Two-Face was once a good man named Harvey Dent, Gotham City's district attorney. But when the Joker disfigures his face, Dent succumbs to madness and becomes a schizoid criminal mastermind. Summing up this transformation, Batman says, "You either die a hero, or you live long enough to see yourself become the villain."

Mental Transformation

Mental transformations refer to a lead character's change in intelligence, creativity, or some fundamental knowledge about the world. We see a significant mental transformation in the character of Caesar in *Rise of the Planet of the Apes*. Caesar is an ape who is injected with an experimental drug that endows him with advanced human intelligence.

Another example is found in the character of Dr. Will Caster, played by Johnny Depp, in the film *Transcendence*. Caster's brain and consciousness are uploaded onto a computer, and his mental abilities then expand exponentially. A similar mental transformation occurs in *Lucy*, in a character played by Scarlett Johansson. Lucy receives a mega-dose of a drug that then allows her to use 100% of her intellectual potential.

Emotional Transformation

Emotional transformations refer to transformations of the heart. A personal change relating to the heart can include the acquisition of courage, compassion, self-confidence, humility, or resilience. Heroes often have to face emotional challenges and dig deep to overcome adversity.

There are an abundance of examples of vast emotional growth in the movies. Bilbo Baggins from *The Hobbit* movie franchise is a vivid example. To achieve his mission, Baggins has to face his fears and show some grit and self-confidence. Louis Zamperini in *Unbroken* is also a dramatic example of growth in emotional strength, courage, and resilience.

We also see emotional transformation in the character of Andrew Neiman in *Whiplash*. Neiman is a budding young drummer who aspires to play in his school's jazz ensemble. The music director, Terence Fletcher, treats Neiman sadistically, and Neiman must develop courage and resilience to overcome Fletcher's brutality.

Another recent example of emotional transformation is shown by Maria Altmann, played by Helen Mirren, in *Woman in Gold*. Altmann must overcome her fear and disgust of Nazi Germany to achieve her goal of reclaiming her family's famous painting.

Physical Transformation

At times, the hero of a story undergoes a significant physical transformation. This transformation can take the form of physical decline, as was the case in the character of Ron Woodroof played by Matthew McConaughey in *Dallas Buyers Club*.

Physical transformations can also include a change toward greater size and robustness. We see this type of transformation in many coming-of-age movies such as *Boyhood*. This movie chronicles the life of a boy, Mason, from the age to 6 to the age of 18. We witness Mason, and his sister, growing up. Superheroes and supervillains can also undergo immense physical transformations as a result of massive exposure to toxins or radiation.

Spiritual Transformation

Spiritual transformations occur when characters undergo a change in their beliefs about the nature of God or the mysteries of the universe. One notable example of a spiritual transformation appears in the 2002 movie, *Dragonfly*. Kevin Costner stars as an atheist doctor whose beliefs about God and the afterlife are forever changed when he begins receiving messages from his deceased wife.

In 2014, there were at least two movies that featured a spiritual transformation. In *God's Not Dead*, the character of Professor Radisson is a fervent atheist who debates a student about the existence of God. It is only when Radisson is dying that he embraces the idea of a divine being.

Not all spiritual transformations are about God, however. In 2014's *Interstellar*, Matthew McConaughey's character, an astronaut named Joseph Cooper, undergoes painful trials that forever alter his beliefs about the nature of the universe. His new insights about the glue that holds the cosmos together can be considered a spiritual revelation.

6. Dimension 3: Quantity

As we noted in our 2014 book, heroes (and villains) can be categorized by their quantity. In the movies, we see a large number of stories in which the hero stands alone in opposing a villain. We also see stories about two heroes joining with each other to overcome villains. And there are times when a group of three or more main characters work together in an ensemble. This year, we augment the quantity dimension of heroism with the *system*: an amorphous group of characters made up of many people, or by nature itself. Let's take a closer look at each of these categories.

6.1. Single

More often than not, heroes and villains proceed along their journeys alone. Occasionally, the hero fights a battle within him- or herself: an inner demon that begs for resolution or healing. This suggests that at times we can be our own villain. Another example of a single is the hero or villain who represents the face of a larger ensemble or system. And we've seen cases where a hero or villain represents a mastermind in control of one or more henchmen. Below we more thoroughly explore the different types of singles.

Lone

The lone hero is no doubt the most common type of hero in storytelling and in the movies. Classic lone heroes in the movies include James Bond, Bilbo Baggins, Indiana Jones, Robin Hood, Atticus Finch, Rocky Balboa, and Oskar Schindler. It is important to recognize that lone heroes still receive assistance from others. Yet we consider them lone heroes for a couple of reasons. First, the movie's focus is primarily on them and their story. Second, even though lone heroes do benefit from some assistance from others, they must achieve their objectives on their own, without a trusty sidekick or group to accompany them at all times.

Lone villains are also abundant in the movies. The movie *Gone Girl* features a ruthless villain, Amy, who frames her husband and torments and murders others to serve her interests. Amy is on her own; she has no trusted friend to confide in, nor does she report to any higher-up. Similarly, in *Big Eyes*, Walter Keane is a lone villain who manipulates and exploits his wife, Margaret. These lone villains may receive occasional assistance, but for the most part, they stand alone in opposing the hero.

Self

At times, heroes and villains must battle their inner demons. These psychological wounds may stem from addiction, early childhood abuse, or some severe emotional problem. Heroes do not let these maladies define them; they find ways to overcome their deficits and triumph. In contrast, villains allow their personal woes to define who they are, and they inflict the same pain onto others that they themselves are experiencing.

An example of a hero's battle with himself occurs in the film *Non-Stop*, starring Liam Neeson. Neeson plays an air marshal named Bill Marks, who is struggling with alcoholism, divorce, and the recent death of his daughter. He is clearly agitated and must pull himself together to overcome a villain onboard the plane who is murdering passengers. Another example of a hero battling himself is found in *Get on Up*, which chronicles the life of legendary musician James Brown. In this movie, we see how Brown heroically must overcome an abusive father and his own abusive tendencies.

The Face of Ensemble or System

A common character type is the person who represents a much larger organizational entity. Because this character usually has minimal screen time, we can infer that he or she is simply a human proxy for the organization.

As we've noted, a hero such as James Bond may represent a larger government organization but Bond is such a deeply fleshed out character that we wouldn't dare call him a simple proxy. Bond is a lone hero for sure. Heroic protagonists are rarely the mere face of an organization. Usually that role is reserved for the villain in a story that is so hero-centric that the villain character doesn't need to be well-developed.

So we frequently encounter a villain in the movies who is the face of large, menacing organization. In *Earth to Echo*, the heroes are a group ensemble of children who are being stalked by a government official posing as a construction worker. This villain is a poorly drawn out character and serves only as the face of an evil (or at least misguided) organization. Two other movies, *The Monuments Men* and *Woman in Gold*, include minor Nazi characters whom we know nothing about other than they are Nazis doing their evil work. They are simply the face of a large villainous machine.

The Mastermind

Our two new categories of singleton characters (masterminds and henchmen) describe individuals who give and receive orders.

One of the most common villains in the movies is the mastermind who pulls all the strings from some remote location and conveniently avoids any of the dirty work. Robert Redford in *Captain America: The Winter Soldier* is just such a character. While at first he appears to be the mastermind of S.H.I.E.L.D., we eventually learn that he has been directing the actions of the Winter Soldier. Redford's character, then, is a mastermind.

We don't often see a hero who is a mastermind, but it does happen. Professor X in *X-Men: Days of Future Passed* is such a character. He directs the action of the other X-Men to accomplish his goals.

The Henchman

We usually think of a henchman as the active arm of an evil mastermind. And in our taxonomy, this is still the case. However, a boss–subordinate power relationship also exists for heroic characters. It is often the case that the hero must deal with an unreasonable boss. In fact the hero's ability to get the job done despite the boss's poor judgment often makes him more heroic. In 2014's *3 Days To Kill,* Kevin Costner answers to a CIA boss named Vivi: a tyrannical femme fatale. She is so dastardly that she withholds a cancer treatment from him until he completes his mission. Even though he is a good and moral man, we call him a henchman hero because he answers to a higher authority.

Then, of course, are the villains who are not at the top of the evil food chain and are doing the bidding of an (often unseen) mastermind. We see this in *The Equalizer* where Denzel Washington's character is pitted against a very nasty henchman named Teddy who answers to the unseen Pushkin. Teddy sends messages to the rest of the mob by killing off anyone who isn't performing at top standards. While he is the villain of the story, we call him a henchman villain because he answers to a higher authority.

6.2. Duo

Often the protagonist role of the story is occupied by two characters. The duo can be a pair of characters who are alike in many ways, or complement each other. We call them the buddy duo. Sometimes the story revolves around two romantically involved characters. We sometimes see one of the duo take the lead and the other act as a sidekick. When they're villains, we see a mastermind-and-henchman pattern. And when they separate at the end of the story, we call them divergent duos. Let's take a deeper dive into each of these classifications of heroes and villains.

Buddy Duos

The classic buddy story often begins with two characters who don't like each other, but come together to solve some problem. By the end of the movie, they are friends and continue a relationship beyond what we see on screen. This year, we expand our understanding of the buddy story to include buddies in the antagonist role.

2014's *Deliver Us from Evil* qualifies as a buddy film, twice in fact as there are two buddy stories here. For the first half of the film, we focus on the buddy cop story between Sarchie (Eric Bana) and his partner, Butler. These two start out together and are clearly in sync. However, Butler dies about halfway through the film and Sarchie takes on a new buddy in the form of Mendoza, a Catholic priest. This pair starts out on opposite philosophical sides, but eventually comes to work together and stay together beyond the end of the film.

Buddy villains are far less common in the movies than buddy heroes. There are plenty of notable examples in movie history. The 1993 film *Pulp Fiction* featured a memorable pair of buddy villains (or more accurately, anti-heroes) in Vincent Vega, played by John Travolta, and Jules Winnfield, played by Samuel Jackson. Another iconic buddy anti-hero movie is the 1973 movie *The Sting*, featuring two buddy con artists named Henry "Shaw" Gondorff (Paul Newman) and Johnny "Kelly" Hooker (Robert Redford).

Romantic Duos

Romantic duos are similar to buddy duos but with the addition of a romantic love component. As with buddy duo movies, romantic films start with two people who dislike each other initially but are forced to work together to achieve a goal and over time develop romantic love for each other. It is not uncommon for the movie to end with romantic duos living happily ever after, as happened in the 2013 movie *About Time*. But some romantic duos go their separate ways, as in *The Theory of Everything* and *The Fault in Our Stars*.

There are, on occasion, villainous romantic duos in the movies. One recent example is the slave-abusing couple, Master and Mistress Epps, in the 2013 film *12 Years a Slave*. Other examples include Bellatrix Lestrange and Lord Voldemort in the 2007 movie *Harry Potter and the Order of the Phoenix*, Honey Bunny and Pumpkin in 1993's *Pulp Fiction*, and Mickey and Mallory Knox in 1994's *Natural Born Killers*.

Hero and Sidekick

In our previous book *Reel Heroes: Volume 1* (2014), we examined protagonist duos where there was a main character and a closely aligned helper. This year, we acknowledge the antagonist version of this. We'll examine the mastermind and henchman in the next section. But first let's look at the protagonists when they are a hero-and-sidekick duo.

In 2013, we met *The Lone Ranger* who had Tonto as a sidekick. While this may appear to be a buddy duo, we consider it a hero and sidekick duo because one character (The Lone Ranger) was the leader of the two. It's important to clarify that the sidekick is not just a secondary character who is helping the hero. The sidekick must be as heroic as the leader. It is a story about the two characters together. Other examples from days gone by include Batman and Robin and Captain America and Bucky.

Mastermind and Henchman

The mastermind and henchman is the villainous dual to the hero and sidekick. This is a duo of villains who are closely aligned in their attempts to thwart the hero. Again, one of the duo is a leader and the other is a follower. As with the hero and sidekick, it is important that the henchman be as important as the mastermind; it's just that the mastermind is the leader and the henchman is the follower.

The 2013 film *Elysium*, hero Max (Matt Damon) is pitted against mastermind Delacourt (Jodie Foster) and her henchman Carlyle (William Fichtner). Max is attempting to get into the Elysium satellite where he can be cured of cancer. But Carlyle has orders to do away with him. Carlyle gets all of his orders from Delacourt, who very much keeps her hands clean of any dirty business. This is a classic example of the mastermind-and-henchman pattern. The mastermind stays in the background and gives orders while the henchman does the work.

Divergent Duos

Another duo type that we examined last year is the divergent duo. In this case, two unlikely characters come together to solve some problem and go their separate ways at the end of the film. This divergence is more than a physical separation. It is usually a philosophical or ideological difference.

Take for example 2014's *Dawn of the Planet of the Apes*. In this case, we have two unlikely heroes working together. Caesar is a chimpanzee who is leading a band of escaped apes finding refuge in the wild of San Francisco Bay. Enter Carver, a human looking to restart a stalled power plant. The two create an uneasy partnership as they try to find a way to bring their two tribes together to live in harmony. But by the end of the film, the mistrust each side has toward the other makes their partnership impossible. The two go their separate ways at the end of the film, each leading their tribe to a divergent future.

It's harder to find villains who diverge at the end of their story. 2014's *Neighbors* stands out as an example of a divergent villain duo. The story revolves around a married couple (a buddy hero duo) who lives next door to a fraternity house. Things are going pretty well until the couple calls the cops on the frat boys for their misbehavior. At first, the frat president (Teddy played by Zac Efron) and his vice president (Pete played by Dave Franco) are aligned in their villainy to destroy their neighbors. But ultimately, Pete leaves Teddy as he realizes that frat life is not the ultimate accomplishment they'll make in their college years. This villainous duo then diverges as their philosophies on life go in different directions.

6.3. Ensemble

There are times when one or two heroes (or villains) is not enough. This collection of three or more characters is called the ensemble. We've identified four types of ensembles. The family, the fraternity or sorority, the police or military, and the team. The ensemble does not have to *literally* fit into one of these categories. For example, in the 2014 film *The Other Woman*, three ladies behave in a sophomoric way as they wreak revenge on a man who betrayed them. They aren't a sorority per se, but they resemble the stereotype.

Family

At times, the members of a nuclear family unit are the heroes in a movie. We see this type of ensemble in the 2013 film, *We're the Millers*, where a small-time crook named David Clark hires a woman and two teens to play the role of his family so that he can complete a drug deal. Another notable example is the 2014 movie *Boyhood*, which chronicles the life of several members of a family over a 14-year time period.

Less common is the villainous family unit. In the 2013 film *The Family*, Robert De Niro stars as a mobster whose entire family is placed under the

FBI's witness protection program. These family members continue their detestable behavior throughout the movie, making them a good example of a family anti-hero ensemble. *The Grand Budapest Hotel*, released in 2014, can also be considered a movie with a family villain.

Fraternity/Sorority

This hero category can include a literal fraternity or sorority, as seen in the iconic 1978 film *Animal House*. But more often than not, a group ensemble is figuratively a stereotypical fraternity or sorority because their behavior is extremely juvenile or slapstick. All three *Hangover* movies are vivid examples of grown men in their 30s behaving like hormonally pumped-up teenagers. As we've noted, the 2014 film *The Other Woman* tells the story of three women who play cruel pranks on a man who betrayed them. These are good examples of fraternity/sorority ensembles.

Although it is rare, a fraternity or sorority ensemble can play a villainous role in a movie. In 2014, the film *Neighbors* is about a young couple who discover that a college fraternity has moved into the house next door. This fraternity makes life very difficult for the couple, and thus the fraternity members are villains. One could argue that 2013's *Pain & Gain* also exemplifies a villainous fraternity group, as it features three guys who bungle a kidnapping and perform one stupid act after another during their crime spree.

Police/Military

An extremely common hero and villain group unit is the police/military ensemble. In the 2014 film *The Monuments Men*, George Clooney stars as Frank Stokes, a museum curator who wants to save valuable works of art from falling into Nazi hands. He handpicks a half-dozen civilian art experts to undergo basic military training to accomplish their mission. The 2012 film *The Avengers* portrays them as a police/military ensemble representing the counter-terrorism agency called S.H.I.E.L.D.

Villains as a police or military unit are also standard fare in the movies. *The Hobbit: The Battle of the Five Armies* features a couple of evil armies who oppose Bilbo Baggins and the heroic dwarves. Another example is found in the 2013 movie *Captain Phillips* in which the captain must overcome an armed group of Somali pirates. Also in 2013, young Ender Wiggin in *Ender's Game* must resist the evil influence Colonel Graff and his military henchmen who are grooming Ender to commit genocide.

Team

This year, we've added the team ensemble. The team is a group ensemble entity of people who work together to achieve a goal. Teams in the movies can be part of a formal organization or be assembled together to meet an urgent short-term need. Sports teams are a typical example, such as the De La Salle high school football team from 2014's *When the Game Stands Tall*.

On occasion, the villains in a story can assume the shape of a team. The 2001 film *Ocean's Eleven* offers a textbook example of a team of anti-heroes who pull off the ultimate heist. More recently, the 2013 film *Now You See Me* features four small-time magicians who appear to rob a French bank of millions of dollars during the middle of their Las Vegas act. Next, they plunder the bank account of their main financial sponsor, and the FBI is in hot pursuit of them. These magicians are clearly a team of anti-heroes.

6.4. System

At times, a heroic or villainous entity is too large and amorphous to be represented by a human face. We call this entity a *system*. Governments, corporations, institutions (such as slavery), and nature itself are classifications of systems that we've observed in movies. Systems almost always assume an antagonist role in movies because moviegoers need a well-developed human character to play the role of the protagonist. Below we expand on how systems offer an oppositional force to protagonists.

Government

A governmental entity is an extremely common system in the movies. In American films, there are two evil government systems in particular that movies repeatedly cast as villains: Nazis and Russians. Nazis as government systems appear in *The Monuments Men*, *Woman in Gold*, *The Imitation Game*, *The Grand Budapest Hotel*, and *Unbroken*. The Russians are the government system villains in *Jack Ryan: Shadow Recruit*, *Red 2*, and *A Good Day to Die Hard*. North Koreans are the evil system behind the takeover of the White House in *Olympus Has Fallen*.

Organization/Corporation

Organizations as antagonistic systems include organized crime families, corporations, armies, and police forces, among others. We see law enforcement agencies play the role of antagonistic systems in movies such as *Labor Day*, *Selma*, *Nightcrawler*, *Dallas Buyers Club*, *Earth to Echo*, *We're the Millers*, *Snitch*, and *Hunger Games*. Corporate systems have played villainous roles in movies such as *St. Vincent* and *The Wolf of Wall Street*.

Institution

An institution refers to any cultural system in place that erects invisible yet powerful barriers that challenge the protagonist to complete his or her mission.

We've identified three common institutions in the movies. The most common is the institution of racism, which we see in its full form in movies such as *42*, *The Butler*, *12 Years a Slave*, and *Selma*. Another institutional barrier is sexism, which we see challenging our heroes in *The Imitation Game* and *Big Eyes*. Another "ism" is classism (or class warfare) on full display in *Hunger Games* and *Divergent*.

Nature

Systems also include forces of nature, which are large and powerful phenomena such as storms, floods, droughts, the passage of time, the force of gravity, and even disease. Storms are an extremely common force of nature, which we've seen in movies such as *Castaway*, *All Is Lost*, *Twister*, and *The Perfect Storm*. At times the natural force is gravity, which appears in movies such as *Gravity* and *Interstellar*.

A natural force that a protagonist fights can be time itself. We see time as a foe in movies such as *Edge of Tomorrow*, *About Time*, and *Interstellar*. Another common natural force is illness and disease, which we see confronting our heroes in movies such as *The Fault in Our Stars* and *The Theory of Everything*.

7. Attributes

The core of our model consists of three main dimensions of movie characters: character type (protagonist vs. antagonist), transformations (moral, mental, emotional, spiritual, physical), and quantity of characters (single, duo, ensemble, system). But a final important consideration should not overlooked: the *attributes* of movie characters.

In our study of movie protagonists and antagonists, we found that heroic and villainous characters can assume one or more attributes that meaningfully define and describe them. These attributes are central to our understanding of the various types of movie characters.

7.1. Competent

In our research on heroes, we've found that people view heroes as either being highly moral, highly competent, or both. So when we refer to lead characters as "good" or "virtuous," this can mean either moral or competent. Competence in heroic characters is seen in the car-driving ability of the two lead characters in *Rush*, or in the baseball ability in the two lead athletes in *Million Dollar Arm*. Morality in heroic protagonists can be illustrated in the character of Frank Stokes in *The Monuments Men*. Stokes is driven by the noble desire to save great works of art from Nazi destruction.

Our greatest heroes are endowed with both morality and competence. A striking example is seen in Martin Luther King, Jr., in *Selma*. King not only aspires to achieve racial equality in America, but also calls upon his vast leadership skills and ability to coordinate a large social movement. Another hero who combines both morality and competence is Alan Turing in *The Imitation Game*. Turing is inspired to defeat the Nazis and must concoct a sophisticated machine that can crack the Nazi codes.

Villains are judged to be immoral, and the greatest villains combine extreme immorality with extreme competence. Consider the diabolic character of Amy in *Gone Girl*. Amy is a ruthless sociopath who murders and manipulates to serve her interests. She is also highly skilled, making her even more terrifying. No doubt the combination of evil and skillfulness is responsible for the enduring appeal of iconic villains such as Hannibal Lecter and Darth Vader.

7.2. Misunderstood/Deceptive

Sometimes the true goodness or badness of a main character is concealed from viewers. We see this pattern with a protagonist in *St. Vincent*, where Bill Murray's character is shown to be a selfish unethical grouch until we learn of all the selfless sacrifices he makes for others. Vincent is what we call a *misunderstood* hero.

At times the true villainy of a character is concealed from viewers. We see this pattern in the character of Amy in *Gone Girl*. During the first half of the movie, Amy is seen as an innocent victim of a brutal crime. Then we, the audience, are supplied with the startling truth, namely, that Amy is a vicious psychopathic killer. Amy is a *deceptive* villain.

We're fairly certain that only heroes are misunderstood, and only villains are deceptive. It would be rare for a hero to be deceptive about his true nature.

7.3. Mysterious

At times, an important character can be shrouded in mystery for a long portion of the movie. The character's name will be mentioned repeatedly by other characters, but we never lay eyes on this person, perhaps ever, or perhaps not until the very end of the movie. In the film, *Ride Along*, the mastermind villain named Omar is referenced repeatedly throughout the movie. But we never actually see Omar until the last few minutes of the film.

7.4. Simple/Mindless/Pure (Evil or Good)

Movies often feature villains that are uniformly pure in their evil. We see this monolithic badness in movies with monsters and aliens. A recent example can be found with the extra-terrestrial creatures called the Mimics in *Edge of Tomorrow*. The Mimics are just nasty aliens with an unexplained desire to kill humans. There is no backstory to explain their evil nature; it's just assumed. Monsters of all sorts are considered pure evil.

Good characters can also be purely virtuous, usually when the good characters are anti-villains who play a minor role as the oppositional force pitted against an anti-hero. Examples here are the law enforcement personnel shown sparingly in *Labor Day* and in *Nightcrawler*, both of which we've covered earlier.

7.5. Catalytic or Mentor

When a hero undergoes no transformation, he usually affects a change in those around him. In this case, the hero acts as a catalyst for change in others. Put another way, the hero is a mentor character to those around him.

We see this in 2013's *42*, the Jackie Robinson story. Robinson starts out a virtuous and positive person at the beginning of the film. He overcomes many obstacles, not the least of which is racism directed at him by fans and teammates. Robinson is essentially the same person at the end of the film as he is at the beginning. However, the fans and his teammates have accepted him. Robinson ushered in a new age of interracial baseball. He was a catalyst for change in the hearts and minds of baseball fans.

7.6. Episodic

The proliferation of movie franchises means that movie-goers are exposed to more episodic film heroes than ever before. But there is a price to be paid for serialized heroes. Just as episodic television heroes tend not to change over time, neither do episodic movie heroes. Episodic heroes tend to resist change because filmmakers don't want to tamper with a successful formula. Movie franchises with episodic heroes include James Bond, Sherlock Holmes, Indiana Jones, and James T. Kirk.

8. Pulling It All Together

Let's illustrate our model using two specific examples of notable characters from movies released in 2014.

8.1. Louis Zamperini in *Unbroken*

We'll start with the character of Louis Zamperini in the 2014 film *Unbroken*. Here is our analysis of Zamperini using the three dimensions of our model including his character attributes.

Character Type: Protagonist

Zamperini is the lead character of the movie, making him the protagonist. He faces two types of antagonists in the film. The main human antagonist is "the Bird," the abusive Japanese prisoner of war camp guard who torments Zamperini. The other antagonist is a system; Zamperini overcomes the powerful force of nature while adrift in a raft for many weeks in the Pacific Ocean.

Transformation Arc: Positive to More Positive

Zamperini starts out as a good, decent person and capable military fighter. After enduring many extraordinary trials, he is transformed into a new and better person. This is the journey of the classic hero.

Transformation Type: Emotional

Zamperini undergoes horrific conditions on the life-raft and is starved and beaten for years as a prisoner of war. To survive these events, he is able to overcome his deepest fears and develop remarkable resilience. His transformation is, therefore, an emotion-based transformation.

Quantity: Single

Zamperini is a lone hero. Like all great heroes, he receives help from his fellow officers and prisoners of war. But for the most part, he travels the hero's journey by himself, without a sidekick, buddy, romantic companion, or group ensemble by his side.

Attributes: Competent

As we've noted, the most powerful heroes in literature and in the movies are heroes who demonstrate high levels of both morality and competence. By virtue of the fact that Zamperini is a soldier who is serving his country and fighting the Nazis, he is a moral hero. To survive on the raft, Zamperini shows skills as a survivalist: he invents methods to fish and catch birds, he develops a procedure for collecting rainwater, and he assumes the role of a leader.

8.2. Walter Keane in *Big Eyes*

We next examine the character of Walter Keane in the 2014 film *Big Eyes*.

Character Type: Antagonist

At the beginning of *Big Eyes*, the character of Margaret is established as the protagonist. She aspires to become a professional artist, and eventually she meets fellow artist Walter Keane. Walter is the antagonist in the movie because he begins taking credit for Margaret's work, thereby preventing Margaret from achieving her goal of establishing her own career.

Transformation Arc: Negative to More Negative

When Walter Keane first takes credit for Margaret's paintings, he reveals himself to be petty and selfish. He promises Margaret that his deception is short-term but soon we realize that Walter's intentions are far more insidious. While pressuring his wife to increase her output, he subjects her to sweatshop work conditions. She is forced to isolate herself from the world and produce her big-eye paintings so that Walter can make money and enjoy fame. Walter's spiral downward toward greater evil makes him an irredeemable villain.

Transformation Type: Moral

Because Walter mistreats and disrespects his wife to an increasing extent throughout the movie, we can say that his descent is a moral one.

Quantity: Single

Walter is a lone villain. He travels the villain's journey by himself, without a sidekick, buddy, companion, or group ensemble by his side.

Attributes: Deceptive

Walter is clearly immoral in his behavior. It is not until the halfway point in the film that we, the audience, are informed that he had a long fraudulent history before he met Margaret. Both Walter and the makers of this film decided to withhold this information from us, making Walter a deceptive villain.

9. Summary

Our new model of heroic and villainous characters is based on our observation that the hero–villain dichotomy in the movies is not the same as the protagonist–antagonist dichotomy. The protagonist in a story is always the lead character, and this person can be either the good guy (the hero) or the bad buy (the anti-hero). Moreover, the antagonist in a story is always the oppositional character, and this person can be either the bad guy (the villain) or the good guy (the anti-villain).

Distinguishing among these four types of characters has allowed us to observe the various types of journeys that they embark on as they perform their heroic or villainous deeds. Their journeys are characterized by a transformational arc that reveals the way their characters evolve over the course of the movie. We've outlined eight transformational arcs that protagonists and antagonists undergo, ranging from no transformation at all to single and even double transformations.

Our new model also reveals the specific nature of those transformations. We've identified transformations as being moral, mental, emotional, physical, or spiritual. In general, the most compelling characters in the movies undergo one or more of these types of transformations. Dull characters, as a general rule, fail to undergo a transformation.

Consistent with our 2014 model, we recognize protagonists and antagonists who operate alone, in duos, or in group ensembles. This year we've added large amorphous systems as another protagonistic or antagonistic unit. These heroic and villainous entities of different sizes can undergo any one of the eight transformational arcs that we've identified. Moreover, these heroic and villainous entities can undergo any of the five types of transformations.

Finally, we've identified a number of key attributes of protagonists and antagonists that truly make their heroic and villainous qualities distinctive. These attributes include the idea that movie characters can be competent, misunderstood, deceptive, mysterious, simple/mindless/pure, catalytic or mentor, or episodic.

9.1. Types of Hero Journeys

We've identified four types of hero journeys based on the nature of the hero's transformation:

1. Negative to Positive (enlightened). This journey shows us a hero who sees the light and shows great personal growth. A form of redemption, we call it *enlightenment*.
2. Positive to More Positive (classic). This classic pattern, first described by Joseph Campbell, is the most common hero's journey in the movies.
3. Positive to Positive (untransformed). This pattern of non-transformation is so common in superhero movies that we could call it the *superhero* journey. These types of heroes are often catalytic (or mentor) heroes. They change those around them, rather than themselves.
4. Positive to Negative to Positive (redeemed). This double transformation shows us the power of redemption. The hero comes full circle, and hence we also call it a *round trip* journey.

9.2. Types of Villain Journeys

We've identified four types of villain journeys based on the nature of the villain's transformation:

1. Negative to More Negative (irredeemable). This is the classic super-villain pattern, as seen in the character of the Joker in *Batman* and the Green Goblin in *Spider-Man*. It's ironic that in superhero movies, the superheroes don't transform but the villains often do.
2. Negative to Negative (untransformed). This pattern may be the most common villain journey, not because filmmakers set out to make dull, unchanging villains but because movies are almost always more about the hero than about the villain. Villains who receive minimal screen time simply don't have the time or opportunity to transform. This is also the villain's journey for monsters.
3. Negative to Positive to Negative (regressed). This double transformation is especially tragic, as the villain once appeared to have redeemed him- or herself.
4. Positive to Negative (fallen). This pattern reflects another type of tragic hero, often seen in Shakespearean plays.

9.3. Differences Between Heroes and Villains

Listed below are our 10 observations about the ways that movie heroes and villains differ from each other. These observations also apply to movie anti-heroes and anti-villains, but for the sake of simplicity we use the terms *hero* and *villain* here. Our observations include the following:

1. Movie heroes are usually (but not always) better developed characters than are movie villains. Filmmakers assume that audiences care more about the details of the hero journey than the villain journey.

2. Heroes find ways to redeem themselves, even when they appear to be irreparably damaged. Heroes transcend difficult circumstances. Villains succumb to them.

3. Heroes discover their missing inner quality and become transformed. Villains never discover that quality and either stagnate or regress.

4. Heroes know they are on the side of good. Villains often don't know they are on the side of bad.

5. Heroes attract benevolent mentors; villains either never get mentored or attract dark mentors.

6. Heroes usually participate in all aspects of their journey. Villains often "outsource" parts of their journey to henchmen or minions.

7. Heroes are on a journey of becoming in union with the world. Villains are on a journey of separation from the world.

8. Sometimes the hero redeems the villain as in *Karate Kid*, *Return of the Jedi*, *X-Men*, and *St. Vincent*. But the villain never redeems the hero.

9. Heroes enjoy a good relationship with their sidekicks. Villains mistreat their sidekicks. The sidekick either defects to the good side or ends up dead.

10. Heroes complete their journey with an act of selflessness. Villains complete their journey with an act of selfishness.

9.4. Conclusions

In 2013, we reviewed 75 films and were able to get a peek into the composition of heroes in movies. At that time, we were focused on the number of characters playing the lead role. In 2014, we reviewed another 52 films and analyzed not just the heroes, but also the villains in the stories. This led us to generalize our taxonomy to encompass both types of lead characters.

This new taxonomy introduces two dimensions of movie characters. Not only are we interested in the quantity of characters, but also their role and their transformation. By including the role of the characters, we are able to generalize our findings to cover not just the hero and villain, but also the anti-hero and the anti-villain.

We're excited with this new taxonomy, as it offers a richer model than before. To our knowledge, this is the first time a classification system has been created that satisfies both the hero and villain. It further supports our initial thoughts that the hero and villain have similar traits and parallel character arcs.

Our work is not yet complete. In 2015, we will be reviewing another 52 films with an eye toward supporting characters. We want to understand how the supporting characters develop and whether they also have an arc. What are the traits of a good supporting cast, and what happens when a movie doesn't satisfy these common elements?

We hope you will enjoy the 52 movie reviews found in this volume of *Reel Heroes*. And we hope you have found some value in our new taxonomy of heroes and villains. Please drop by our website at http://ReelHeroes.net and follow our blog as we continue to review movies and analyze their reel heroes and villains.

Part II.

Reel Heroes
Movie Reviews
2014

22 Jump Street

Starring	Channing Tatum, Jonah Hill, Ice Cube
Director	Phil Lord, Christopher Miller
Screenplay	Michael Bacall, Oren Uziel
Genre	Action/Comedy/Crime
Rated	R
Running Time	112 minutes
Release Date	June 13, 2014
Schmidt & Jenko Protagonist	Duo, Untransformed Positive Moral (Untransformed Buddy Heroes)
Mercedes Antagonist	Single, Untransformed Negative Moral (Untransformed Mastermind Villain)

(Dr. Scott Allison, Professor of Psychology, University of Richmond)

Greg, it's looking like Jump Street is a much longer road than we thought.

(Greg Smith, Founder of Agile Writers of Richmond, VA)

And I enjoyed the ride a lot more than I imagined I would. Let's recap:

Our two heroes from *21 Jump Street*, Morton Schmidt (Jonah Hill) and Greg Jenko (Channing Tatum) are assigned the task of going undercover at a local university. Apparently, the use of a new illegal drug called WHY-PHY (work hard yes, play hard yes) has reached epidemic proportions and recently killed a young coed. Captain Dickson (Ice Cube) wants Schmidt and Jenko to locate and arrest the suppliers of this drug.

Schmidt and Jenko arrive on campus and immediately try to merge into the local scene. They are doing well despite looking older than their peers. Schmidt befriends a young woman (named Maya, played by Amber Stevens) who happens to have been the across-the-hall neighbor of the deceased coed. Meanwhile, hunky Jenko is embraced by a local fraternity where he is becoming best buds with the captain of the football team (Zook, played by Wyatt Russell). This new pairing is splitting up our buddy cops and is the bromance portion of our story.

Greg, although there are some occasionally amusing moments in *22 Jump Street*, I just couldn't muster up much enthusiasm for this movie. The story and premise are pretty much pointless. Now I will admit that I've enjoyed some pointless comedies in the past, but for a pointless movie to be enjoyable, some elements must truly stand out as excellent. The jokes have to be stellar and consistently good throughout the movie, or the characters must be particularly memorable. I didn't see that here.

22 Jump Street features some clever humor at times, as when our two heroes remark that Ice Cube's office looks like a cube of ice. But these moments of cleverness are in short supply. One long-running joke is that the two main male friendships in the movie (between Schmidt & Jenko, and between Jenko & Zook) have some of the characteristics of a gay relationship. This joke isn't very funny and actually becomes painful to watch as it's milked repeatedly over 90 minutes. Another tired joke is that Schmidt and Jenko look too old for their roles. Yes, we get that – over and over again.

I liked this film a lot more than you did, Scott. This was a very clever look at the typical buddy-cop sequel. There are constant references made to how "this case is exactly like the last one." And how Schmidt and Jenko must stop trying to do something different and solve this case just like they did last time. In other words, we all know this is a sequel. We all know that the audience expects a retread of what they've seen before. Now just go out there and give it to them.

Within that context, the movie delivers a very sardonic look at the state of movies and their sequels. There are so few new concepts in Hollywood. Last year of the 75 movies we reviewed, 15 were sequels. That's a whopping 20%. *22 Jump Street*'s writers knew what was expected of them - to do the same as last time only bigger. But they didn't - they delivered a perfect send up of the Hollywood sequel. I think it was a very smart movie.

 As much as I like Jonah Hill and Channing Tatum, they aren't funny. At least not to me. They are likeable and amusing, but that's it. So the running jokes fell flat for me, and not much was going on that held my interest. *22 Jump Street* is not only a movie that is constantly winking at itself, it is a movie that is winking at it's own winking. This isn't the first film that pokes fun at itself and its genre, and it isn't close to being the funniest, either.

As you might expect, the buddy hero story here is inconsequential. Goofball comedies aren't designed to deliver any kind of meaningful message about life or about how people grow or change. So we're presented with a parody of how buddy cops grow apart and then in the course of events are brought closer together at the end. The characters aren't meant to be taken seriously, so there isn't much meaningful analysis we can do here.

Which is exactly the point of this spoof. It takes a look at the buddy-cop hero archetype and plays it to the extreme. For every earnest attempt at creating a buddy-cop movie, there is a joke in *22 Jump Street* that pokes fun.

And there are other side jokes that are great. The duo are seeking out a man with a tattoo on his bicep who is the drug supplier. Jenko is on the tail of a college football player (by going undercover as one of the players) only to learn that the tattoo his suspect has is of a wait for it red herring. Not the tattoo they were looking for.

The villains are like typical villains we've seen in other buddy-cop stories - virtually invisible until we need a chase scene to wrap up the story. And *22 Jump Street* delivers on that as well. The villains are painfully ordinary and typical and just what you'd expect. But there's a twist on who the kingpin is - just as most buddy-cop movies might deliver. Even in creating their villains, *22 Jump Street* is keenly aware of the fact that they're in a sequel making fun of sequels.

 22 Jump Street is a movie that I wanted to like but just couldn't. I have to give them credit – the filmmakers put a lot of effort into this movie, almost as if they realized they had almost nothing to work with and therefore had to pull out all the stops. I give them an "A" for effort here. But the movie deserves only one and a half Reels. I'll generously round up and make it 2 out of 5.

The buddy heroes were not terribly memorable people, nor was their journey a notable one at all. The less said the better here. Again, I'll give them 2 out of 5 Heroes. As you note, Greg, the villains play a peripheral role in the movie. But I do need to give a shout-out to the stand-out performance delivered by Jillian Bell who plays the student roommate villain. She is by far the most interesting character in the movie, as well as the funniest. I wish we could have seen more of her in the film. Overall, I'll give the villains a rating of 2 out of 5.

Movie: Villains:  Heroes:

I had the opposite opinion - I expected to hate this film but was dragged into its farce kicking and screaming - with laughter. You're right, this is a film that knew a sequel would be ridiculous - so the filmmakers made it ludicrous. And good for them. Still, the joke can only go so far. While I enjoyed myself, grudgingly, I can only award 3 out of 5 Reels for a comedy that satisfied both those who wanted a sequel and those who dreaded one.

The heroes are not really superb - they are the typical buddy-cops we've come to expect from such films. They don't inspire us to great heights or warn us of great depths. I can only award these caricatures 2 out of 5 Heroes.

I have to agree with you on the villains. The typical bad guys are boring and perform their role. It's only the introduction of the roommate from hell that makes the villains rise above complete worthlessness. I can only give her 1 Villain out of 5, however.

Finally, if you have any doubt about whether *22 Jump Street* in any way takes itself seriously, just sit around for the ending credits. It will definitely fill you in on what is yet to come.

Movie: 🎞️🎞️🎞️ Villains: 🤠 Heroes: 🦸

3 Days to Kill

Starring	Kevin Costner, Hailee Steinfeld, Connie Nielsen
Director	McG
Screenplay	Adi Hasak, Luc Besson
Genre	Action/Crime/Drama
Rated	PG-13
Running Time	117 minutes
Release Date	February 21, 2014
Renner Protagonist	Single, Positive to More Positive Moral (Classic Lone Hero)
Albino Antagonist	Single, Untransformed Negative Moral (Untransformed Henchman Villain)

(Dr. Scott Allison, Professor of Psychology, University of Richmond)

Greg, good things come in threes. The musketeers, the little pigs, the stooges, etc.

(Greg Smith, Founder of Agile Writers of Richmond, VA)
It seemed like I had three hours to kill watching *3 Days to Kill*.

We meet Ethan Renner (Kevin Costner), a CIA assassin agent who is dying of cancer. He moves to Paris to spend his last few months near his ex-wife and teenage daughter, from whom he's been estranged for five years. While in Paris, Renner is assigned the task of killing a man nicknamed "The Albino" (Tomas Lemarquis), who is plotting to unleash a smart bomb on the general public. Meanwhile, Renner discovers that his ex-wife and daughter want little to do with him.

To give Renner ample incentive to complete the job, Vivi, (Amber Heard) his diabolical boss lady, offers him an experimental serum that will cure him. It has strange side effects, however and leaves Renner incapacitated without warning. Back home, ex-wife Christine (Connie Nielsen) is going on a business trip and needs Renner to watch over daughter Zoe (Hailee Steinfeld) for three days. Hilarity ensues when the CIA hit man must juggle the duties of daily spy work with fatherly responsibilities.

Greg, we all try to find a balance between our work lives and our personal lives. This struggle is the main recurring theme of *3 Days to Kill*, with the added twist that the hero of the story is a CIA assassin on assignment who is dying of cancer. Renner tries to reconnect with his daughter while hunting his villainous prey, and the movie tries to be a bit too cute by including scenes where he is literally on the phone parenting his child while dodging bullets.

A curious yet appealing element of this movie centers on the family of squatters who take over his apartment. They are quirky and culturally different, and the elder among them ends up sharing his wisdom with Renner. This is a nice nod to the classic mentor figure in hero tales, a figure who is typically deviant and mysterious. Another mentor character is Renner's ex-wife Christine, who also imparts wisdom to Ethan about life's priorities. She helps Renner, a long-time assassin, transform himself into a loving, pacifistic family man.

The film does a pretty good job of balancing action and humor.
Unfortunately for me some of the scenes were a bit far-fetched. At
one point Renner is at a party with his daughter who wanders off
with a boy. Then an all-out gun fight ensues and somehow she is never the
wiser. And there are the scenes where the snitch is in the trunk and Zoe is in
the front seat and seems not to notice the sounds of a man banging around in
the back. It's all a bit far-fetched. If this were a comedy it would be funny but
it's a thriller so it's just eye-rolling material.

Renner is pretty good hero material. He's dedicated to his work and is trying
to mend a strong inner hurt (that of being estranged from his daughter and
having little time to reconcile). He's rugged and charismatic. Despite the
fact that he has to lie about what he does, he's an honest guy. And he's as
reliable as he can be given that people are always out to murder him, which
causes him to be late for father-daughter appointments every so often. And
he ultimately reconciles with his daughter so he resolves that missing inner
quality. Renner's not a complicated hero but he does fit the mold of what we
look for in a good hero.

 I agree, Greg. And Costner deserves credit for delivering an understated performance that allows us to forgive (mostly) the ill-attempt
of the movie to balance silly humor with life-threatening bullies and
bullets.

But what of the villains? These villains have hackneyed nicknames like the
wolf and the *albino*. Another stereotypical character is Ethan's beautiful and
rather villainous CIA boss Vivi, who is just as ruthless as the story's Russian
villains. She coerces Ethan to work for her by threatening to withhold treatment for his cancer, leading us to wonder (and perhaps Ethan to wonder, too)
who exactly are the good guys here? All three of these villains are oversimplified yawners who are constructed to look menacing and pose danger. But
in the end they are uninteresting.

I agree Scott. Vivi struck me as a sort of anti-villain because she
is working for the "good guys" but is just as corrupt as the "bad
guys." Sometimes it's hard to tell the difference between a hero
and a villain. As Joseph Campbell once said, "A hero will do anything to get

what he wants, at his own expense. Whereas a villain will do anything to get what he wants, at someone else's expense." And by that definition Vivi falls squarely into the category of villain.

 3 Days to Kill is a surprisingly entertaining movie about a dying man's attempt to juggle his work life and his personal life. Kevin Costner delivers a solid, sympathetic performance as man who is out to redeem himself both professionally and personally. The film features a pretty well-crafted hero's journey with our hero's descent into a dark world of cancer and assassins, a recovery of our hero's missing humanity, and several redemptive acts of triumph at the end. This movie will not win any awards but it is endearing in its own simple way. I give it 3 Reels out of 5.

As mentioned above, the hero journey is solid in its arc and with its inclusion of several key allies, love interests, mentors, and villains. I hereby award Renner 3 Heroes out of 5.

The villains were disappointing and dragged the film down. Had the villains been interesting or endowed with some kind of depth, *3 Days to Kill* might have been a very good movie. But we're given simple cartoon-like characters who are almost laughable in their stereotypical minimalism. I generously award this film 2 Villains out of 5.

Movie: Heroes:  Villains:

Scott I think we're pretty well-aligned here. Any father with a teen-aged daughter will feel the pull of work versus family that Renner has to deal with. Most of us don't have to literally fight to get home at the end of the day so seeing Renner take fatherhood to the absurd extreme made for light entertainment. I also award 3 out of 5 Reels for an entertaining thriller wrapped in a family conundrum.

The hero here is pretty basic and as you point out Costner plays the role casually, and that works for him. We're satisfied with the resolution as he reunites with Zoe. So I give Renner 3 out of 5 Heroes.

So often we measure our heroes by the quality of their villains. The villains here were mostly offscreen and were mere shadows of characters. The real villain here was Renner's ties to his work, which many men feel. Vivi is the physical manifestation of that conflict. But she's a typical femme-fatale that we've seen before. The villains don't give Renner much to play against and so I give them just 2 Villains out of 5.

Movie: Heroes: Villains:

The Amazing Spider-Man 2

Starring	Andrew Garfield, Emma Stone, Jamie Foxx
Director	Marc Webb
Screenplay	Alex Kurtzman, Roberto Orci, Jeff Pinkner, James Vanderbilt
Genre	Action/Adventure/Fantasy
Rated	PG-13
Running Time	142 minutes
Release Date	May 2, 2014
Spider-Man/Peter Protagonist	Single, Untransformed Positive (Untransformed Episodic Hero)
Electro/Max Antagonist	Single, Positive to Negative Moral (Fallen Lone Villain)
Green Goblin/Harry Antagonist	Single, Positive to Negative Moral (Fallen Lone Villain)

(Dr. Scott Allison, Professor of Psychology, University of Richmond)

Greg, it looks like Marvel Comics has just spun another web of super-heroism and super-villainy.

(Greg Smith, Founder of Agile Writers of Richmond, VA)
My spider senses are tingling! Let's recap.

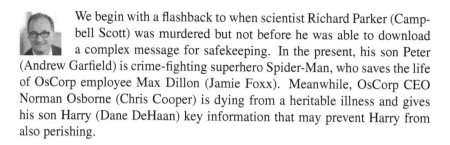

We begin with a flashback to when scientist Richard Parker (Campbell Scott) was murdered but not before he was able to download a complex message for safekeeping. In the present, his son Peter (Andrew Garfield) is crime-fighting superhero Spider-Man, who saves the life of OsCorp employee Max Dillon (Jamie Foxx). Meanwhile, OsCorp CEO Norman Osborne (Chris Cooper) is dying from a heritable illness and gives his son Harry (Dane DeHaan) key information that may prevent Harry from also perishing.

Max is obsessed with Spider-Man. At work he is tasked with fixing an electrical connection and accidentally falls into a vat of genetically altered electric eels. He is transformed into the super villain Electro. Meanwhile, when Norman Osborne dies, Peter visits old pal Harry and they rekindle their friendship. However, Peter's relationship with the beautiful Gwen Stacy (Emma Stone) is on the rocks as Peter cannot reconcile a promise he made to her father on his death bed - a promise to keep Gwen safe by not seeing her.

Greg, *The Amazing Spider-Man 2* is an ambitious work of art, a three-pronged story of heroism endowed with two heavy-weight villains. I say "three-pronged" because our hero has three missions in this film to restore his father's good name, to resolve his conflict with his girlfriend Gwen, and to defeat the supervillain Electro. These goals are intertwined and some might say that they somewhat over-complicate the movie. In any good superhero film, vanquishing the villain is the primary mission and this film is no exception, even with the two other main storylines taking place.

In most superhero stories, the superhero rarely shows much character transformation, remaining as solidly virtuous as a character can get from start to finish. One could argue that this shortcoming, if you could call it that, occurs in *The Amazing Spider-Man 2*, although we do witness Peter Parker learn a lesson or two about the perils of falling in love, possibly with the wrong woman.

We're introduced to a young Chris Kyle (Bradley Cooper) who wants nothing more than to be a cowboy. But he's hampered by the fact that real cowboys exist only in the past. Instead he's a rodeo cowboy riding bucking broncs and steers. One day he watches the bombing of an American embassy on TV and he signs up for the Navy. It's not enough to just join the military, he wants to be the best and toughest, so he signs up for the Navy Seals.

 Kyle undergoes rigorous Seal training and meets his future wife Taya (Sienna Miller) in a bar. They fall in love and get married, but then Kyle is sent on his first tour of duty in Iraq. While sniping at the enemy, Kyle earns a reputation as the best and deadliest shooter in the armed forces. He earns the nickname "The Legend". When he returns stateside, Taya notices that he is emotionally distant and shows worsening signs of PTSD.

Scott, *American Sniper* is the true-life story of the deadliest sniper in American military history. Director Clint Eastwood uses all his experience to create an accurate recreation of what it is like to be a modern American warfighter. We are witness to the extreme conditions that our service men and women have to endure to keep America safe. In one scene, we see the kind of dedication Kyle has to his profession. After a full day of maneuvers, Kyle's commander climbs to the top of a building where Kyle has been sniping and proclaims that it stinks. And stink it does because Kyle hadn't moved from the spot all that day and had relieved himself right there.

 Greg, *American Sniper* is one of the most emotionally powerful movies of 2014. The movie holds no punches in depicting the horrors of war in graphic and stunning detail. Some viewers might believe that this movie glorifies American honor, valor, and patriotism. Perhaps it does. But the true take-home message of this film is that war exacts a horrible toll on all participants and that there is no winning, only degrees of losing – and everyone loses in a horrid, senseless way.

Bradley Cooper deserves kudos for his remarkable portrayal of a man who is assigned the task of killing people with his sniper rifle. And no one does it better. The hero story here is a fascinating one in that Kyle undergoes at least three transformations. The first is a transformation from a raw, unskilled recruit to a master of sniping. He must sacrifice plenty to get there – his freedom, his family, and his emotional well-being. We then witness Kyle's second transformtion – his acquisition of PTSD. Then, in a final transformation, we watch him recover from this disorder. The hero's journey is packed and powerful.

You're right, Cooper makes a complete transformation into Kyle. Kyle represents all that is good in heroes. He is the best at what he does. He is protective of everyone - his family, his men, and his country. He has a strong moral code. He risks everything to be the protector. There's a scene early in the film that explains why Kyle is so protective. He gets in a fight defending his brother from a bully. At dinner that night his father explains that there are three types of people: sheep, wolves, and sheepdogs. The sheep can't protect themselves, the wolves prey on the sheep, and the sheepdogs protect the sheep. And he made it clear, in no uncertain terms, that in his house he was raising sheepdogs. Rarely do we get to see the seeds of heroism as it is portrayed here.

 You're exactly right, Greg. This film gives us insight into the origins of Kyle's brand of heroism. We see his dad's influence on the development of his moral code, which is strong on loyalty, country, family, and saving others who need help. We see how the terrorist attack of 9/11 helped shape his patriotic zeal and how sniping was his perfect calling. We see how adapts to the role of "Legend" with natural ease yet remains uncomfortable with any idolatry directed his way.

The villains in this story are primarily the Al Qaeda fighters who are shooting and bombing American troops. But another villain is the disease of PTSD that Kyle must also fight and overcome. The enemy fighters are undeveloped characters who are less interesting in this movie than the PTSD, which emotionally cripples Kyle and other soldiers.

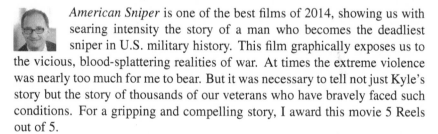

Kyle has a compulsion to return to Iraq over and over again to fight the terrorists. He is obsessed with protecting his flock. Eastwood puts a face on the villainy in Iraq. One such face is "The Butcher" who is a lieutenant to al-Zarqawi - a leading insurgent in Iraq. We see The Butcher maim and kill helpless women and children. There is also a Syrian sniper they call "Mustafa" who kills one of Kyle's friends. Kyle is determined to kill Mustafa. It takes him four tours to do it and he risks the lives of all the men in his command when he does it.

You're right about PTSD as another faceless villain in this film, Scott. We see its effect on Kyle. When Kyle returns home he visits a Veteran's Administration hospital where the doctor recognizes Kyle's disorder and recommends he talk to some of the other soldiers who have come back from the war. Kyle finds that he can help them recover from their disabilities through the discipline of target shooting. In helping others, Kyle finds a way to continue protecting his military brothers. In giving this protection, he finds his way back into civilian life - and he heals his PTSD.

American Sniper is one of the best films of 2014, showing us with searing intensity the story of a man who becomes the deadliest sniper in U.S. military history. This film graphically exposes us to the vicious, blood-splattering realities of war. At times the extreme violence was nearly too much for me to bear. But it was necessary to tell not just Kyle's story but the story of thousands of our veterans who have bravely faced such conditions. For a gripping and compelling story, I award this movie 5 Reels out of 5.

Kyle's hero story is a complex one in its portrayal of his transformation into a legendary marksman, and also his transformation from an emotionally traumatized veteran to a recovered healthy civilian. Like all good heroes, Kyle receives assistance along the way both within the military and beyond it. His wife Taya and his children are instrumental in helping him adapt to normal life back home. Kyle's hero story merits 5 out of 5 Heroes.

The villainy in *American Sniper* is less well-developed than the storytelling and the development of the heroic characters. We aren't given any details about the origins of the enemy army or their motivations. We do witness the slow progression of PTSD in Kyle but there we aren't privy to the details of the disorder's onset, progression, or treatment. This film only paints its villains with minimal brushstrokes and so I can only award the villains a rating of 3 out of 5.

Movie: Villains: Heroes:

American Sniper is not just a great story about a real American hero, but one of the best-made movies we've seen this year. Clint Eastwood spends just the right amount of time in Kyle's backstory so that we understand where he comes from. Then he propels us with Kyle into the special world of being a sniper in Iraq. Kyle's first kill is a small child and we see both the necessity of the act, and the conflict it creates within him. It's a crucial moment in the film and Eastwood captures it skillfully. It's just one of a dozen such well-crafted moments. I give *American Sniper* 5 out of 5 Reels.

Bradley Cooper is unrecognizable as he completely transforms himself by gaining muscle mass and taking on the mannerisms and vocalisms of Kyle. We truly see Chris Kyle on the screen, not Cooper. We're taken on the complete arc of the hero's journey in this movie. We start out with Kyle as a boy being instilled with the heroic values of protecting those weaker than himself. We watch as he becomes a good, then great sniper. And we witness his descent into obsession and affliction with PTSD. Finally, we see him overcome his PTSD and go on to help others. I give Chris Kyle 5 out of 5 Heroes.

There are several villains in this movie. The main villain is the Iraqi bad guys who Kyle is fighting against. We don't see much of them and I get the sense that director Clint Eastwood assumes we know this villain and it needs no introduction. Still, he gives us a sense of the terrorists by showing us The Butcher and Mustafa who are the face of villainy in *American Sniper*. We don't get much of the villain's journey - but that's not what this movie was about. For Kyle to be the hero, it's sufficient to have the mindless evil of terrorism. We're given even less information about the PTSD villain. We see some of its effects on Kyle, but PTSD is not what this movie was about. I can only give 3 out of 5 Villains for the bad guys in *American Sniper*.

Movie:  Villains: Heroes:

Big Eyes

Starring	Amy Adams, Christoph Waltz, Krysten Ritter
Director	Tim Burton
Screenplay	Scott Alexander, Larry Karaszewski
Genre	Biography/Drama
Rated	PG-13
Running Time	106 minutes
Release Date	December 25, 2014
Margaret Keane Protagonist	Single, Positive to More Positive Emotional (Classic Lone Hero)
Walter Keane Antagonist	Single, Negative to more Negative Moral (Irredeemable Deceptive Lone Villain)

(Greg Smith, Founder of Agile Writers of Richmond, VA)

Scott, I thought we were going to see a movie about Big Guys?

(Dr. Scott Allison, Professor of Psychology, University of Richmond)

No, Greg. This movie is about popular paintings of oversized ocular cavities. Let's recap.

We're introduced to divorcee and single mother Margaret (Amy Adams) who draws caricatures for a dollar on the boardwalk. It isn't long before fellow painter and realtor Walter Keane (Christoph Waltz) takes an interest in Margaret's work. She paints waifs with mournful, oversized eyes. Walter and Margaret soon marry and Walter starts selling his own paintings and hers in a local jazz club. Through a misunderstanding, Walter sells one of Margaret's paintings as his own (they are signed "Keane" after all).

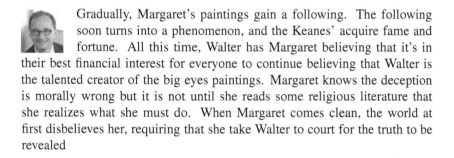

Gradually, Margaret's paintings gain a following. The following soon turns into a phenomenon, and the Keanes' acquire fame and fortune. All this time, Walter has Margaret believing that it's in their best financial interest for everyone to continue believing that Walter is the talented creator of the big eyes paintings. Margaret knows the deception is morally wrong but it is not until she reads some religious literature that she realizes what she must do. When Margaret comes clean, the world at first disbelieves her, requiring that she take Walter to court for the truth to be revealed

Scott, *Big Eyes* is a nice, quiet, engaging look at the artist behind a marketing genius. While the main character is Margaret Keane, it's her evil husband Walter who makes things happen. Undeniably, Margaret is a rare talent. But it isn't until she meets Walter that her art makes an impact on society. Walter is a liar and a cheat. He tries to pass off some French painter's street paintings as his own - and then does the same with Margaret's work. At first Margaret sees Walter as a savior, but as the movie moves along, Walter relegates Margaret to the attic where she hides her work not only from the public, but her own daughter. Margaret begins to take on the appearance of a sweatshop slave with no friends and few acquaintances.

Big Eyes was eye-opening is its portrayal of the subjugation of women prior to the feminist movement of the 1960s. Our hero Margaret finds her life and career constrained by a society that empowers White men at the expense of women. In some ways, I see parallels to *Selma*, another fine movie that we've seen and reviewed this year. Both these movies focus on how a hero goes about achieving justice. Margaret must break down barriers, both societal and personal, that are denying her proper recognition for her work.

The hero story in *Big Eyes* emerges quite nicely. Margaret starts out lacking self-confidence and thus allows herself to be mistreated and taken advantage of by her morally bankrupt husband Walter. She begins to derive strength and chutzpah from her best friend DeeAnn (Krysten Ritter) and from her teenage daughter Jane (Madeleine Arthur). These mentoring figures, along with a pair of evangelicals who arrive at her doorstep at the right time, help Margaret find the courage to stand up for herself. My only quibble is that the movie never shows us the aftermath of Margaret's final courtroom redemption.

I found *Big Eyes* a very paint-by-numbers biopic. While you're right that there is a transformation for our hero, Margaret, it comes from a very strange place - and occurs late in the film. I found it odd that Jehovah's Witnesses were the catalyst for Margaret's decision to finally divorce her husband and petition the courts for her share of their fortune. They are known for their belief that women should be subservient to their husbands, so it was an ironic turn.

The villain in this film is clearly Walter Keane and he undergoes an interesting transformation himself. While he always comes off as a sort of used-car-salesman-type, he seems genuinely caring for Margaret at first. It isn't until his marketing talents bring in millions for the couple that he becomes evil. At one point he threatens Margaret with her life and even attempts to burn her house down. This convinces Margaret that she has to leave the relationship and moves to Hawaii.

At first I thought Walter might be the type of transforming villain who starts out as mildly evil but then grows increasingly evil as time goes on. We've seen this type of evil transformation in an earlier movie from 2014 called *Nightcrawler*. But the scene in which we discover that Walter has faked his paintings of Parisian streets changed my mind about

Walter. It turns out he was a scumbag from the start, but we just didn't know it. Certainly Margaret didn't know it until far too late.

Walter is simply a lone villain with sociopathic tendencies who exploited his wife to achieve his own selfish aims. Perhaps he can be categorized as somewhat of a mysterious villain in that we don't know the extent of his evil ways until the latter half of the film. We don't gain much of an understanding of why Walter is such a lousy schmuck but then this movie isn't about him as much as it is a story of Margaret's transformation from doormat to courageous hero.

Big Eyes is an entertaining movie about an artistic phenomenon of the 1960s. While Amy Adams does a fine job in the role of Margaret Keane, I thought Christoph Waltz really stole the show with his rich interpretation of Walter Keane. This is where art imitates life as it was Walter who overshadowed Margaret in real life. I enjoyed myself in this film, but I don't think I'd get much more from it on a second viewing. I give *Big Eyes* just 3 out of 5 Reels.

Margaret Keane is a quiet hero with not a lot of backbone. We see her transform from an acquiescent, obedient wife to a woman of her own. I was happy to see her overcome her insecurities and realize her self-worth. I give her 3 out of 5 Heroes.

Walter Keane was the more interesting character in my mind. He was colorful, extraverted, and entrepreneurial. There was a lot to admire about his accomplishments. But he gained his wealth and status at the expense of Margaret's talents. He was talentless and built himself up on Margaret's skills. I liked the emergence of Walter's behavior from somewhat shady to downright evil so I give him 4 out of 5 Villains.

Movie: 🎬 Villain: 👿👿👿👿 Hero: 🦸🦸🦸

 Big Eyes is an interesting examination of how easily women could lose their identities and their dignity in the era of male chauvinism and gender inequality. It is also a fine story of a woman's ability to muster up the moral and physical courage to confront male evil and defeat it. This movie is entertaining and features great performances from all involved, particularly Amy Adams. I award this film 4 out of 5 Reels.

As I've noted, the hero story is capably constructed as it features Margaret's transformation from a frightened and exploited sweatshop worker to a fierce social and legal champion of her own rights. The hero journey is not portrayed to the fullest extent yet still merits 4 Heroes out of 5.

The villain Walter Keane is quite a selfish bastard who gets his comeuppance in a final courtroom scene that reveals him to be laughably inept. I enjoyed watching Walter rise in his evil ways and then fall and shatter like Humpty Dumpty. Still, we aren't told much about what made Walter such a douchebag and so I must limit my rating of his villainy to 3 out of 5 Villains.

Movie: ⬤⬤⬤⬤   Villain: 👒👒👒   Hero: ◈◈◈

Birdman

Starring	Michael Keaton, Zach Galifianakis, Edward Norton
Director	Alejandro González Iñárritu
Screenplay	González Iñárritu, Nicolás Giacobone, Alexander Dinelaris, Armando Bo
Genre	Comedy/Drama
Rated	R
Running Time	119 minutes
Release Date	November 14, 2014
Riggan Protagonist	Single, Positive to More Positive Emotional (Classic Lone Hero)
Riggan Antagonist	Single, Positive to More Positive Emotional (Self Villain)

(Dr. Scott Allison, Professor of Psychology, University of Richmond)

Well, Greg, Michael Keaton once played *Batman*. Now he plays *Birdman*.

(Greg Smith, Founder of Agile Writers of Richmond, VA)

It's uncanny the parallels between reality and fantasy in this surreal depiction. Let's recap.

In the opening scene, we meet an aging actor named Riggan Thomson (Michael Keaton) who is levitating in a room while practicing meditation. Riggan once starred in the movies as a superhero named Birdman but he has since fallen on hard times. He is now trying to resurrect his career by writing and starring in his own Broadway play called *What We Talk About When We Talk About Love*. Riggan uses his telekinesis abilities to arrange for a light fixture to fall on the play's co-star who is doing poorly during rehearsals. Riggan and the play's producer (Zach Galifianakis) are now desperate for a name-brand actor to step in and attract an audience.

Enter Mike (Edward Norton), boyfriend to another actor in the play, Lesley (Naomi Watts) who suggests he take the role. Mike is just off another project and needs a job. Riggan is desperate and can use Mike's popularity to boost the attendance. Mike wastes no time changing his lines and giving directorial suggestions - not to mention hitting on Riggan's just-out-of-rehab daughter Sam (Emma Stone). Riggan has a lot on his plate trying to get through the first rehearsal when Mike succumbs to an outburst because Riggan switched his vodka for water. After all, Mike wants everything on stage to be real, and if his character is drunk, so should he be.

Greg, I'll come right out and say it: *Birdman* is one of the year's best films. The movie is probably not for everyone; it is odd, edgy, and stylish. *Birdman* pulls us into the tortured life of our hero Riggan Thomson, grabs us, and never lets go. Director González I/ nárritu's use of continuous, seamless transitions between scenes is partly responsible for the relentless power of this movie. But mostly we're riveted because of the Pulp-Fictionesque intensity of the characters and their dialogue.

Birdman's themes are dripping with irony. Thomson is well-accomplished yet haunted by an inner-emptiness. On Thomson's mirror is a placard that reads, "A thing is a thing, not what people say about the thing." Yet Riggan is obsessed with what fans and critics think of him and he is most known for the Birdman role that hid his true identity. He saves a note that he received many years earlier from a fan who admired his honesty, yet Riggan wears a toupee and acts for a living. The enigmatic subtitle of this film (*The Unexpected Virtue of Ignorance*) hints at the value of self-oblivion, but we're left unsure. This is a movie of such depth that it begs to be seen twice.

Scott, *Birdman* is the type of movie that makes you feel stupid for watching it. There are so many references to the Broadway scene, hidden meanings (like the sign you mentioned), and inward winks to itself that I couldn't really follow what was going on. It was so sly and self-aware that it left me dangling trying to understand what the film-makers were trying to say. Everything was some sort of mystical symbol for something else. Riggan obviously didn't have the ability to levitate or move things with his mind, but there it was. Was it symbolic of something? I don't know. And was he able to fly? There were several scenes where it looked like he could - or at least believed that he could.

And then there's the Birdman character itself that is constantly inside Riggan's head. He's there to expose the doubts that Riggan has about himself. Then later, the Birdman appears to Riggan. The Birdman keeps reminding Riggan that he should have done that *Birdman 4* sequel. This is fine with me, I can follow the symbolism of the Birdman being the voice of doubt for Riggan. But what does it mean when, at the end of the film, Riggan seems free of the voice, but when he looks in the mirror, he sees Birdman taking a shit on the toilet? Is this some sort of high-brow-low-brow commentary? I don't know. It's beyond my capabilities to understand.

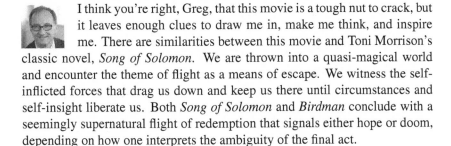

I think you're right, Greg, that this movie is a tough nut to crack, but it leaves enough clues to draw me in, make me think, and inspire me. There are similarities between this movie and Toni Morrison's classic novel, *Song of Solomon*. We are thrown into a quasi-magical world and encounter the theme of flight as a means of escape. We witness the self-inflicted forces that drag us down and keep us there until circumstances and self-insight liberate us. Both *Song of Solomon* and *Birdman* conclude with a seemingly supernatural flight of redemption that signals either hope or doom, depending on how one interprets the ambiguity of the final act.

The villain structure appears to fall under the category of *Man versus Self*. As you mention, Greg, Riggan is haunted by the voice of his alter-ego Birdman and tries, mostly unsuccessfully, to rise above the dark commands of the voice. Earlier in our review of *Whiplash* we observed the villain to be a dark mentor figure, and one could say that Riggan's inner Birdman voice serves as a dark mentor. In this way we have within the same character both a heroic persona and a villainous mentor character.

I think it's more than just a tough nut to crack, I think it's purposely cynical both about the audience and the Hollywood system that will nominate it for an Oscar. This is a very slickly produced story that tries so hard to have meaning that the meaning is lost. Which is exactly what is going on in Riggan's life. He desperately wants the respect of the theater but is still seen as Birdman despite his best efforts.

This is a film that was made for the Hollywood elite to show how much the film-makers understand the inner psyche and problems of Hollywood - how actors are stuck in their roles. But the film is filled with so much introspection that the rest of us are merely along for the ride. In my opinion the purpose of a movie is to entertain the audience, not to share a wink and a nod with your peers. I have no doubt the academy will nominate and possibly even award an Oscar for this film. But for the rest of us, it begs the question: What is this about?

Our hero is a man caught between two worlds. We have his daughter who is telling him that what he really wants to be relevant. But the problem is that none of us is relevant. But then she goes to the extreme and tells him that to be relevant he has to appear on YouTube or Twitter. In other words, get with the times. At the other extreme he's faced with the movie critic who has vowed to kill his play with the swipe of her pen because he's not a legitimate actor, just a celebrity. And "we don't want your kind in our town."

If there is a physical villain here, it might be Mike. He's constantly getting in Riggan's way. Riggan wants to make a play with meaning and Mike keeps telling him to amp-up the reality. I agree with you that Riggan is at war with himself. In the end, he tries to destroy himself, only to create a spectacle that raises him to higher heights. That makes him a redemptive hero.

Birdman is a complex and gripping piece of cinematic art. It is exhilarating, thoughtful, and complex. We are treated to intelligent character exchanges and nimble camera direction. Most notable about *Birdman* are the extraordinary performances from the cast. Keaton and Norton deserve Oscar nods for their portrayal of two men attempting to overcome powerfully neurotic, loveless lives. These are men who dive into the acting profession because it is a reprieve from the facade of reality. The themes of authenticity and flight to freedom sustain our attention and encourage a second visit to the theater. For me, it's a no-brainer awarding this film 5 Reels out of 5.

The character of Riggan Thomson is one of the most memorable characters in the movies in 2014. With the death of Robin Williams earlier this year, we are reminded of how actors use their craft to mask their inner demons. For me, Greg, *Birdman* doesn't wink at us as much as it winces in pain at us. Riggan's journey rings true to me and his flight of triumph at the end suggests a successful end to his heroic journey. Again, I give the highest rating of 5 Heroes out of 5 here.

The Birdman villain residing with Riggan is the semi-human face of one's anchors and limitations. We're not given much backstory about the origins of Riggan's inner demons, but we do know that the our hero is burdened by a ruthless absence of self-worth and self-validation. The dark self-mentor figure residing within Riggan lacks the depth of Riggan himself and thus only earns a respectable 3 Villains out of 5.

Movie: Villain: Hero:

For me I couldn't figure out what I was supposed to follow. It was life-imitating-art-imitating-life in a tight spiral. I wanted to like this film but it just seemed so interested in being clever that I never got a chance to appreciate it. The camera work was great. It appeared to be shot on one unending reel. So, well-done. But if you want me to enjoy myself at the movies, you need to think about me when you make your work. To paraphrase that great philosopher Peter Griffin, *Birdman* insists upon itself. I give it just 3 out of 5 Reels.

Riggan is a tortured hero who is wrestling with real existential demons. He's tormented about his past, and about how he's forever tied to decisions he made as a younger man. While the past is gone, no one will let him move on. And as he looks to the future he realizes that the number of days ahead of him are much fewer than the days past. If ever he's going to do something with his life, now is the time. This is a hero I can appreciate. Riggan gets 5 out of 5 Heroes.

If Riggan is at war with himself then the Birdman inside his head is the manifestation of his inner villain. Birdman torments Riggan mercilessly to the point of insanity. I have to admit I don't know how to rate such a villain. I've already rated the hero a full 5, can I rate his mirror image any less? I don't think so. I award Birdman 5 out of 5 Villains.

Movie: Villain: Hero:

Boyhood

Starring	Ellar Coltrane, Patricia Arquette, Ethan Hawke
Director	Richard Linklater
Screenplay	Richard Linklater
Genre	Drama
Rated	R
Running Time	165 minutes
Release Date	August 15, 2014
Mason Protagonist	Single, Positive to More Positive Emotional/Physical (Classic Lone Heroes)
Alcoholism Antagonist	System, Untransformed Negative (Disease Villain)

(Dr. Scott Allison, Professor of Psychology, University of Richmond)

Greg, we just saw a summer film that is about as different from any other summer movie as we've ever seen.

(Greg Smith, Founder of Agile Writers of Richmond, VA)

Boyhood was made over 12 years with all the same actors. Let's recap...

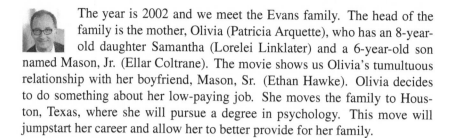

The year is 2002 and we meet the Evans family. The head of the family is the mother, Olivia (Patricia Arquette), who has an 8-year-old daughter Samantha (Lorelei Linklater) and a 6-year-old son named Mason, Jr. (Ellar Coltrane). The movie shows us Olivia's tumultuous relationship with her boyfriend, Mason, Sr. (Ethan Hawke). Olivia decides to do something about her low-paying job. She moves the family to Houston, Texas, where she will pursue a degree in psychology. This move will jumpstart her career and allow her to better provide for her family.

Boyhood follows young Mason from age 6 to 18 in twelve vignettes depicting his life as he grows from boyhood to young manhood. This is not a conventional story. There is no "aha moment" where Mason makes the transition from boy to man. There is no "main goal" for Mason to attempt to acquire. This is the deliberate telling of a young man's life as a series of moments in time.

Strangely, *Boyhood* is a sort of period piece as it chronicles what it is like to be a boy in each of the 12 years the movie was filmed. We're shown the elements of Mason's life that were important at that time. For example, Mason graduates from watching *Dragonball-Z* to playing Gameboy to playing with a Playstation. Normally a filmmaker would have to dig around in the archives of some movie production house for these time-sensitive relics. But for director Richard Linklater, he was simply documenting what was happening at the time he was filming a particular chapter in Mason's life.

Greg, this is a movie that requires patience. There aren't many fascinating moments in this film, and in fact most of the scenes in this movie are depictions of simple moments and mundane details. But that's one of the main points of *Boyhood*. A person' life is an accumulation of many such moments, and they matter. We learn that everyday moments may seem trivial but they may later carry great significance. These simple life snippets pave the way from boyhood to adulthood.

For example, there is one telling scene in which Mason at age 13 is hanging out with a friend and a few older boys at a construction site. The older boys are full of bravado about women and drugs, and they taunt and dare Mason and his friend to partake in their debauchery. The tension in the scene is magnified by them all taking turns violently tossing a blade saw onto a wood plank. Experiences like this are a right of passage for all young men as they test their mettle against their own fears and society's constraints. This is *Boyhood* at its finest.

It's hard to say there are any real villains in this story. Although Mason's mother has a tendency to pick drunk, abusive men for husbands. Mason's stepfathers start out nice enough but fall into the "a**hole" zone pretty quickly.

I have to say that as a one-off movie this is a pretty neat novelty act. Getting a group of actors to regroup year after year to perform scenes together is a logistical marvel. But as a complete story, it leaves something to be desired. *Boyhood* has its place in cinema history, but its message that life is a series of moments took a long time (nearly 3 hours) to tell. Watching the young man transform from a boy to a man was entertaining, yet I can't help but get a feeling of watching home movies rather than a coherent story.

As a family hero ensemble, several themes emerge that are central to their journey. One theme is the importance of redemption in family life. The father, Mason, Sr., is mostly a ne'er-do-well with an almost debilitating immaturity problem. As the years go by, we are surprised by his growing sense of responsibility as a father and later as a husband to his next wife. Similarly, Olivia takes charge of her life and assumes a responsible position as a college professor. Throughout the movie every adult figure seems to be imploring Mason, Jr., to become more responsible, but of course we witness him learning responsibility the hard way, like all of us do, through a series of mistakes. *Boyhood* excels in showing us how redemption and responsibility unfold across the human lifespan.

Alcoholism is a primary villain in this story. The jerks in this story are afflicted with this addiction and behave atrociously toward our family of heroes. One scene in particular is difficult to watch, as it involves Professor Bill (Marco

Perella) behaving abusively while in a drunken rage toward everyone at the dinner table. While we see redemption in many forms in this movie, we never get the sense that anyone overcomes alcoholism. This is a sad lesson of the movie albeit not an unrealistic one.

I enjoyed *Boyhood* but I won't be rushing back to the theater to see it again. It was long and for me held little message. It's an unusual story as it doesn't follow the usual pattern. Which is a refreshing change of pace. Still, I think it is the novelty of this approach to storytelling that is the appeal, and not the story itself. I give *Boyhood* 4 out of 5 Reels.

Mason ends up surprisingly well-adjusted after living a life with a variety of fathers and homes. He's a bit of a zen buddhist in his attitudes toward life. Despite all the advice to be responsible, he is in fact among the most responsible people in the movie. He settles on photography as a passion and has little interest in his scholastic assignments - yet he goes to college to study art. He's very much an ordinary young man by the end of the story. His arc is a long one and comes to a nice completion point. I give Mason 4 out of 5 Heroes.

The villains in the story are of the type we might encounter every day. As Scott points out, the men in the story give Mason little guidance and a lot of reasons to become a problem child. Still Mason overcomes these villains. Unlike most of the villains we see in the movies, these villains are not complicated puppeteers. And they're not intrinsically bad. We get some background to them and we see where their villainy comes from. I give them 4 out of 5 Villains.

Movie: Villain: Hero:

Boyhood is a remarkable cinematic achievement for the way it patiently portrays a family's dramatic story unfold over the course of a dozen years. There are no cheap thrills, fancy CGI effects, or scintillating costuming here. There are only real emotions, real family crises, real tears, and moving moments of redemption. We see not just a boy grow up but an entire family blossom, leading me to wonder why this movie isn't called *Family* or *Familyhood*. I admired this film greatly and give it 4 Reels out of 5.

The heroes were an impressive group of people who took punches, rolled with them, grew nicely, and became better people as the result of their heartaches. There is plenty of growth, mentoring, loving, crying, mending, and healing. In short, *Boyhood* has just about every aspect of the hero's journey, and each aspect is depicted with searing realism. I believe these heroes deserve 5 Heroes out of 5.

There are a few detestable people that our heroes must navigate through on their journey, and the worst of the characters are afflicted with alcoholism. *Boyhood*'s depiction of alcoholism is a by-the-numbers stereotype of the disease and offered an incomplete view of its progression. The addiction and its effect on the men in Olivia's life could have been better fleshed out, and as a result I limit my rating here to 3 Villains out of 5.

Movie: Villain: Hero:

Captain America: The Winter Soldier

Starring	Chris Evans, Samuel L. Jackson, Scarlett Johansson
Director	Anthony Russo, Joe Russo
Screenplay	Christopher Markus, Stephen McFeely
Genre	Action/Adventure/Science-Fiction
Rated	PG-13
Running Time	136 minutes
Release Date	April 4, 2014
Captain America Protagonist	Single, Untransformed Positive Moral (Untransformed Lone Hero)
Pierce/Brock Antagonist	Duo, Negative to more Negative Moral (Irredeemable Mastermind/Henchman Villains)
Winter Soldier Antagonist	Single, Untransformed Negative Moral (Untransformed Henchman Villain)

(Greg Smith, Founder of Agile Writers of Richmond, VA)

Well, Scott, it's our patriotic duty to review *Captain America: The Winter Soldier*.

(Dr. Scott Allison, Professor of Psychology, University of Richmond)

It's going to be hard writing a review with my right hand over my heart and the other hand saluting. But I'll give it an All-American try.

We meet our intrepid hero, Steve Rogers (aka Captain America played by Chris Evans) running laps around newcomer Sam Wilson (Anthony Mackie). The two exchange army stories and Rogers is driven off by beautiful spy-woman Natasha Romanoff (aka Black Widow played by Scarlett Johansson). Rogers rushes away to a mission where he and Romanoff rescue hostages on a S.H.I.E.L.D. secret ship. Along the way they pick up a thumb drive of super secret information.

Back at S.H.I.E.L.D. headquarters, Rogers confronts director Nick Fury (Samuel L. Jackson) about being kept in the dark about Black Widow's separate mission. Fury is later ambushed by a formidable masked soldier (Sebastian Stan) who appears to kill Fury. Using data from the thumbdrive, Rogers and Romanoff discover a vast underground bunker containing the intelligent e-remains of Arnim Zola (Toby Jones), who reveals a vast evil operation inside S.H.I.E.L.D. that has badly compromised the organization.

Scott *The Winter Soldier* delivers a fast-paced, action packed sequel to 2011's *Captain America: The First Avenger.* Not only was it a great action movie, but it also had an interesting take on modern-day warfare. You see, Nick Fury and S.H.I.E.L.D. director Alexander Pierce (Robert Redford) are building these mega-drones which are designed to pre-emptively kill anyone S.H.I.E.L.D. deems is a threat. If it sounds a bit like our drone program and President Obama's "kill list," that's no accident. Writers Marcus and McFeely were aiming at just that.

Fury tries to read the thumb drive Romanoff acquired and finds it has been encrypted by S.H.I.E.L.D. itself - which makes Fury think that S.H.I.E.L.D. has been compromised. After the attempt on his life, Fury makes his way back to Rogers' apartment and hands the device over to him and warns him not to trust anyone. Then Fury dies. Now the race is on for Rogers and Romanoff to discover who killed Fury, what is on the thumb drive, and who is the mole inside S.H.I.E.L.D.

I agree, Greg. This movie is a winner. *Captain America: The Winter Soldier* is a good movie on several different levels. First, the casting is as rock solid as Steve Roger's biceps, with Samuel L. Jackson, Scarlett Johansson, Chris Evans, and Robert Redford all charismatically bringing their characters to life. While the hero story itself is not terribly standout, the villain tale may be the best we've seen this year. In fact, from where I stand, the villain story carries the movie.

I don't mean to disrespect Captain America; he is a stalwart hero. Rogers is more than worthy of the hero label, embodying every single trait in the great eight attributes of heroes - he is *smart, strong, resilient, reliable, caring, selfless, charismatic*, and *inspiring*. Ironically, this perfection may also be Captain America's weakness. There is no room for development or transformation in his character, and we know that hero transformation is the quintessential characteristic of a good hero.

Rogers is working on some demons of his own, Scott. He's still not at home in the new millenium. He feels uncomfortable in his soft bed and is still getting the hang of the internet. He confides these feelings to new friend Sam Wilson who is a war veteran and runs a local Veterans Administration support group. While Rogers is every bit the hero, he can still be vulnerable. In fact, Romanoff keeps trying to set him up with co-workers back at S.H.I.E.L.D, but Rogers isn't ready. In many ways, he's still the embodiment of a 1940's corn-bred, down-home, American boy. So, there's room for growth. But I have to agree, he's pretty much fully-formed as a hero.

We've seen this in other hero stories from Marvel as well. We reviewed last year's *The Wolverine* and *Thor: The Dark World* and noted that episodic heroes rarely make gains in the personal development area. We need our heroes to return to us at the end of the story quite as we found them at the beginning. This way we know what we're getting when we return next time.

There were other supporting heroes in this movie as well. And kudos to the actors as well as the writers and directors for giving everyone equal screen time. Black Widow is just as kick-ass in this installment as in 2011's *The Avengers*. Scott, we're always looking for great female heroes and Black Widow doesn't disappoint. Although she's not Rogers' physical equal, she's plenty strong and very smart. Also, newcomer Sam Wilson emerges as Falcon. I'm looking forward to seeing more of him in Marvel's universe.

 Greg, you're absolutely right that we have a stellar ensemble cast here. Somehow, despite the fact that there are a multitude of characters, the movie smoothly takes all the complex pieces and weaves a coherent tale that never leaves us confused. This is excellent filmmaking and directors Anthony and Joe Russo deserve great kudos.

Best of all, the film weaves a complex and multi-layered tale of villainy. I detected three very different types of villains, and each one of them was fun to watch. First, we once again encounter a mastermind-muscle pairing with Alexander Pierce as the mastermind and Brock (Frank Grillo) as his goon who carries out the dirty work. Second, Pierce plays the role of the *insider* or *defector* villain, who unexpectedly defects from the side of good and becomes a villain. In my second book on heroes, we call this a *transposed* hero-villain character.

Third, there is the villain who doesn't voluntarily defect from the good guys but who is captured and brainwashed into becoming a villain. The *brainwashed* villain here is Bucky Barnes, and he follows the usual pattern of snapping out of his brainwashed state by clever reverse psychology from the hero Steve Rogers. In what is perhaps the most emotionally moving scene in the film, Rogers is about to be beaten to death by Barnes and invokes their relationship loyalty as a reason why Barnes should finish him off. This is a powerful scene.

Good observations on the villains, Scott. I also detected the hidden villain in the form of Dr. Zola. We saw this in this year's *Ride Along* and *Non-Stop*. He is hardly seen in the traditional sense but was pulling levers the whole time. He also gets credit for the usual "Evil Gloating" trope in this film as he explains where everything comes from and how S.H.I.E.L.D. was corrupted.

We do see the mastermind-muscle villain pair quite a lot in movies. *The Grand Budapest Hotel* had that one too. It seems pretty popular with filmmakers to have a villain who doesn't like to get his hands dirty but sends others to do his dirty work. Interestingly, we don't see that pattern among heroes. Usually the hero is front and center with the action. Even in *The Winter Soldier*, Nick Fury sends others to do his bidding, but he is plenty active in this film.

Captain America: The Winter Soldier is an entertaining movie that is more than mere mindless fun. The movie has layered, complex relationships among its characters, and it features some of the most well-developed villain characters that we've seen in the movies in a long time. *The Winter Soldier* is a film that I'd see twice, which is high praise coming from a guy who is rarely impressed with comic book superhero flicks. The movie comes close to earning all 5 Reels but falls just short. I give it 4 out of 5 Reels.

As I've noted, our hero Steve Rogers is pretty darn perfect from start to finish. He's a terrific character, a man caught out of time but who manages to morally outshine everyone he encounters in the modern era. Because I don't see a whole lot of character transformation, I can only award the good Captain a respectable 3 Heroes out of 5.

The villains carry this movie and give it some unexpected heft and depth. I saw 3 villain types and Greg observed a 4th as well. I applaud any movie that intuitively knows that audiences thirst for an understanding of evil almost as much as they do an appreciation for good. I give all these terrific villains a rating of 4 Villains out of 5.

Movie: Heroes:  Villains:

I agree, to a point. *Captain America* doesn't let up on the action and the all-star cast was well-played. I *did* see it again and enjoyed it even more the second time around. I give *Captain America: The Winter Soldier* 4 out of 5 Reels as well.

I liked Steve Rogers more than you did, Scott. I agree that he is a pretty well-stacked hero character from the beginning. He measures really well on your Great Eight scale. And I saw dimensionality in his relationships that we don't often see in super heroes. I give Steve Rogers 4 out of 5 Heroes.

I have to disagree with your villain rating. These were good villains, but not great. We got a variety of villainy but these are the same villains we've seen before. Little backstory, little dimension. We have yet to see a villain that transforms. But I predict that by the end of the summer one or two Marvel films will have more deep villains worthy of your high praise. I can only give these bad guys 3 out of 5 Villains.

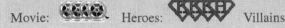

Movie: Heroes: Villains:

Dawn of the Planet of the Apes

Starring	Gary Oldman, Keri Russell, Andy Serkis
Director	Matt Reeves
Screenplay	Mark Bomback, Rick Jaffa, Amanda Silver
Genre	Action/Drama/Science-Fiction
Rated	PG-13
Running Time	130 minutes
Release Date	July 11, 2014
Caesar & Malcolm Protagonist	Duo, Positive to More Positive Moral (Classic Divergent Heroes)
Koba, Dreyfus Antagonist	Single, Untransformed Negative Moral (Untransformed Lone Villains)

(Greg Smith, Founder of Agile Writers of Richmond, VA)

Well Scott, here comes another performance capture movie starring Andy Serkis. It truly looks like he's playing another Sirkis animal!

(Dr. Scott Allison, Professor of Psychology, University of Richmond)
Sirkis is chimply marvelous in this role. Let's recap.

It's been ten years since Caesar (Andy Serkis), the genetically modified chimp from *Rise of the Planet of the Apes* escaped into the forests of San Francisco. A lot has happened. There was an outbreak of simian flu that decimated humanity leaving only a handful of humans who were genetically immune to the disease. Meanwhile, Caesar has freed hundreds of apes from human captivity and taught them to communicate by sign language. They've created an entire culture separate from the humans. Then, one day, a human named Carver (Kirk Acevedo) in search of a hydroelectric dam happens upon a couple of apes and he shoots one of them.

 Caesar warns the humans never to venture into ape territory again. But the humans need to get the dam operational to regain electrical power. They send Malcolm (Jason Clarke), his wife Ellie (Keri Russell), and a few others, including Carver, to negotiate access to the dam. Caesar agrees, but only if the group gives up their guns. Carver hides a gun and threatens Caesar's infant son with it, causing an uproar that is only quelled by Ellie's willingness to provide medical treatment to Caesar's wife. Meanwhile, an ape named Koba (Toby Kebbell), who will not accept any peace with the humans, sabotages relations between the two groups by secretly setting fire to the ape settlement and attempting to assassinate Caesar.

Scott, this was a much better film than 2011's *Rise of the Planet of the Apes*. There were some real personalities here and some real conflict. We see two sets of characters at play - the humans and the apes. On the side of the humans we have Malcolm who wants peace with the apes. On the other side is Caesar who looks at the dam agreement as their one chance for peace with the humans.

But both sides have their hawks as well. The humans have Dreyfus (Gary Oldman) who is so mistrustful of the apes that he starts hoarding weapons. This, of course, inflames the ape Koba (Toby Kebbell) who has reason to distrust humans as he was the victim of experiments at the hands of human scientists. This creates a great conflict both between human and ape as well as between hawks and doves.

Sadly, Keri Russell isn't given much to do here except "stand by her man." And the female chimp (Caesar's wife) does little more than give birth and get sick. Apparently, the future is still male-dominated.

Dawn of the Planet of the Apes is a complex film. Admittedly, it does have some of the telltale signs of a summer blockbuster - flying bullets, daredevil stunts, and plenty of explosions. But these superficial trappings of summer popcorn bely the true meaty core of this very measured and thoughtful movie. *Dawn of the Planet of the Apes* made me *think*, and it's been a long time since I've had to really turn my brain on at the movies.

First and foremost, this is a movie about the very real and very demanding challenges of resolving intergroup conflict. We learn that sometimes good leadership isn't enough. There must also be good *followership* in that a critical mass of people being led need to be on board with the vision of an effective leader. As you point out, Greg, we have peace-loving leadership on both sides but only a few bad apples can undermine all the good intentions.

The hero structure looks like (what we describe in our book *Reel Heroes: Volume 1*) a divergent duo. They start out as separate characters, opposed to working together. But with time, they form a bond. They work together toward a common goal. During this period they are buddy heroes. But in the end, they go their separate ways. Destiny has played its hand and humans and apes cannot be friends - war is their ultimate demise.

Good call on the heroes in this movie being divergent heroes, Greg. I'm beginning to believe that divergent hero stories are my favorite kind of stories because they provide two separate hero tales for the price of one. Often, the two separate hero journeys become intertwined in surprising ways. Last year's *Philomena* comes to mind, for example. In *Dawn of the Planet of the Apes*, Caesar and Malcolm are wise and well-intentioned, yet they are brought down by forces beyond their control that rage all around them. The joy of the movie is watching how our two heroes act on their virtuous characteristics, and how they respond to the treachery of their sidekicks.

One of my beefs with this movie centers on the character of Carver. *Dawn of the Planet of the Apes* begins with Carver needlessly shooting one of the apes. He's a racist hothead who should never have been chosen to go on the expedition in the first place, and yet, inexplicably, he's chosen *again* to accompany Malcolm on the trip to repair the dam. Surely there are more even-keeled and reasonable alternatives to Carver. Yes, we need Carver's misbehavior to help add dramatic tension, but it stretched the bounds of believability for me.

I have to agree with you on that. I was really impressed with the quality of the CGI in this film. There's a point where Caesar and Malcolm touch foreheads and you cannot see any dividing line between them. Caesar's hair becomes matted down by Malcolm's head. It's simply amazing. And the full articulation of the facial features is wonderful. This is an order of magnitude better than the original Gollum character that Sirkis created for *Lord of the Rings*.

The villains in this story are driven by their fear - the heroes are driven by their vision. It's a compelling difference to watch. As you point out, Carver is the bigot who cannot see past the limitations of stereotypes he's been taught. Koba, the hawkish ape, has been harmed so badly by humans that he cannot see past his pain. And Dreyfus is intent on saving what's left of humanity. He doesn't have the space to work toward a peaceable trust. This was an interesting collection of villains, with just enough depth to make them interesting.

 What I appreciate most about the heroes and villains in this movie is the fact that they exist on both sides of the dispute. There are ape heroes and ape villains. And there are human heroes and human villains. This film could have taken the easy route and made one side all good and the other side all bad, but it decided that nuance and realism were more important than the usual oversimplification we see at the movies.

I also appreciate the complex motives that drive the villainous behavior. Besides the usual racist ethnocentrism, there is fear that drives both sides to aggress against the other. There is also the bitter memory of past oppression, which fuels Koba's hatred of humanity. And finally there is pure ignorance. The humans underestimate ape intelligence, and the apes underestimate human goodness. Again, this film really nails the genesis of intergroup conflict.

Dawn of the Planet of the Apes is an intelligent and intelligently crafted science fiction thriller that examines the heart of war. At 130 minutes long, it tested my attention in places. However, it is the best of the *Apes* franchise and I give it a hearty 4 out of 5 Reels.

The heroes in this story are interesting and deeply drawn. The emotive power of Sirkis' Caesar was simply amazing and helped to tell the full story. The duo/divergent heroes is a pattern we've seen before, but played especially well here. I give Malcolm and Caesar 4 out of 5 Heroes.

Finally, the villains were not as strong as the heroes. Carver plays the typical purely bad guy. Koba is at least given a decent backstory to motivate his hatred. Dreyfus as the leader of the humans will do whatever he can to ensure the survival of his people, but is too blind to see the larger picture. I wish the villains were as detailed as the heroes, so I give them only 3 out of 5 Villains.

Movie: Villains: Heroes:

 Greg, we're on the same page on two of the three ratings. *Dawn of the Planet of the Apes* is a refreshing reprieve from the usual summer mindless popcorn fare that infects movie theaters. This film is a thought-provoking look at human conflict, how it begins, how hard it is to avoid, and how difficult it is to stop once it has started. Yes, this movie reeks of patriarchy, and once again the limited role of women in a Hollywood film is disappointing. Still, I enjoyed this movie very much and give it 4 out of 5 Reels.

Our two divergent heroes are a joy to watch, not just because they time and again show wisdom and compassion, but because their journeys are arduous and realistic. Are they transformed by their journeys? Yes, and in profound ways. Caesar has certainly learned the true value of family and friends, and he pays a dear price for holding naive views of ape goodness and human trustworthiness. Like you, I'll give our pair of heroes 4 out of 5 Heroes.

We disagree about the villains, Greg. Most movies devote little time to fleshing out the details of villains' motives and backstory. With Koba, we see the origins of evil; the past torturing of Koba may not justify his actions but it makes them understandable. The human leader, Dreyfus, also has a history and set of motivations that leave us understanding his aggressive behavior but not condoning it. The villains here are complex and fascinating. I'm happy to give them a full 5 out of 5 Villains.

Movie: Villains: Heroes:

Deliver Us From Evil

Starring	Eric Bana, Édgar Ramírez, Olivia Munn
Director	Scott Derrickson
Screenplay	Scott Derrickson, Paul Harris Boardman
Genre	Crime/Horror/Thriller
Rated	R
Running Time	118 minutes
Release Date	July 2, 2014
Sarchie & Mendoza Protagonist	Duo, Positive to More Positive Emotional (Classic Buddy Heroes)
Satan Antagonist	Single, Untransformed Negative Moral (Untransformed Pure Evil Mastermind Villain)

(Greg Smith, Founder of Agile Writers of Richmond, VA)
Scott, I was afraid I'd want to be delivered from this film. But it wasn't bad.

(Dr. Scott Allison, Professor of Psychology, University of Richmond)
There were some bad odors, Greg. Straight from the bowels of hell. Let's recap.

We're introduced to Bronx Police Officer Sarchie (Eric Bana) and his partner Butler (Joel McHale). The duo are investigating a strange event at the zoo. A woman has thrown her child into the moat surrounding the lion's pit. A strange hooded man (Sean Harris) is painting the walls of the pit when Sarchie gives chase. The man escapes but not before he sicks the lions on Sarchie.

 Sarchie escapes harm and discovers that the hooded man, named Santini, was painting over the same kind of cryptic Latin writing that was found at another crime scene. Sarchie meets an unconventional Catholic priest named Mendoza (Édgar Ramírez) who has spent years hunting down violent demonic spirits at work in the city. Skeptical at first, Sarchie ultimately becomes convinced, and he teams with Mendoza in hunting down and expelling the malevolent spirit that has taken over Santini's body.

Scott, I'm not a fan of horror movies. I find they use cheap tricks to pull you in and then throw things into your face (in 3D, quite literally). They are all about shock value and appeal to the basic fears we all tuck away inside our reptilian brain. I just don't find that entertaining.

But *Deliver Us From Evil* really had me in its grip right from the beginning. It is based on Sarchie's actual experiences on the streets of New York City which makes it all the more compelling. Unlike last year's *The Conjuring*, *Deliver Us* is a smart and compelling story that makes the unbeliever think twice about dismissing the demonic world.

 I agree, Greg, that *Deliver Us From Evil* is a more effective horror movie than last year's *The Conjuring*. There are several things working in its favor, and chief among them are stellar performances by Bana and Ramírez, an unlikely pairing with great chemistry. Their terrific acting delivers us from boredom, which is the worst kind of evil for us movie critics.

This film also scores high on the creep-o-meter scale. Yes, there are the usual assortment of cheap frights and false scares, but there are enough meaty, gruesome chills and thrills to keep us in terrific suspense. *Deliver Us From Evil* knows how to yank our chain in all the right ways.

Oh yeah, like the corpse that was found behind a wall that had been sitting there for two weeks. It was all full of gruesome flies and maggots - perfectly hideous.

I compare all horror movies to the classic *The Exorcist* and the two films shared many features in common. There was the little girl that was stalked by evil demons. There was the unlikely priest who specialized in demonic possession. An evil demon that just couldn't leave people alone. And a great exorcism in the end.

Eric Bana performed well as the NYC cop with a Jersey accent. He starts out as a skeptic and is slowly turned into believer. He's a tortured soul with a deep secret that will be his undoing as the demon can use it against him. He's a good hero character as he lives to protect and serve not just the people of New York, but also his little family. While he has a partner in the form of police officer Butler, this is more of a Hero and Sidekick affair rather than a buddy cop film. In fact, Mendoza (the priest) works out as the Mentor, leading Sarchie around the special world of demons and possession. Ultimately, though, it looks like Mendoza graduates from his Mentor role into one of the buddy.

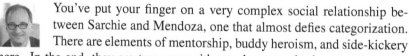

You've put your finger on a very complex social relationship between Sarchie and Mendoza, one that almost defies categorization. There are elements of mentorship, buddy heroism, and side-kickery here. In the end, they are two men with equal status who have complementary strengths – Sarchie is the law enforcement expert while Mendoza has the PhD in demonology. In this movie, Sarchie assumes more of the primary hero role, and he in fact is the one who undergoes the greatest transformation on his journey here.

The villains in *Deliver Us From Evil* are an interesting assortment of hellish henchmen of Satan, or of one of Satan's main operatives. In other reviews of movies released in 2014, we've discussed a common pattern of villainy that features a central mastermind villain who outsources his evil tasks to underlings who do all the dirty work. This film appears to follow that same pattern, as poor Santino and two other characters are compelled by devilish forces to perform horrific acts. There isn't a lot of depth to the villains in this movie, nor is there much backstory. Still, they are effective in their own bloodthirsty way.

I liked that the demon in this film is not always an unseen evil. Santino's possession gives us something to focus on as the villain in the story. But as you point out, there isn't much depth here. I don't think they ever even named the demon - only that it came from Iraq.

As I said, I was pleasantly surprised by this film. It had more characterization than other films of the genre and the acting was pretty good. I can happily give it 3 out of 5 Reels for keeping me interested and a little grossed out without stepping over the line that makes most horror films look ridiculous.

The hero is nicely molded here. He's a good cop and a good father who is stretched to his limits. He has a dark backstory and a strong desire to do right. He overcomes his past transgressions and is redeemed in the end. A very nice hero's journey that I can give 3 out of 5 Heroes.

The villain is pretty nasty and performs as the typical mastermind/puppeteer that we see in most films these days. We don't get much detail about why the demons exist or what their goals are - they're just evil. This is a pretty unidimensional evil and I award just 2 Villains out of 5 for the possessed Santini.

Movie: ●●● Villain: Hero:

Deliver Us From Evil delivers exactly what you'd expect – a scary, creepy story of demonic possession that derives much of its appeal from the claim that it is based on a true story. There's not a lot of new ground broken here, but I was captivated by the outstanding performances of our two unlikely buddy heroes and by the strong "ick" factor in several scenes involving various gooey bodily fluids. Like you, Greg, I believe that this film deserves 3 solid Reels out of 5.

The complex relationship between our two heroes is fun to watch, as each brings different strengths to the game and grow in their interdependence. With help from Mendoza, Sarchie's heroic transformation unfolds before our eyes and is absolutely necessary for him to crack the case. The heroes are a commendable pairing, thus producing a rating of 3 Heroes out of 5.

As you point out, Greg, the villain here isn't developed terribly well or with much depth, but then again we neither expect nor want a movie that delves into Satan's childhood woes that led to his evil lifestyle. All we really crave is for Satan to behaviorally manifest his bad-ass ways, which this movie allows him to do with gory flair. A rating of 2 Villains out of 5 seems about right here.

Movie: Villain: Hero:

Divergent

Starring	Shailene Woodley, Theo James, Ashley Judd
Director	Neil Burger
Screenplay	Evan Daugherty, Vanessa Taylor
Genre	Action/Adventure/Science-Fiction
Rated	PG-13
Running Time	139 minutes
Release Date	March 21, 2014
Triss Protagonist	Single, Positive to More Positive Emotional/Physical (Classic Lone Hero)
Jeanine Antagonist	Single, Negative to more Negative Moral (Hidden Irredemable Villain)
Eric Antagonist	Single, Untransformed Negative Moral (Untransformed Lone Villain)
Peter Antagonist	Single, Positive to Negative Moral (Fallen Villain)

(Greg Smith, Founder of Agile Writers of Richmond, VA)

It's time for our weekly diversion and review *Divergent*.

(Dr. Scott Allison, Professor of Psychology, University of Richmond)

It's great that we can converge to review *Divergent*.

We're introduced to 16-year-old Beatrice (Triss) Prior (Shailene Woodley) who lives in dystopian Chicago. In the future, all Chicagoans are divided into 5 factions: Abnegation (selfless), Amity (kind), Candor (honest), Erudite (intelligent) and Dauntless (brave). Beatrice is a member of the Abnegation and she has come of age and must choose which faction she will live in for the rest of her life. She takes a simulation test which is supposed to tell her which faction she is most inclined to. The problem is, her test is inconclusive. This is unheard of. Everyone is supposed to be aligned with one faction or another. People who are not aligned are called "Divergent." And Divergents are the most feared of people because they can think for themselves.

 As a Divergent, Beatrice is in danger. The Erudite are attempting to gain control of the city and are intent on exterminating all Divergents. At the choosing ceremony, Beatrice opts to become a member of the Dauntless and must prove herself worthy of this warrior group in a series of grueling initiation tests. Her first step toward redefining herself is to assume the name 'Triss'. She then must overcome a cruel bully leader of the Dauntless (Jai Courtney) and then must take steps to hide her Divergent status from the head Erudite, Jeanine (Kate Winslet), who is on a ruthless quest to seize the leadership role from the Abnegation.

Scott, I had read the book this movie is based upon. It was over 480 pages in length and took me 11 hours to listen to the audiobook. I was concerned that the movie wouldn't be able to do justice to the book. I was pleased that the movie was actually better than the book in many ways. The book spends about 75% of the story focused on the initiation of Triss into the Dauntless. The movie balanced the beginning, middle, and end.

Having said that, I found the story to be derivative of other stories we've seen on the big screen in recent years. The division of society into basic groupings was used in the Harry Potter series where the students were divided into four houses: Gryffindor, Hufflepuff, Ravenclaw, and Slytherin - each with its own personality. In *The Hunger Games* Katniss' country of Panem was divided into 13 Districts - each with its own speciality. This division into and belonging to a group is prevalent in Young Adult novels and movies.

 Greg, I was impressed by *Divergent*. The movie manages to capture the most appealing elements of both *Hunger Games* and *Enders Game*. These two films, along with *Divergent*, feature a strong young hero who is thrust into a dark world run by corrupt elders. The young hero must pass arduous tests and harrowing simulations. The neophyte hero then encounters real hazards that require an abundance of guts, grit, and resourcefulness to overcome. Underdog stories such as these have a natural, universal allure.

Shailene Woodley is outstanding in her role as Triss, a young woman on a voyage of self-discovery. I found her character to have far more depth and nuance than Katniss in *Hunger Games*. Triss spends this movie trying to reconcile others' expectations of her with her own quest for self-knowledge and self-growth. There is everything one would want in a hero journey here. Triss attracts allies among the Dauntless and is mentored by both her mother and Four (Theo James), who also serves as a love interest. Challenges both physical and intellectual in nature are met and resolved in sometimes surprising ways. The hero journey is packed to delicious satisfaction.

The world Triss lives in is more interesting to me. The five factions seem to represent the five divisions of society. The Abnegation serve the factionless (aka homeless). They are the politicians and public servants. The Amity represent the workers, Candor are the legal entity, Erudite are the academics and Dauntless represent the police and military.

Triss let me down as a hero. When compared to Katniss we find that she is constantly relying on the beneficence of others, namely her love interest Four. When she's in trouble, he comes to her rescue. Katniss, on the other hand was constantly saving Peeta from his demise. While it's true that Triss took initiative, she never really overcame her fears. On the contrary, her "special power" is that she is fearless already. I grant you that Triss is on a journey of self-discovery, but that is true of most young adult heroes. Triss offers nothing special in that regard.

Au contraire, Greg, I could be wrong but I believe that Triss saves Four's life as many times as he saves her's. There is one particular brilliant scene toward the end of the movie that stands out. Four has been brainwashed to attack and kill Triss, who ingeniously realizes that the only way to save them both is to point the gun at herself with Four's finger on the trigger. She forces Four to look her in the face, when she knows he cannot fire the gun, and in this way she spares her own life while snapping him out of his hypnotic state. It's a daring move and is quite possibly the most powerful scene in the movie.

There is great chemistry between Triss and Four, with far more sizzle than we see with Katniss and Peeta in *The Hunger Games*. I'm not sure I can disagree with you about her journey of self-discovery being all-too common in movies about young adult heroes. With youth comes naivete and it could be argued that it's a tiresome missing quality in youthful heroes. But this science fiction setting puts a unique and refreshing spin on this journey. I enjoyed it considerably.

There were a handful of villain characters in this movie, too. First was Eric (Jai Courtney) the drill sergeant of the Dauntless. He was intent on driving out any weakling initiate and he didn't care if they died in the process. Another was Peter (Miles Teller), the over-zealous initiate who would do anything to rise to the top of rankings. Finally, there was

Jeanine, the leader of the Erudite who was driven to take over the Dauntless and destroy the Abnegation.

I think we see three distinct types of villain here. Jeanine is very much the "invisible" villain we've seen in other films. She really doesn't have much to do in the main flow of the movie, but is revealed in the end to be very corrupt. Like the villains we've seen in *Non-Stop* and *Ride Along*, she exposes her evil plot to the audience in the climax of the film. Eric represents the "clear and present" villain - one who is constantly in the face of the hero and the one the hero has to deal with. We saw this in *3 Days to Kill* and *Jack Ryan: Shadow Recruit*. Finally, Peter represents the villain within the group. This is the arch rival in such films as last year's *Ender's Game*.

 Good observation about the layerings of the villains, Greg. The head villain, Jeanine, is in some ways a strong character but in other ways she seems to disappoint. Her strength lies in her believability; Jeanine's motives are not entirely evil although they are certainly grossly misguided. Her cold-heartedness is almost understandable given the rigidity of the system of which she is a product. It pains me to say that at the ripe old age of 38, Kate Winslet is cast to play a misguided elder of her society, a symbol of an archaic system that brainwashes and brutalizes its young.

Although I admire this aspect of Jeanine's villainy, I was left disappointed with the one-dimensionality of her character. We are never told of her backstory, and in fact we know little about her other than she is willing to commit Abnegation genocide in order to raise her faction's ruling power. Winslet does the best she can with her character but has little to work with. It seems this is the plight of the villain in most movies they have the depth of cardboard and meander in the film's periphery until it is time for the hero to topple them.

I found *Divergent* to be a nice diversion but lacked the coherence of the film it will be forever compared to: *The Hunger Games*. It was longish at 2 hours and 20 minutes - necessary to encompass the origin story and dispatching the villain. The screenwriters were challenged to pack everything in the book into the movie. However, they made some excellent choices in reducing the complexity of the book. I give *Divergent* 3 out of 5 Reels.

Triss was a good hero for her growth and depicting the angst of young adults trying to fit in both in society and within a social group. I thought she lacked the kind of independence I'd like to see in a young female hero. Even in the end of the movie she needed help from Four to climb onto her escape train. I give her 3 out of 5 Heroes.

I liked the multiple levels of villains in this story. While we have yet to see a fully formed complex villain character this year, I enjoyed watching Triss deal with Peter as a peer villain, Eric as the leader-villain, and Jeanine as the omnipresent invisible villain. I give them 3 out of 5 Villains.

Movie: Hero: Villain:

 Divergent offers a fun and psychologically rich story about a young woman's journey toward self-discovery and self-actualization. This movie sends us into a fascinating world that lumps its citizens into oversimplified categories that fulfill rigid social roles. Once again we have a story along the lines of the *Hunger Games* that questions a societal status quo that permits and encourages human suffering and injustices. I enjoyed *Divergent* and recommend it very much. I give it 4 Reels out of 5.

The hero story was outstanding for many of the reasons I've already stated. Triss starts out uncertain of her self-identity and is forced by circumstances to undergo a satisfying personal transformation. By the film's end, she knows her place in the world and how she can engineer positive social change. In addition, her journey contains all the relevant stages of the mythic hero journey. I award Triss 5 Heroes out of 5.

Once again, the villains were a significant notch (or two) below the heroes in their depth and quality. They did fulfill the function of a good villain but didn't particularly stir me with their personalities or backstories. A month from now, I probably won't remember them at all. For this reason I'll give them a mere 2 Villains out of 5.

Movie: Hero:  Villain:

Draft Day

Starring	Kevin Costner, Chadwick Boseman, Jennifer Garner
Director	Ivan Reitman
Screenplay	Scott Rothman, Rajiv Joseph
Genre	Drama/Sports
Rated	R
Running Time	109 minutes
Release Date	April 11, 2014
Weaver Protagonist	Single, Untransformed Positive Moral (Untransformed Lone Hero)
Weaver Antagonist	Single, Untransformed Positive Moral (Untransformed Self Villain)

(Dr. Scott Allison, Professor of Psychology, University of Richmond)

Greg, it feels a little cold in this room.

(Greg Smith, Founder of Agile Writers of Richmond, VA)

Well shut the door to stop the draft. It's time to review *Draft Day*. Let's recap.

It's the day of the 2014 NFL draft, and Cleveland Browns general manager Sonny Weaver (Kevin Costner) has the 7th pick in the first round. The Seattle Seahawks have the first pick and are expected to draft the highly heralded hotshot quarterback Bo Callahan (Josh Pence). Seattle's general manager contacts Weaver and offers Cleveland it's first round pick but the price is too high and Weaver declines. Soon Weaver's boss, Browns' owner Anthony Molina (Frank Langella) pressures Weaver to make a big "splash" with the draft pick, hinting that he'd welcome Callahan to the fold.

So Sonny calls the Seahawks back and takes the deal. He isn't sure about the deal and sets his staff to investigate Callahan's background. Meanwhile, Sonny's girlfriend Ali Parker (Jennifer Garner) (who is also on the Browns staff as a lawyer) reveals that she is pregnant with his child. This being the biggest day of the football year, Sonny isn't thrilled with the news. And now the stage is set as Sonny Weaver must decide if his first-round draft pick will be for his favorite player or for the hotshot quarterback with a shady past.

 Greg, the best word I can generate to describe *Draft Day* is that it's a pleasant movie to watch. The formula for a pretty decent movie is well in place – we have a genuinely good heroic leading man in Sonny Weaver, who faces a number of challenging circumstances beyond his control and struggles to cope with them. These circumstances include the recent death of his father; an owner who demands a splashy first-round pick; the quarterback who trashes his office; the head coach who wants more control over player personnel than he deserves; the mother and ex-wife who criticize him; and the girlfriend who wants to take their relationship to the next level.

All this makes for a good hero story, as we, the audience, are eager to see if Weaver can overcome these challenges. As with any good hero story, Weaver gets some support and assistance from key characters and does manage to rise to the occasion. As I said, *Draft Day* a pleasant movie – it features an interesting situation and these are characters we care about. Costner, moreover, is effective in his role. I can't use a word more enthusiastic than 'pleasant' because no new ground is broken here and I doubt I'll give this movie a second viewing.

I think you've summed it up pretty well. This movie was almost made-for-TV quality with its split-screen phone conversations and Lifetime subplot. Costner really phoned in his performance. I think I've been forever spoiled by 2011's *Moneyball*. I'm not a sports fan, so *Moneyball*'s ability to pull me into the world of Major League Baseball and make me care about what happens in that world impressed me greatly. *Draft Day* looked like it wanted to be *Moneyball* for football and failed miserably. I was lost for the first thirty minutes because I don't follow football (let alone the annual draft picks).

Costner's Sonny Weaver was a terse, no-nonsense sort of man's man. He is living in his father's shadow who was the former coach of the Browns. This is Sonny's first opportunity to shine as his own man. He has pressures from all around and manages them as best as he can - although he is prone to throwing laptops through the wall. As a hero, Sonny Weaver is no surprise, yet still no embarrassment either.

 Greg, I'm curious to hear your thoughts about the villains in this movie. There really aren't any, and so that eliminates the 'Man vs. Man' villain-type that we discuss in our explanation of our villain ratings. This leaves us with the other two options – 'Man vs. Self' or 'Man vs. Nature." Sonny Weaver faces daunting circumstances, and you could argue that these somewhat natural stressors serve as the "villainous" opposing forces in the movie. This suggests 'Man vs. Nature."

But Weaver's challenges are also internal ones can he overcome his past, can he focus his thoughts, can he will himself to think clearly and make the right call? These factors suggest a 'Man vs. Self' villain type. So we may have a hybrid operating here, with our hero struggling with both environmental and personal oppositional forces.

I can see your conflict here Scott. I think it's because the villains are so poorly drawn. We do have a couple "oppositional" characters that are in the foreground then some lesser ones bringing up the rear.

I think the Brown's owner Molina is playing the villain character in this film. He's the one pressuring Sonny to go against his better judgement and risk it all to draft the hot-shot quarterback. Also, the head coach played by Denis Leary is in Sonny's face demanding to be given the team he wants to play. These two characters are the faces of Sonny's external challenges. The lesser villains here are the managers from the other teams who are making deals with Sonny and trying to get the better of him. Arguably, Sonny's mother is an oppositional character as well as she attempts to distract him from the biggest day of his career with his dead father's last wishes.

 I don't see Molina or the head coach as villains. They're good men trying to do their jobs, and they have honest disagreements with Sonny. Plus, in the end, none of them are defeated the way villains are usually defeated at the end of a movie. The only things that are defeated are Sonny's vulnerabilities and insecurities, suggesting that his major foe was himself.

The one unsavory person in the movie is the quarterback Bo Callahan. But even Callahan is just an immature college football player who is hardly the force of evil that we typically see in movie villains. The mother isn't a villain; she's merely one of many distractions. So I guess I'm leaning toward the "self" as the major oppositional force in this movie. Weaver is in the pressure cooker and is compelled to muster all his strength to steer his way through all the pressure.

This was a weak movie all around, Scott. You called it 'pleasant' but I'd call it bland. There was not much tension in the film and that is due largely to Costner's understated delivery. I spent the first act just trying to understand the significance of Costner's draft day dilemma. I give *Draft Day* a mere 2 out of 5 Reels.

Costner plays a "darned-good-guy" in this film, as he does in most of his films. He's likable as Sonny Weaver but I never feel his pain or stress. I give him only 2 Heroes out of 5.

The villains in this story were difficult to see because everyone appears to be on the same team (pun intended). I give them just 2 Villains out of 5 as well.

Movie: Villain: Hero:

 I enjoyed this movie more than you did, Greg, perhaps because I'm a big football fan, although you are correct in pointing out that *Money Ball* proved that a good sports film should appeal to a broad audience. *Draft Day* is good mindless fun and takes viewers on a roller coaster ride inside the sports world. The movie is a bit too formulaic but Costner's pleasant (there's that word again) demeanor and winning spirit carry us forward. I give this movie 3 Reels out of 5.

There's a decent hero story here, with Weaver thrown into a dark unfamiliar world without his father and with intense pressure from family and work. Weaver doesn't so much change or transform himself as much as he is forced to dig deep to become the effective general manager that Molina hired him to be. Sometimes finding our true selves amidst the chaos of life is our greatest challenge. For a pleasing hero story, I award Weaver 3 out of 5 Heroes.

We couldn't agree on the nature of the villains, but I don't think that this is a weakness of the film. Instead, I see it more conceptually as a blurred line between challenges that heroes face because they are weak-minded versus challenges they face because circumstances make them appear weak. I come down on the side of viewing Weaver as conflicted and tormented, thus making this movie an example of 'Man vs. Self.' Overall, I'm willing to give these oppositional forces 3 out of 5 Villains.

Movie: Villain: Hero:

Dumb and Dumber To

Starring	Jim Carrey, Jeff Daniels, Rob Riggle
Director	Bobby Farrelly, Peter Farrelly
Screenplay	Sean Anders, Mike Cerrone
Genre	Comedy
Rated	PG-13
Running Time	109 minutes
Release Date	November 14, 2014
Harry & Lloyd Protagonist	Duo, Untransformed Positive Mental (Untransformed Buddy Heroes)
The Pinchelows Antagonist	Ensemble, Untransformed Negative Moral (Untransformed Family Villains)

(Dr. Scott Allison, Professor of Psychology, University of Richmond)

Greg, we've been waiting twenty long, painful years for this sequel to *Dumb and Dumber*.

(Greg Smith, Founder of Agile Writers of Richmond, VA)
And watching it felt like another 20 long painful years. Let's recap:

Twenty years after Lloyd (Jim Carrey) has had his heart broken by a woman in the previous movie, we learn that the shock of the breakup has caused him to be institutionalized for two decades. We also learn that he was faking the trauma as a practical joke directed at Harry (Jeff Daniels). Harry has a damaged kidney and needs a friend or family member to donate one. Harry's parents are poor candidates because they are Asians and adopted him. But as fate would have it, Harry learns that he fathered a child twenty years earlier. The two men set out to find the child (now grown) and her kidney.

Scott, *Dumb and Dumber To* is impressive not in its content, but in the commitment its two stars put into their roles. This movie has a very loose plot held together with some very outrageous jokes and slapstick. There are some running gags left over from the original film (young Billy and the birds are back). And some new ones (the cat named Butthole, because, you know, cats have butt holes).

This is a classic buddy hero story with Lloyd and Harry on a quest to find Harry's long lost daughter. But as heroes these guys leave a lot to be desired. They can be mean (as when they heckle a scientist at a TED-type talk), they are selfish and self-centered, and they are not the least bit reliable. They are poor examples of human beings. Still, they care for each other. Harry has been visiting his old friend in the nursing home for 20 years. And Lloyd is committed to getting his friend a new kidney, regardless the cost. What they lack in visible heroism, they make up for in loyalty.

 Greg, *Dumb and Dumber To* is one of those movies that defies any kind of serious analysis, and yet here we are as movie reviewers writing about these characters as if they matter. The truth is, this movie falls in the same category of throwaway movies as Adam Sandler's *Grown Ups* films. *Dumb and Dumber To* is pure farce, and I use the term farce because it almost sounds like fart. Most of the humor here is about butts, butt cracks, and butt holes. You mention, Greg, that these are buddy heroes but I think you meant butty heroes.

Our two heroes are not bad people, Greg. They are just stupid people. What psychologists know about human nature is that nothing makes us feel better about ourselves than witnessing others people who are dumber than us. In fact, that's what this movie franchise should be called: *Dumber Than Us*. And what's most disturbing about this movie is that I found myself laughing at many of the jokes. I've never felt so much shame in my entire life.

Not only are they not very smart, but not very mature. Imagine, if you will, two ten-year-olds with drivers licenses. When you look at *Dumb and Dumber To* in that light, it all starts to make sense. This is the mentality of all the Farrelly Brothers films (*Dumb and Dumber*, *The Three Stooges*, and *Movie 43*). There's nothing wrong with that, but if your characters start out as children, and end up as children, there's not much growth (or transformation) going on.

The villains were a pretty plain lot too. All of them were painted pretty broadly and with no real dimension. The evil wife character Adele (Laurie Holden) is slowly poisoning her husband to get his fortune and is in cahoots with her adulterous boyfriend Travis (Rob Riggle). This is a simplistic plot device in a simplistic movie. Later, Travis is replaced with mercenary Captain Lippencott who is another "pure evil" character with little other explanation. This is all pretty tame fare designed as scaffolding for a series of (as you put it) butt jokes.

 You're right about the villains, Greg. These may be labeled *Family* villains, as described by Paul Moxnes and his model of both good and evil family social roles. Despite being thousands of IQ points smarter than Harry and Lloyd, these villains somehow are vanquished by our two butty heroes. Much of the humor of this movie stems from the ways that Harry and Lloyd experience one unlikely (and purely lucky) triumph over a villain after another. As you point out, our two heroes are hardly good people, but compared to Adele and Travis, they are pure of heart and thus we have no trouble rooting for them. Sort of.

Still, I had a good time at *Dumb and Dumber To*, due in large part to the 100% commitment of Carrey and Daniels. Both actors have much better things to do with their time than make such low-brow comedy. But I did fall in love with the Harry and Lloyd's innocence. In the end (sorry) that is where the heart of this movie lies. For an enjoyable 100-minute ride, I'll give *Dumber and Dumber To* 3 out of 5 Reels. And for our naive heroes 3 out of 5 Heroes. The villains left me wanting, but surely didn't distract me, so I'll give them 1 Villain out of 5.

Movie: Villains: Heroes:

 I also enjoyed *Dumb and Dumber To*, Greg. Jim Carrey and Jeff Daniels were born for these toilet roles. They clearly enjoy doing these movies and it shows. Sometimes it shows a bit too much, as when Daniels displays more butt-cleavage than Dolly Parton. I didn't learn a thing and grow in any way as a result of watching this film, but I did enjoy connecting with my innermost potty-humor self. Like you, I award this movie 3 Butt-Reels out of 5.

The hero story is inconsequential and there is no growth or change in our heroically stupid characters. Apologies to Joseph Campbell, who is probably turning over in his grave. There is no Great Eight, only a Great Taint. I'll kindly award these two goofballs 2 Heroes out of 5. The villains were ridiculous, as they allowed themselves to be defeated by a couple of cheeky (sorry), empty-headed losers. One Villain out of 5 sounds about right.

Movie: Villains:  Heroes:

Earth to Echo

Starring	Teo Halm, Astro, Reese Hartwig
Director	Dave Green
Screenplay	Henry Gayden
Genre	Adventure/Family
Rated	PG
Running Time	89 minutes
Release Date	July 2, 2014
Kids Protagonist	Ensemble, Untransformed Positive Moral (Untransformed Fraternity Heroes)
Government Antagonist	System, Untransformed Negative (Untransformed Government Villain)

(Dr. Scott Allison, Professor of Psychology, University of Richmond)

Greg, it's hard to believe that it's taken 35 years for Hollywood to attempt to re-capture the magic of *E.T. the Extra-Terrestrial*.

(Greg Smith, Founder of Agile Writers of Richmond, VA)
Earth to Scott: They still haven't! Let's recap.

We meet three 13-year-old kids from in Nevada who live on a street that's about to be demolished to make room for a new superhighway. The kids are Tuck (Astro), Alex (Teo Halm), and Munch (Reese Hartwig). They have a crush on a girl in school, Emma (Ella Wahlestedt), who seems out of their league. One day their cell phones begin displaying a strange, amoeba-like image. They somehow discover that the image is actually a map of a remote part of the Nevada landscape 20 miles away.

When they arrive (by bicycle) they find an object that contains a living (?) mechanical alien they dub "Echo." Echo is trying to col- lect all the pieces to his spacecraft and sends a sequence of maps to the boys' cell phones. Each map leads to another missing piece. Meanwhile, it turns out that there are some evil government types who are chasing after Echo too. Will the boys find all the pieces in time to save Echo and send him home? Or will the evil adults find him first and do mean nasty experiments on him?

 Greg, as your opening line in this review suggests, *Earth to Echo* in no way approaches the quality or playful spirit of *E.T. the Extra-Terrestrial*. I don't mean to imply that *Earth to Echo* is a failure. If the goal was to create a pleasant diversion for kids that isn't terribly offensive for adults to sit through, then this movie is a success. Personally, I wasn't bored but I wasn't dazzled or entertained to any great degree, either.

The quality of a predictable movie like this one truly depends on the casting of the main actors. Unfortunately, the ensemble of child actors is a rather forgettable lot, despite an obvious attempt to manufacture a *Breakfast Club*-like grouping. There's a nerd, a misfit, a bad-boy, and a cute girl, and together they exude little chemistry or flair. A few months from now I'm far more likely to remember their smartphones than their personalities.

Harsher words were never more true, Scott. *Echo* is a painfully slow quest for missing pieces. The characters just go from place to place and don't have much of an adventure. There is a nice little lesson - you can be friends despite the distance - but it is mostly just tossed in at the end. It tries a bit too little to be a *Stand by Me* for millennials with its coming of age theme. I think 2011's *Super 8* is a better film with the same themes. Surely, the shaky-cam first-person effect are reminiscent of such films as *The Blair Witch Project* and *Cloverfield*.

As a hero story, it looks like we have a nice ensemble / fraternity cast with the addition of a tomboy thrown in for diversity. The foursome are on a quest and each has their own quirks but nobody seems to overcome any missing inner qualities. As such, the heroes fall flat and leave us wanting more substance.

 And speaking of flat substances, our group of heroes encounter an odd, dirty-looking piece of equipment in the desert, and it turns out to be an alien creature in disguise. The kids name him Echo and I suppose we're supposed to think he's cute in the same way we fall for E.T. in *E.T. the Extra-Terrestrial*. But I felt no such emotional connection to Echo. He's sort of a mechanical Tweety Bird who lacks any of Tweety Bird's adorable qualities. Echo possesses the power to move inanimate objects when doing so advances the storyline but not when it doesn't.

The villains in the story are the humans who want to capture Echo, and they are disappointingly unidimensional and uninteresting. The one human who interacts with the kids is a government official posing as a construction worker. The man has all the charm of Atilla the Hun and exists solely as a hateful figure who wants to do harm to Echo. I guess it's decided that that's all we need to know about him. Very disappointing.

It's true. The villain in this story was none other than Jason Gray-Stanford who played Detective Randy Disher on the TV show *Monk*. He's a pretty non-threatening-looking guy. His only pur-pose is to represent all adult people in the universe as being both unfeeling and, well, stupid.

This is pretty much a movie for the younger crowd, Scott and so there aren't many tense moments. It's pretty safe for your 5-10 year olds who look up to 13-year olds. However older kids will see through the saccharine and find it silly. I can only give *Earth to Echo* 2 out of 5 Reels.

The heroes in the story don't offer us much, but I did like the way they reminded me of the *Goonies*. They get just 2 out of 5 Heroes.

And the villains were nearly non-existent. Just one adult chasing after Echo and the kids and he was pretty mild fare. I give him just 1 Villain out of 5.

Movie: Villains: Heroes: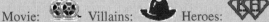

 Greg, you've aptly summed it up. I considered giving this film a single insulting Reel out of 5 but as we've already mentioned, *Earth to Echo* caters to a young crowd and probably delivers to them exactly what they're looking for. The movie is flimsy in just about every way that's important to us, but we're adults and certainly not the target audience. Two out of 5 Reels is about right.

The heroes are a forgettable collection of kids who are predictable and uninspiring. Even Echo himself does his home planet a disservice by lacking sophistication and charm. These heroes do go on a journey and are not totally lacking in redeeming qualities, and so they manage to eek out a rating of 2 Heroes out of 5.

The villains are about as awful as villains can get in a movie, and by "awful" I don't mean that they are evil or dastardly or the kind of villain that we love to hate. I mean that they are just poorly constructed and an insult even to the intelligence of a 5-year-old kid. I was so thoroughly disgusted by the villains here that I give them a big fat zero rating. That's right, zero out of five for me, Greg.

Movie: Villains: 0 Heroes:

Edge of Tomorrow

Starring	Tom Cruise, Emily Blunt, Bill Paxton
Director	Doug Liman
Screenplay	Christopher McQuarrie, Jez Butterworth
Genre	Action/Science-Fiction
Rated	PG-13
Running Time	113 minutes
Release Date	June 6, 2014
Cage Protagonist	Single, Negative to Positive Moral (Enlightened Lone Hero)
Mimics Antagonist	System, Untransformed Negative Moral (Untransformed Nature Pure Evil Villains)

(Dr. Scott Allison, Professor of Psychology, University of Richmond)

Greg, I would say 'let's review this movie' but I'm pretty sure we've done it already.

(Greg Smith, Founder of Agile Writers of Richmond, VA)

It's deja-vu all over again. Let's recap Tom Cruise's new film *Edge of Tomorrow*.

We meet Major William Cage (Tom Cruise), the spokesperson for the United Defense Forces, a combined military force that is attempting to repel an extraterrestrial invasion by a species known as the Mimics. Cage is sent to General Brigham's office and is surprised when Brigham (Brendan Gleeson) orders him to participate as a soldier in a wide scale invasion of Mimic-occupied France. When Cage resists and attempts to blackmail Brigham, the General has him arrested and sent to an English base as a private about to be deployed to France.

Cage is outfitted with a mechanical exoskeleton and lifts off in a heli-transport with his new troop of soldiers bound for a D-Day sort of invasion. They crash land and are met with overwhelming forces - as if the Mimic enemy knew they were coming. Cage is all thumbs with his new gear and is quickly killed in combat.

He then immediately wakes up back at the base where he was shanghaied and relives the experience of meeting the soldiers, flying into battle, crashing, and getting killed. On his third incarnation, he meets up with Rita (Emily Blunt) - a soldier who is well-known as the fiercest of the Army's warriors. He relates his experiences to her and she tells him to find her when he wakes up.

When he wakes up at the beginning of his day again, he seeks out Rita and relates his experiences to her. Much to his surprise, she believes him. She relates that she herself had been infected with the ability to "reset the day" but had lost it. Rita tells him that he must go into training to help them find the "Omega" alien who, once killed, will destroy the enemy and save the Earth.

 Greg, I have a confession to make. I'm a sucker for time travel movies, especially ones that are smartly made and contain all the elements of a good hero story. One of my criticisms of previous Tom Cruise movies has been that his characters rarely show any change or growth. Because *Edge of Tomorrow* is one of those repeating time-loop movies, much like *Groundhog Day*, William Cage absolutely must change in order to break the temporal cycle. So we're given a satisfying story of personal growth that redeems not only the character but saves the world as well.

Cage starts out a coward and a fool. We don't like him very much, and when we learn that he is squeamish it doesn't seem likely he can survive countless blood-soaked battles with the Mimics. Dire circumstances, however, gradually transform Cage into an invincible warrior. What we have is a dark *Groundhog Day* on steroids, a film that works on many different levels, including the all-important emotional level.

Scott, I'm glad you mentioned *Groundhog Day* because that is the criticism I have of *Edge of Tomorrow*. It takes the central idea of Bill Murray's film and applies it to war. Since *Groundhog Day* is such a well-known film, the filmmakers must offer something above and beyond what we already know must happen. We already know that the hero will recycle through his life experiences and learn and relearn lessons until he becomes proficient. *Edge* does offer one new thread which is the ability for the hero to lose the gift of time travel. However, once this fact is mentioned in the story, you know there has to come a point in the film where the hero *must* lose the power. It made *Edge* rather predictable.

I'll agree with you on Cage's growth in this film. He starts out as a wimp and a coward and when he finds himself in the predicament of reliving his life over again daily. We see him become a better man. He comes to care for his platoon-mates and falls in love with Rita, the beautiful war veteran. By the end of the film we are treated to a redefined man, one we hardly recognize.

 Another difference between this film and *Groundhog Day* centers on what has to happen for the hero to escape from the time loop. Bill Murray's character has to become a good man, but Tom Cruise's character must do more than just change his nature; he must also destroy the Omega. In both *Groundhog Day* and *Edge of Tomorrow*, a woman is the central instrument of the man's change. I think it's no coincidence that the woman's name is Rita in both movies.

The villains in *Edge of Tomorrow* – the Mimics – are somewhat novel in both their appearance and in their behavioral characteristics. The creatures are a strange spider-reptile hybrid that moves at hyper-speed. They also have the ability to use time travel to anticipate their enemy's next moves. The Mimics are also disappointing in some ways, and I'll let you, Greg, describe why this is the case.

Thanks, Scott. Apparently the Mimics suffer the same malady that aliens from across time and space suffer from - that of being controlled by a singular, central mind. When Cage destroys the "Omega" beast, all the "Alpha" and "Drone" aliens also stop working. This is a tired plot device that we've seen in such movies as *Independence Day*, *Divergent*, *RoboCop*, and *Transcendence*, just to name a few.

Edge of Tomorrow recycles a few old ideas but offers two rock-solid hours of fun and adventure. Tom Cruise turns in one of his best performances in years here, and for a refreshing change he plays a character who evolves throughout the course of the film. Because the movie is very well done and because I love sci-fi stories that utilize time travel effectively, I'm happy to award *Edge of Tomorrow* 4 Reels out of 5.

The hero story in this film is appealing on several levels. Cage embarks on a dangerous journey in an unfamiliar world, and to achieve his mission he must undergo a transformation that is satisfying to watch. We're treated to several key features of the hero's journey, such as Cage's encounter with Rita, a remarkably strong female character who plays a mentoring role in helping Cage discover his missing inner quality. Rita is the key to Cage's redemption and also steals his heart. In my view William Cage is a worthy hero who deserves a rating of 4 out of 5 Heroes.

As you point out, Greg, the two formidable forces that Cage must overcome are the Mimics and his own weakness of character. There are also a few other oppositional characters who get in Cage's way, such as General Brigham and Sergeant Farrell. Pardon the pun, but the Mimics unfortunately do mimic prior sci-fi extra-terrestrials. But the good news is that the Mimics also have a unique look and intriguing time-shifting abilities. Overall, the villainous components of this movie are used to great effect, leading me to conclude that *Edge of Tomorrow* deserves a strong rating of 4 Villains out of 5.

Movie: Villains: Heroes:

I really hate to say this, but I didn't have the same impression of this movie as you did, Scott. The graphics and battle scenes are definitely worth the price of admission. But *Edge of Tomorrow* borrowed so many plot devices from other movies that I can only give it 3 out of 5 Reels.

Cage as the hero undergoes a good transformation which is gradual and believable (in the context of the sci/fi elements). But we've seen this done before exceedingly well in *Groundhog Day*. One redeeming element that I found in *Edge of Tomorrow* was Emily Blunt as a completely believable female warrior. We don't see that everyday. Still, I can only give Tom Cruise's character 3 out of 5 Heroes.

Finally, we're so far apart on the villains here. The Mimics are such a retread from other movies and have so little to offer other than being evil, mindless, bad guys that I can't give them such a lofty score as you did. I'll grant you that there are other oppositional forces in play, but in my mind, it's the Mimics who are the main villains and they simply don't measure up to other fine villains we've seen this year (witness *The Amazing Spider-Man 2* and *X-Men: Days of Future Past*). I give the Mimics just 1 Villain out of 5.

Movie: Villains: Heroes:

The Equalizer

Starring	Denzel Washington, Marton Csokas, Chloë Grace Moretz
Director	Antoine Fuqua
Screenplay	Richard Wenk
Genre	Action/Crime/Thriller
Rated	R
Running Time	131 minutes
Release Date	September 26, 2014
McCall Protagonist	Single, Untransformed Positive Moral (Untransformed Lone Hero)
Teddy Antagonist	Single, Untransformed Negative Moral (Untransformed Henchman Villain)

(Dr. Scott Allison, Professor of Psychology, University of Richmond)

Greg, after seeing *The Equalizer*, I want to stay on Denzel Washington's good side.

(Greg Smith, Founder of Agile Writers of Richmond, VA)

I thought he was going to balance my stereo system. I was wrong. Let's recap...

We meet Robert McCall (Denzel Washington), a retired special forces agent who works at a large Home-Mart hardware store in Boston. Robert enjoys helping people, such as his buddy Ralphie (Johnny Skourtis), who aspires to become a security officer at the store, and a young woman named Teri (Chloë Grace Moretz) who sits in the same coffee shop that Robert frequents in the middle of the night. Teri is a prostitute working for the Russian mob, and one night Robert sees Teri's pimp abuse her.

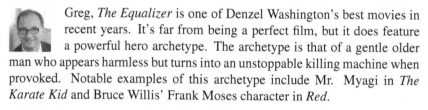
That's when Robert decides to *equalize* the odds. He strides into the office of the head mob bad guy and lays down $9800 to buy Teri's freedom. The head guy not only refuses Robert's offer, but tells him he can have Teri only after he's "used her up." That's when Robert locks the door behind him, starts his stopwatch, and begins to lay some serious hurt on the bad guys.

Greg, *The Equalizer* is one of Denzel Washington's best movies in recent years. It's far from being a perfect film, but it does feature a powerful hero archetype. The archetype is that of a gentle older man who appears harmless but turns into an unstoppable killing machine when provoked. Notable examples of this archetype include Mr. Myagi in *The Karate Kid* and Bruce Willis' Frank Moses character in *Red*.

As an audience, we apparently love highly moral heroes who have supremely powerful abilities and who have the wisdom to hide those abilities from just about everyone – except very, very bad men who deserve to get their butts kicked. Denzel plays this role to the hilt. We can't help but love the man who looks out for others and who only uses his immense talents when someone he cares about is in grave danger.

Denzel does this well. We like McCall because he is altruistic: he gives his time and experience to younger people to help them better themselves. As such, he plays a mentor role as well as the hero.

McCall also has a deep inner pain as a man who lost his only true love - his wife. He made a promise to her not to indulge in his super-spy ways. But when evil is done to an innocent, as McCall would say, he makes an exception.

We also like McCall because he has a few social tics that make him relatable. He's focused on finishing the 100 books his wife started reading but died before she could complete them. Also, he is a bit obsessive compulsive: timing his every activity, laying out his dinnerware just so, and at the mob's office, aligning a row of glass skull ornaments on the bad guy's desk. These quirks make our super hero more human, more sympathetic.

And since we're talking about the villains, the mob guys are typical bad guys. Tattooed, rotten teeth, wife-beater-wearing thugs. But when word of McCall's dispatching of the thugs reaches the head Russian mobster (Pushkin), he sends a more interesting villain. He sends Teddy - and we don't mean Teddy Bear.

 The Equalizer gives us a villain whose level of evil matches the level of good in our hero. Teddy (Marton Csokas) is a true sociopath who ruthlessly hunts down our hero Robert McCall. Teddy is handsome, smart, charming, and relentless. We can't help but admire his tenacity and brutal efficiency. Greg, this movie needed a villain we could revile and it delivered.

Once again, we have an evil mastermind (Pushkin) who lurks behind the scenes and sends his henchmen to do his dirty work. This hierarchical structure to villains appears to be common in the movies. I do have a few criticisms of the choices made by director Antoine Fuqua, including the degree of senseless violence shown by Teddy toward his victims. We don't need to see as many blood-splattering blows to the face as this film shows. Decades ago, Alfred Hitchcock showed us that when it comes to violence, less is more.

Scott, Teddy is the villain we've been looking for all year. His demeanor is calm and collected in presentation. But when he wants to send a message, he is savage. And the bigger the message, de- meanor he gets. We're also given a backstory to this villain. McCall has done his research and learns that Teddy was a troubled child taken in by a virtuous man. But the young Teddy couldn't fathom the generosity he was shown. So, rather than accept his new reality, he killed his benefactor before he could disappoint him. That's a really cold story.

Overall, I liked this movie but found it pretty uncomplicated. And in places, it was completely impossible to believe (McCall apparently has the faculties to destroy an entire oil tanker). I was entertained from beginning to end, but there were no surprises. I give *The Equalizer* just 3 out of 5 Reels.

McCall is a great hero and I suspect we'll be seeing more of him (there is a planned sequel). He embodies all the great elements of the hero including altruism, intelligence, and mastery. And, in an interesting turn, he never fires a weapon. However, he lacks a transformation that would give him a nice story arc. Still, he is a catalyst for change in the people he helps. I give McCall 4 out of 5 Heroes.

The majority of the bad guys in this film are typical stereotypes: Russian mafia hit men and cops gone bad. But Teddy really saves this story from being a run-of-the-mill action flick. He is everything his heroic counterpart is, but lacks any empathy. This makes him a villain worth fighting against. I give Teddy 4 out of 5 Villains.

Movie: Villain: Hero:

Greg, I like *The Equalizer* a bit more than you did. Perhaps it's my admiration for Denzel Washington, who wields his talents here in impressive fashion. Perhaps it's the type of hero he portrays, the older gentleman whose hands are lethal weapons, whose wits are unmatched, and whose morals are in all the right places. *The Equalizer* is a very good film well worth seeing if you enjoy a classic battle between good and evil. Director Antoine Fuqua makes some poor decisions here and there, but overall this movie provides great entertainment. I happily give this film 4 out of 5 Reels.

The character of Robert McCall is one of my favorite hero types and most certainly is thrown into a different world where he must triumph over a formidable villain. But it's not the strongest hero story for a few reasons.

While Robert must kill the bad guys to accomplish his mission, does he really need to use corkscrews and power drills? Like Teddy the villain, Robert's level of violence seems a bit over-the-top. Second, there is no classic hero transformation here. Robert is a benevolent bad-ass when the movie starts and he remains one by the movie's conclusion. As much as I love Denzel, I can only give a hero rating of 3 out of 5 here.

I agree with you, Greg, that Teddy is a terrific villain. The scene you mention in which Robert converses with Teddy in the restaurant is a fabulous piece of work; the scene is tense, taught, and meaningful for our understanding of what's going on with these two powerful characters. All the bad guys and henchmen were fun to watch and had my full attention at all times. There is a fascinating backstory to Teddy that helps us understand his horrific disregard for human life. Like you, Greg, I give Teddy and his associates a meritorious 4 out of 5 Villains.

Movie: Villain:  Hero:

The Fault In Our Stars

Starring	Shailene Woodley, Ansel Elgort, Nat Wolff
Director	Josh Boone
Screenplay	Scott Neustadter, Michael H. Weber
Genre	Drama/Romance
Rated	PG-13
Running Time	126 minutes
Release Date	June 6, 2014
Hazel & Gus Protagonist	Duo, Positive to More Positive Emotional (Romantic Divergent Classic Heroes)
Cancer Antagonist	System, Untransformed Negative (Nature Mindless Villain)

(Greg Smith, Founder of Agile Writers of Richmond, VA)

Scott, there's not a flaw in *Fault In Our Stars*.

(Dr. Scott Allison, Professor of Psychology, University of Richmond)

There are no faults but plenty of stars. Let's recap.

We're introduced to teenage cancer survivor Hazel (Shailene Woodley). She's had thyroid cancer and it damaged her lungs so she must travel with an oxygen tank. Her mother encourages her to go to a cancer counseling meeting where she meets slightly older Gus (Ansel Elgort) who lost a leg to cancer the previous year. Hazel is trying to keep her distance but Gus is persistent and with humor and charm wins Hazel's affections.

 Hazel's dream is to speak with the author of her favorite book. She has many questions to ask this man, Peter Van Houten (Willem Dafoe), but he lives in Amsterdam and won't answer her queries unless she travels to The Netherlands to meet him. At first her medical condition and her parents' limited finances prevent her from traveling overseas, but Gus arranges with a make-a-wish foundation to make her dream of meeting Van Houten come true. The journey yields bittersweet surprises as the two star-crossed lovers attempt to meet their many challenges.

Scott, I didn't know what to expect from this movie. I knew it was based on a Young-Adult novel that was very popular. I kind of expected a saccharine, glossed-over presentation of young love in the shadow of cancer.

I was pleasantly surprised when the story unfolded to reveal a thoughtful and charming story about young love that was tinged by the shadow of cancer. We last saw Shailene Woodley in last Spring's *Divergent* where she played a young girl in a dystopian future world. So much of today's Young Adult fiction is cast in just such a world that to find a story that dealt with real people in real situations was refreshing and welcome.

 Greg, I agree that the quality of this film is surprising. Given the topic, the movie could easily have devolved into a forgettable made-for-TV level product. But it didn't. We're treated to two stellar performances from Shailene Woodley and Ansel Elgort, whose moving depiction of two cancer-ridden teens in love is deeply inspiring. These are two great characters whom we like for their intelligence, courage, and *realism*. They were highly convincing in these difficult roles to play.

Hazel is the primary hero of the story, although one could argue that she and Augustus are duo heroes. I think of Hazel as the main hero because she narrates the story and also because she is the character who grows and evolves as events unfold all around her. Hazel is transformed by Augustus and also by Anne Frank, whose recorded voice in Amsterdam inspires Hazel to hold onto hope and savor the beauty and love all around her. The hero journey evokes painful emotions but somehow manages to be uplifting, too.

I agree. Hazel is the hero of the story and she is acted upon by her catalyst Gus. She starts out as isolated and wanting not to get involved in people's lives. She considers herself to be "a hand grenade waiting to explode," taking the lives of those around her in her wake. It is Gus's determination to love Hazel whether she wants him to or not - and that cracks her shell. Once he gets under her skin she starts to grow and flourish.

The villain here is either time or cancer. Of course, the two are connected. We feel that Hazel can't survive very long in her condition. And we also witness her laboring to climb the stairs at the Anne Frank house and wonder if she'll make it.

Regardless of whether time or cancer is the villain, I was pleased that the storytellers gave Hazel and Gus a true opposition character in the form of author Peter Van Houten. He is a recluse after having written his novel based on the death of his daughter from cancer - a book that Hazel is obsessed with. When she meets him he is rude to the extreme and completely self-absorbed. He was a good villainous character, but not the main villain of the story.

 Greg, it is true that cancer is the villain of this story. It is tempting to say that the author whom Hazel adores, Peter Van Houten, plays a villain role. But Van Houten is very much a character reminiscent of Angelina Jolie's character in *Maleficent*. Like her, Van Houten is embittered by loss and is redeemed by love. His rude, jerky behavior actually helps bring Hazel and Gus together, as they consummate their love shortly after their dark encounter with him.

Yes, nothing says redemption like teenage sex. I really enjoyed this film, despite the crowd of weeping teenage girls in the audience. Many have called *The Fault in Our Stars* the *Love Story* for a new generation. And I agree. It was a thoughtful and masterfully crafted story (based on the real life of Esther Earl whose video blogs can still be found on YouTube despite the fact the she succumbed to her cancer in 2010). I give *Fault* 5 out of 5 Reels.

The hero story is hard to deny. Hazel starts out pushing everyone away and ends up loving more than ever. I hate to say that the ending is telescoped from the beginning, but still it was a powerful drama worthy of viewing by those of any age. I give Hazel 4 out of 5 Heroes.

I'm having a tough time rating cancer on our villain's scale. It follows the pattern of the hidden villain, never becoming visible yet affecting our heroes at every turn. It is an insidious disease (or cluster of diseases) and is hard to wrap your mind around it. The cancer we see on-screen is muted and sugar-coated. Compared to the profound presentation of other diseases we've seen recently (witness *Dallas Buyer's Club*) I can only give cancer as depicted in *The Fault in Our Stars* 2 out of 5 Villains.

Movie: Villain: Hero: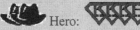

 The Fault In Our Stars directly tackles two of the heaviest themes in storytelling: Love and Death. Such a jarring collision with these topics could have yielded sappy, disastrous results, but this movie has the biggest heart of any film I've seen in years. Woodley and Elgort carry the show masterfully and made everyone in the theater cry. I give this film a heartfelt 5 out of 5 Reels.

Every hero sets out on an important journey, and in *The Fault In Our Stars* Hazel's blossoming relationship with Gus and trip to Amsterdam transforms her on many different levels. Hazel is an unforgettable hero, and Gus is her unforgettable mentor, lover, friend, and symbol of life and hope. The hero and her friends, allies, and companions are all present in full-form and are quite moving. I give Hazel 5 out of 5 Heroes.

As you note, Greg, the film's villain, cancer, is hard to evaluate. Cancer doesn't have an intriguing backstory like a human villain would have. Cancer doesn't have interesting facial expressions, quirky mannerisms, henchmen, or a diabolical laugh. But cancer is the Adolf HItler of diseases, a horrific affliction that attacks and torments its victims on every conceivable level. *The Fault In Our Stars* does a fine job illustrating all the terrible ways that cancer destroys a human. It's hard to assign a villain rating but I'd say this film's effective depiction of cancer deserves 4 out of 5 Villains.

Movie: Villain: Hero:

Get On Up

Starring	Chadwick Boseman, Nelsan Ellis, Dan Aykroyd
Director	Tate Taylor
Screenplay	Jez Butterworth, John-Henry Butterworth
Genre	Biography/Drama
Rated	PG-13
Running Time	138 minutes
Release Date	August 1, 2014
Brown Protagonist	Single, Positive to More Positive Emotional (Classic Transformed Hero)
Brown Antagonist	Single, Positive to More Positive Emotional (Redeemed Self Villain)

(Greg Smith, Founder of Agile Writers of Richmond, VA)

Scott, it's time to get on up and review the James Brown biopic.

(Dr. Scott Allison, Professor of Psychology, University of Richmond)

May the funk be with us. Let's recap.

Get On Up tells the story of the great James Brown (Chadwick
Boseman) in a non-sequential set of vignettes starting out in the
1970s and flashing back and forth between Brown's childhood and
his emergence as one of the most diverse and unique musical talents of the
20th century.

Brown grows up in a shack in Georgia in the 1930s. His father is abusive both
to him and his mother and she eventually leaves James behind. This is an
event that would scar James Brown for life. His father realizes he can't take
care of the boy or himself and enlists in the army during World War II, leaving
James in the care of an aunt who runs a brothel. Here, young James learns to
attract soldiers with song and dance. He is also exposed to gospel music at a
local church.

 As a young man James meets Bobby Byrd (Nelsan Ellis), who leads
a gospel group. Bobby recognizes James' talent and invites him
into the group. Soon they are known as the *Famous Flames* and
are picked up by a record label. Ben Bart (Dan Aykroyd) becomes James'
manager and convinces James to become the point man for group, diminishing
the role of the other Flames. The group walks out on him, but Bobby Byrd
remains loyal to James. We witness the rising fame and fortune of James
Brown, but also volatile periods involving tax evasion and odd brushes with
the law.

Scott, one of the things we look for in the hero's journey is transformation. And nobody transforms more than James Brown. He
starts out with literally nothing but a pair of shoes he stole from a
corpse and rises to be a great star. He is mentored by some unlikely people as
he grows.

In prison, when it looked like he was doomed to a life of crime, he meets
Bobby Byrd who helps to get him paroled and on the track of gospel music.
Later, he meets a pre-fame Little Richard who advises him to know the devil
when he sees him and to take the deal he offers. This advice bears fruit when
James is given the deal to become a single star and leave the Flames behind.

And finally, his business manager and close friend Ben Bart guides James in the ways of the special world of rock and roll stardom.

And this is where James exceeds his tutors. James turns the tables and becomes a disrupter, shattering the traditional methods of promotion and goes directly to the people. This ability to work outside the system makes James not just a star, but a very rich man.

 Get On Up is an illuminating look at the turbulent yet triumphant life of singer James Brown. The movie pays homage to the uniqueness of every facet of James' life, from his singular personality to his penchant for deviating from the musical norms of his day. James Brown was truly one-of-a-kind, a man who revolutionized music in strange yet brilliant ways. *Get On Up* does a nice job of showing the many seismic shifts in James' life, some very painful, each helping unearth his many gifts.

Chadwick Boseman as James Brown is simply superb here, demonstrating remarkable vocal mannerisms and range, not to mention some seriously slick dance moves. With his stellar performances in last year's *42* and this year's *Draft Day*, Boseman has emerged as one of the most versatile young talents in the movie industry. I wouldn't be surprised to see Boseman garner an Oscar nomination for Best Actor here.

There are some villains for James to overcome along the way as well. His father is a strong influence on him as a boy and also a very abusive man. This abusive nature is passed from father to son as we see later in James life.

While the record producers are depicted as men who are trying to help James, they are really out to help themselves. James realizes this early on and makes plans to extricate himself from the grip of the record companies so that he can create the kind of music he want to make.

Greg, you mention that our hero undergoes a significant transformation, but I'm not so sure. It seems to me that throughout most of his life, James is just a more professionally successful version of his father. He has trouble with relationships and physically abuses at least one of his wives. He has run-ins with the law and is a pure narcissist. We do get a glimpse of some change at the very end when James finally reaches out to Bobby Byrd. Perhaps in his old age he has finally softened and now recognizes the social world beyond himself.

As for the villains, I agree with you that James has plenty of oppositional forces to overcome, including the disadvantaged environment in which he was raised and the racist society that handcuffs him (sometimes literally). James has plenty of inner demons to conquer, all of them nudging him toward self-destruction. His success is a testimony to his immense talent, which pulls him through the maze of the adversity that he faces.

Get On Up is not just a biopic but a legendary rags to riches story. James Brown was an American original whose disruptive approach to music and the music industry had far reaching impacts on musi- cians and society alike. Boseman's depiction of Brown is spot on. He channels Browns mannerisms, dance moves, and vocal stylings which adds to our immersion into the story. I give *Get On Up* 4 out of 5 Reels.

James Brown was a man who was constantly transforming himself. His style and music changed with the decades. However, he was self-destructive and narcissistic. These qualities threatened to destroy him at every turn. Still, he overcame these personality flaws and grew as a man. I give James Brown 4 out of 5 Heroes.

James Brown was probably his own worst enemy. Time after time he created situations that brought him to the edge of disaster. His personality flaws and obsessive nature often pushed away the very people he needed to help him succeed. Otherwise, there were very few true opposition figures in the film. We didn't see much of the racial forces that were present in the 60's, 70's, 80's and beyond. The oppositional forces that were presented were usually "old white men" who posed no real threat to James and were out to help him.

Without strong villains, James' struggle is lost to the audience. I give James and his weak opposition just 3 out of 5 Villains.

Movie: Villains: Heroes:

 Get On Up is an enjoyable and informative movie that portrays the making of a true legend in the music industry. The film meanders at times, but despite an occasional lapse in focus, I recommend *Get On Up* for all fans of music and for movie fans who will appreciate the vast talents of actor Chadwick Boseman. I'm happy to award 3 Reels out of 5 to *Get On Up*.

The hero story follows a pretty classic pattern and reveals to us a powerful underdog story. James Brown had so much to overcome that it's a miracle that he found ways for his funkworthiness to prevail. Certainly his talent, his mentors, and his stratospheric self-confidence helped pave the way. I'm willing to give James Brown a rating of 4 out of 5 Heroes.

The villainous people and constraining forces that impeded James Brown were numerous but not always fleshed out to a satisfactory degree. We do see in vivid and heart-wrenching detail the atrocious conditions in which he was raised, but the people in his life who stood in his way are portrayed somewhat stereotypically. I'll give the villains a rating of 3 out of 5.

Movie: Villains:  Heroes:

The Giver

Starring	Brenton Thwaites, Jeff Bridges, Meryl Streep
Director	Phillip Noyce
Screenplay	Michael Mitnick, Robert B. Weide
Genre	Drama/Science-Fiction
Rated	PG-13
Running Time	97 minutes
Release Date	August 15, 2014
Jonah Protagonist	Single, Positive to More Positive Emotional (Classic Lone Hero)
Chief Elder Antagonist	Single, Untransformed Negative (Untransformed Lone Villain)

(Greg Smith, Founder of Agile Writers of Richmond, VA)

Scott, it's time for us to give our review of *The Giver*.

(Dr. Scott Allison, Professor of Psychology, University of Richmond)

Unfortunately, *The Giver* was a taker of two hours of my time. Let's recap.

In *The Giver* we're introduced to young Jonah (Brenton Thwaites)
on the eve of his "Ceremony of Growth" where he and all the other
18-year-olds will be assigned their jobs. One by one Jonah's peers
receive jobs like caregiver or fighter pilot, but Jonah is left to the last. He is
told he is going to be the *Receiver*. This is a role selected once a generation.
As the Receiver he will be given all the knowledge of previous generations.
In Jonah's "community" they have eliminated all emotion and memory of the
past - even the idea of color. It is the job of the Receiver to advise the elders
based on the inherited knowledge. This knowledge is passed on to Jonah by a
man known only as the *Giver* (Jeff Bridges).

 Jonah begins to receive some of the community's early memories from the Giver, and these images are difficult and sometimes
painful to deal with. One of the emotions that he experiences for
the first time is the feeling of love. Eager to share this new emotion, Jonah
begins to warm up to one of the girls in the community whose name is Fiona
(Odeya Rush). Illegally, he takes her on a mock sled ride and then encourages
her to skip taking her daily injection designed to deny her emotional experience. Eventually, Jonah and the Giver decide that it is best for the community
to break through the barrier of "Elsewhere" to restore the entire community's
memories.

The Giver is YA dystopian fiction. And when I say "YA" I don't
mean "Young Adult," I mean "Yet Another." It starts out as so many
of today's young adult stories do - a young person in a dreary future
where they are being categorized and put into a social class that is selected for
them by adults. We saw it in *Harry Potter* (the sorting hat), *The Hunger
Games* (districts 1-12), and in this year's *Divergent* (which has an opening
scene almost identical to *The Giver*'s). *The Giver* may actually lay claim to
this pattern as it is based on a book that is 20 years old. But it is quite the YA
trope now.

The story starts out in black and white. As Jonah starts to gain an awareness of how things truly are, the color starts to come into focus - both in his

mind and on-screen. It's a nice effect, but we've seen it before in movies like *Pleasantville*.

The main goal for Jonah is to escape from the community and cross the barrier of Elsewhere which will somehow magically restore everyone's memories. This device is really hard to swallow as there are no explanations for how this happens. The Giver merely says it is so and it becomes part of the physics of that universe. I found it hard to accept and it made the ending seem contrived.

 Greg, what a shame that this movie arrives on the heels of so many other films with a similar premise, theme, and moral message. Even if *The Giver* is based on a book that preceded all the other films, it still comes across as derivative. To make matters worse, this film does an inferior job of addressing those same themes compared to what we've seen over and over again in works such *Hunger Games*, *Divergent*, and others. When you and I saw the opening selection ceremony, we looked at each other in the theater and said, 'Not again!' at the exact same time. How unfortunate. Perhaps YA stands for 'Yawn Again.'

The Giver does feature a decent hero's journey. I'm trying not to hold it against poor Jonah that we've seen his story many times in the past couple of years in other films. After all, it's a classic tale of a young person who has a limited view of the universe but then grows in his understanding to the point of realizing that his universe must be overthrown in order for justice, truth, beauty, and the American way to prevail. The Giver himself is the obvious mentor to Jonah, and Fiona is his obvious love interest. Jonah's hero journey is so common and predictable that the key to its success is for the filmmakers to portray it in an uncommon and/or exemplary way. Alas, the filmmakers did not succeed in achieving those goals.

I got a lot of confused messages from this story. At one point we learn that babies who are not fully conformant (by way of weight, intelligence, or social development) are put to death by unthinking doctors. So I thought this was some sort of hidden message about the evils of abortion. But then, the villain character (the lead elder played by Meryl

Streep) makes a speech about how people cannot be given the right to choose, because they make bad choices. Which is an argument against choice. So I was very lost as to what the point of this film was. I give *The Giver* just 2 out of 5 Reels.

Jonah is a common hero and plods along the hero's journey with no surprises. The characters in the story are all going through the paces without thinking about what they are doing. Jonah sees this and decides to make a change. He wants to give people back their autonomy. It's a noble mission. I give Jonah 3 out of 5 Heroes.

The villain here was the lead elder who wanted to maintain the status quo. She liked the world without color, variety, or the messiness of love, hate, and above all, choice. She wasn't played as an evil overlord, but more as a obstructionist - motivated by the fear of returning to things that had lead the world astray. It wasn't a profound role and I wasn't inspired one way or the other. I give the elder just 2 Villains out of 5.

Movie: Villains: Heroes:

The Giver breaks no new ground in its presentation of a future world in which people have been robbed of their emotions and their freedom of choice. We understand that such a sterile and totalitarian universe will prevent war and we also get the fact that sometimes peace comes at too high a price. *Star Trek* dealt with these themes in the 1960s and other more modern treatments are scattered throughout the sci-fi canon. We do get a very nice performance from Jeff Bridges, but as in the case with last year's *RIPD*, Bridges is a great actor trapped inside a mediocre movie. I award *The Giver* a mere 2 Reels out of 5.

As I noted above, the hero's journey is hardly new and can only succeed by adding some new element or twist, or by being exceptionally noteworthy. Jonah is a capable hero and shows great growth as a character, but we've been down this road too many times to be subjected to a routine treatment of his type of journey. I can only give poor Jonah a mere 2 Heroes out of 5.

The great shock of *The Giver* is the appearance of Meryl Streep, who is terribly underutilized as the Cruella DeGiver character here. Why Streep took on this part is a complete mystery to me. Her vast talents are as well-hidden as the clouded land of "Elsewhere" in the movie. There is little to learn about villainy from her evil character, and her role exists only for the purpose of being a vapid obstacle for Jonah and the Giver to conquer. Cruella gets a mere 2 Villains out of 5.

Movie: Villains: Heroes:

Godzilla

Starring	Aaron Taylor-Johnson, Elizabeth Olsen, Bryan Cranston
Director	Gareth Edwards
Screenplay	Max Borenstein, Dave Callaham
Genre	Action/Adventure/Science-Fiction
Rated	PG-13
Running Time	123 minutes
Release Date	May 16, 2014
Ford Protagonist	Single, Untransformed Positive Moral (Untransformed Lone Hero)
Mutos Antagonist	System, Untransformed Negative Moral (Untransformed Pure Evil Villains)

(Dr. Scott Allison, Professor of Psychology, University of Richmond)

Greg, after watching this movie, I'm beginning to believe that size matters.

(Greg Smith, Founder of Agile Writers of Richmond, VA)

And that thermonuclear devices are the cure to all ills. Let's recap.

Godzilla opens with old film clips of nuclear bomb testing in the South Pacific Islands. These clips, however, show mysterious jagged spikes coming out of the ocean near the bomb blasts. We flash forward to 1999 in the Phillippines, where a gigantic fossil of an unknown creature is unearthed. Workers discover that an egg pod is missing. Meanwhile, in Japan, a nuclear reactor is being rocked by unnatural seismic activity. Plant supervisor Joe Brody (Bryan Cranston) sends a team of workers led by his wife Sandra (Juliette Binoche) to investigate.

The reactor collapses but not before Joe escapes, but not so lucky was his wife. We flash forward again another fifteen years to present day where Naval explosives expert Ford Brody (Aaron Taylor-Johnson, the now grown son of Joe and Sandra) has just returned from overseas duty. He's no sooner home than he gets a call that his father has been arrested in Japan for attempting to gain access to the closed nuclear reactor site. Ford takes off for Japan to collect his demented father.

In Japan, Joe convinces Ford that there is something alive beneath the surface of the power plant. They stealth their way into the facility and find an enormous egg which has fed on the radiation of the spent nuclear power plant. It hatches, demolishes what is left of the power plant, and kills Joe Brody in process. Ford is made a believer that there are greater things on this planet than he at first thought and attempts to return home to his family.

Greg, *Godzilla* is one large beast of a movie. Going into the theater, you pretty much know who the star of the show is going to be. Of course it can't be any of the humans who are fighting the monster or who are fleeing from it. The star has to be Godzilla himself. (Or is it herself?) I'm not sure of the gender, but that doesn't matter. What does matter, to any audience, is whether Godzilla is the kick-ass monster we want and expect him (or her) to be.

This film succeeds wildly in producing not just one giant monster but three of them, one of whom is of course Godzilla. These creatures have awe-inspiring size and an astronomically high MQ (Menace Quotient). A couple of the beasts sport a facial look that is just a bit too reminiscent of Ridley Scott's *Alien* from 1979. I'd say this similarity is more of a tribute to the timelessness of *Alien* than it is a criticism of *Godzilla*.

I think last year's *Pacific Rim* foreshadowed *Godzilla*. That was a sleeper that featured giant reptiles that had to be vanquished by giant robots. But, unlike *Godzilla*, that movie focused on the char- acters in the story. The giant robots and giant lizards were just the backdrop to the ongoing human drama. *Godzilla* misses that mark completely. While we do have some human characters in this story, there is little drama between them. They seem to be merely tossed around by the actions of the monsters.

There is a problem with who is the hero of this film. On the one hand, the elder Brody, Joe, kicks off the film as the lead character. Then, after a prologue of sorts, younger Ford Brody joins his father in Japan. Then, at about the one-third mark, Joe dies and it is Ford who carries the rest of the film. But Ford doesn't really have any goals to speak of. He at first just wants to get home to his family. Then he takes responsibility for a young Japanese boy who is separated from his parents. Then he is distracted by joining a military group to arm a bomb (he is an explosives expert after all). His motivations are all over the map and it makes the movie hard to follow.

 I agree, Greg. The hero story is a bit of a disappointment. At the beginning, we get attached to Joe Brody, whose feisty, tragic edginess captures our attention and attracts our sympathy. But just as we've bonded with him, the poor man is fatally crunched by a monster and we're seemingly left hero-less. Fortunately, Joe's son Ford takes over the hero role, but Ford is less interesting as a character. Ford's a bit plastic and a somewhat forgettable compared to his emotionally tortured father.

So we're left with a movie that gets an A+ grade for it's CGI effects of mammoth reptilian beasts destroying model trains and skyscrapers, but this occurs at the expense of a meaningful hero story. The decision to kill off Joe Brody so early in the movie is truly baffling, Greg. He was a good character and at the very least he could have buddied-up with his son to kill off the creatures. It's a poor decision on the filmmakers' part and it cost this movie a chance to be more than just a creature-fest.

Which leads us to review the villains in this story. Godzilla him- self seems to be a savior as he dispatches the evil winged pair of monsters in the end. But at what cost? The city is destroyed with massive loss of life. The two pterodactyl-type monsters were clearly the bad guys as they killed everything in sight. But these monsters were just the obstacles to Ford's heroic acts. He never really deals with them face-to-face. You might argue that this is a "man-vs-nature" story with Ford as the man and the winged MUTO (Massive Unidentified Terrestrial Organism) as nature. But it was dull from beginning to end with Ford running after the creatures and the creatures wreaking havoc wherever they went.

You're right, the villains in this story turn out not to be Godzilla but the two MUTO beasts who really have no evil qualities unless you call a very healthy self-preservation instinct 'evil'. These behemoths do wreak havoc on large human populations in their quest for food and reproductive success. One problem with the MUTOs is that we aren't privy to the reasons behind their existence, nor do we every truly understand their relationship to each other or to Godzilla. They're big and they're bad, and the filmmakers have decided that that's enough for us.

Scott, compared to other movies in this genre, *Godzilla* disappoints. For a longish, boring, CGI fest with no brains and pointless brawn I give this movie 2 out of 5 Reels. There is no clear hero and what we are offered is either a poor human meandering through the film or a questionable monster (Godzilla) who saves the day. I give these guys just 2 Heroes out of 5. And the flying MUTO are little more than beasts who want to reproduce and humanity is getting in the way. They get just 1 Villain out of 5.

Movie: Heroes: Villains: 🤠

I enjoyed *Godzilla* a bit more than you did, Greg. Sure, it was two hours of pointless destruction, but this pointless destruction was a cinematic delight to behold. Never have there been more awe-inspiring creatures on the Big Screen. Yes, the story was thin and the hero was a disappointment, but these heavyweight reptiles held just enough interest to earn 3 Reels out of 5.

For a wafer-thin hero who was a snooze-fest to me, and for the boneheaded decision to kill off the one man who would have made a far more interesting hero, this movie deserves only 1 Hero out of 5.

The villains are the true star of the film, although you are correct that they are mere animals who lack the depth that a human villain would have. But I'm not going to penalize this movie for having a shallow villain any more than I would penalize *Jaws* for its simple-minded shark or *Twister* for its brainless tornado. These remarkable monsters, with their radiation fetish and fire-breathing capabilities, held my interest and deserve at least 3 Villains out of 5.

 Movie: Heroes: Villains:

Gone Girl

Starring	Ben Affleck, Rosamund Pike, Neil Patrick Harris
Director	David Fincher
Screenplay	Gillian Flynn
Genre	Drama/Mystery/Thriller
Rated	R
Running Time	149 minutes
Release Date	October 3, 2014
Nick Dunne Protagonist	Single, Untransformed Positive Moral (Untransformed Lone Hero)
Amy Dunne Antagonist	Single, Untransformed Negative Moral (Untransformed Deceptive Lone Villain)

(Greg Smith, Founder of Agile Writers of Richmond, VA)

I just went to see *Gone Girl*. I guess that makes me a *Went Boy*.

(Dr. Scott Allison, Professor of Psychology, University of Richmond)

And when you went, you made quite a mess. Let's turn our attention to this interesting Ben Affleck-flick. Go ahead and recap, Went Boy.

We're introduced to Nick Dunne (Ben Affleck) - an unemployed author married to the woman of his dreams - Amy (Rosamund Pike).
He comes home to find his wife has gone missing. And all the clues
point to Nick as the culprit. Local Detective Rhonda Boney (Kim Dickens) is
tracking Nick's activity and is building a case against him. There's blood on
the kitchen floor and on the walls. There's Amy's insurance policy that was
doubled in recent days. There's the nosey neighbor who claims Amy said the
marriage was on the rocks - and Amy was pregnant. But without a corpse,
there cannot be a murder. Then, Boney finds a diary where Amy lays out a
story of a marriage gone bad and a husband she fears.

 As public opinion turns against Nick, he senses his imminent arrest.
Wisely, he seeks the legal counsel of Tanner Bolt (Tyler Perry),
who attempts to rehabilitate his public image. A big setback occurs
when Nick's adulterous affair with a college girl half his age is revealed. But
wait, a bigger reveal is that Amy isn't dead after all. We learn that Amy is
a psychopath who has orchestrated what appears to be the perfect frame and
set-up of Nick. Amy's plan is dealt a huge blow when she is robbed of all her
cash and must turn to an old boyfriend (Neil Patrick Harris) for refuge.

Scott, this is a great story. We're pulled in by the story of the perfect
relationship. Then the relationship sours. We are lulled into the
sense that Nick is the typical terrible husband. That he just might
be capable of murder after all. And just when we, like everyone else in the
movie, believe he is guilty - we learn that Amy isn't dead. In fact, she's setting
Nick up for her own murder.

This premise is easily as frightening as *Basic Instinct* or *Fatal Attraction*. Nick
has scorned Amy and now she uses every intimate detail she knows about Nick
to implicate him in a terrible crime. It's anyone's worst nightmare - that all
the secrets you share with the person closest to you can be used against you in
the court of public opinion.

The greatest element of this story is the turnabout of the villains. The first
half of the movie sets Nick up as a dreadful man (and to a certain degree it's
a deserved reputation). Then at the halfway point, the tables are turned and
Nick becomes the victim to Amy's villain.

You got that right, Greg. *Gone Girl* is a dark movie. It's dark in showcasing the worst of humanity and also dark in the way that darkness conceals things. There are hidden agendas of varying degrees throughout the movie, and they keep us guessing and re-guessing. This film is a chess game on steroids, with chess pieces moving methodically along the board in surprising and sinister ways. I've never been a big fan of Ben Affleck's acting ability, but here he is a master of exuding mixed signals, rendering us uncertain of his culpability and character.

Nearly all of this film's darkness emanates from the story's main malevolent character, Amazing Amy herself. For me, Amy is the most memorable female character in the movies since Lisbeth Salander in *The Girl With the Dragon Tattoo*, released in 2011. Amy is sexy, smart, confident, and accomplished. We cannot even imagine her attaining the level of diabolical evil that she reaches. But reach it she does. We're left aghast and appalled while admiring her stunning, disturbing intelligence.

Ben Affleck as the hero of the story is severely flawed. He is childish, a philanderer, and actually not that bright. We're given a tale of him as villain first and when the tables turn he is the victim. The story follows him center stage from beginning to end. It's his conversion from the controlling husband to the one controlled that we are witnessing. He's different from any other hero we've studied thus far. He is transformed, but this time, not for the better.

Amy is likewise a complex villain. At the start of the film she is painted as the dutiful wife who does whatever her husband wants to do. But at the halfway point we come to realize that she's the one who is controlling Nick. She becomes the villain. And again, unlike any villain we've studied so far, she is more capable, more cunning, and more powerful than the hero of the story. She is the ultimate villain.

 Nick is not your typical hero. He's not a terrible man but he's not a good man, either. He goes through hell in this movie yet we hardly see signs of change or growth in his character. He becomes wiser but appears not to use his wisdom to better himself or the world around him. I think this is the point of the movie. We learn that dark people do dark things, and if they're smart enough, they'll get away with murder, literally. We need heroes to stop them but in *Gone Girl* the heroes are neither smart enough nor virtuous enough to rid the world of its darkness.

I do believe that Rosamund Pike is outstanding in her role as Amy and deserves Academy Award consideration for her performance here. There is a multi-dimensionality to her acting, ranging from demure sweetness to true psychopathological rage. I agree with you, Greg, that she is the ultimate villain, making everyone around her look foolish as they try to keep up with her true motives or her next move. Amy is a force unto herself, literally; there are no henchmen or henchwomen to aid her. She is a true lone villain, perhaps the most formidable force of evil that we've seen this year at the movies.

Gone Girl clocks in at two and a half hours - and none of it was wasted. I was getting a little bored by the time we got to the midpoint where the tables are turned. Then I was riveted. This is a completely engrossing tale told spectacularly well by all members of the cast and crew. I give *Gone Girl* 5 out of 5 Reels.

Nick is a flawed hero as we have discussed. He's not altogether bright nor altogether virtuous. He lets women mold him into whatever they want him to be (his mother, other girlfriends, then Amy). We really don't have much sympathy for him as a victim. At the end of the movie he has a way out, but he isn't strong enough to take it. This is a complex protagonist that is difficult to score on our usual scale. I give Nick a 4 out of 5 Heroes.

Amy is the most manipulative, spiteful, vengeful, cunning and controlling villain we've ever seen. If there were a Villain's Hall of Fame, I'd nominate her for it. Her "unreliable first person" narration first paints her as the victim, but in the end we realize she's the one in control. I give Amy 5 Villains out of 5.

Movie:  Villains: Heroes:

Gone Girl is one of the year's best movies with it's stylish portrayal of love, treachery, and murderous revenge. This film drags us through the muck of human relationships and the nadir of human conduct. I enjoyed this movie despite the fact that afterward I was left feeling alarmed and ashamed of the human race. At film's end, there are hints of a sequel, which I would dread seeing with great anticipation. While not a perfect movie by any means, it is engrossing enough to merit a full 5 Reels out of 5.

The hero Nick is confident, handsome, and charismatic, but he's not terribly admirable. He blunders his way through the movie without evolving or learning from the disastrous choices he's made (and continues making). The fact that at the end he remains married to Amy is a horrifying testimony to his lack of heroism. That he even survives his arrogance and foolishness is a miracle – or perhaps it is grist for a sequel. The near absence of heroism in this movie is unfortunate but probably necessary to drive home the film's bleak message about humanity. Generously, I award the rather hapless Nick 3 out of 5 Heroes.

As you point out, Greg, Amy is a force to be reckoned with, one of Hollywood's most formidable and memorable villains we've seen in years. I believe her level of malevolence rivals that of Hannibal Lecter. I hope none of our readers take this the wrong way, but I'd enjoy seeing her tear up additional flesh in future sequels. Because of her magnetism, her backstory, and her ability to surprise us with one chilling act of evil after another, I'll also award her 5 Villains out of 5.

Movie:  Villains: Heroes:

The Grand Budapest Hotel

Starring	Ralph Fiennes, F. Murray Abraham, Mathieu Amalric
Director	Wes Anderson
Screenplay	Wes Anderson
Genre	Comedy/Drama
Rated	R
Running Time	100 minutes
Release Date	March 28, 2014
Gustave/Zero Protagonist	Duo, Positive to More Positive Emotional (Classic Hero/Sidekick)
Dmitri/Jopling Antagonist	Duo, Untransformed Negative Moral (Mastermind/Henchman Villains)

(Dr. Scott Allison, Professor of Psychology, University of Richmond)

Greg, are you Hungary to review *The Grand Budapest Hotel*?

(Greg Smith, Founder of Agile Writers of Richmond, VA)

You keep *pest*ering me to do it, so let's recap!

The movie begins with a young girl admiring a statue of a man simply known as 'The Author.' She begins reading one of his books that describes a trip he made in 1968 to the Grand Budapest Hotel. At that time the drab, outdated hotel attracted very few customers. During his stay, the Author (Jude Law) encounters the owner, Zero Moustafa (F. Murray Abraham), who is anxious to tell his story of how he came to own the Grand Budapest.

That causes another flashback to 1932 where a young Zero is taken under the wing of concierge extraordinaire M. Gustave (Ralph Fiennes). Gustave is quite the lady's man - if by lady you mean elderly widow. One of his "friends" has died and left him a fortune in the form of a priceless painting *Boy with Apple*. However, the children of the deceased are not willing to let the painting go that easily. They frame Gustave and he escapes from prison. Now the chase is on as Gustave and Zero are on a mission to clear his name and recover the painting.

Greg, *The Grand Budapest Hotel* is a strange movie about strange people. The movie tells the story of a man, Gustave, who is overly polite and loquacious in situations that call for neither quality. Gustave is a mentor figure for a young lobby boy named Zero who appears incapable of showing any facial expressions. The duo get caught up in a dangerous plot with many other equally strange people, each of whom has some quirky or menacing mannerism.

Wes Anderson-world is stylistically surreal and cartoon-like. Pastel colors tend to dominate and actors are instructed to master the art of nonverbal minimalism with their bodies, faces, and movements. There seems to be an exaggerated attempt to create and nurture caricatures of people and situations. Sometimes the effect is comical; at other times it is merely odd. If the goal was to make the movie sets and characters memorable, in a way that a bottle of Pepto-Bismol is memorable, then the goal has been achieved.

I enjoyed *Budapest* very much. Wes Anderson always delivers an
experience that you won't find in other films. Last year's *Moonlight*
Kingdom was another standout movie by Anderson. The characters
are always likable and innocent in their own way.

If I have a complaint about *Budapest* it is that it dragged on in the second act.
The film clocks in at just 100 minutes, but it felt like much longer. Another
complaint was the appearance of too many cameos. There is a hotel shootout
that had so many luminaries pop into frame that I was distracted from the
story.

 Ironically, within a movie that is as unconventional as a movie can
get, we have a rather conventional hero-sidekick combination. This
is not to say that these dual heroes are uninteresting. Far from it,
in fact. Gustave does a fair amount of mentoring of Zero, who grows from a
youthful innocent boy into an informed and experienced young man. Gustave
relishes his role as a mentor to Zero, and while I'm not sure that Gustave
changes much during the course of the movie, he certainly has plenty of heroic
traits. In fact, he dies performing an act of self-sacrifice.

I agree, Scott. In our book on heroes in the movies *Reel Heroes:*
Volume 1 we lay out the Hero/Sidekick as one of the types of duo-
heroes. Gustave and Zero play this pattern to full force. Zero knows
nothing of the world of hotels yet Gustave feels sorry for the boy because he
is a refugee. Here, the hero is the mentor to the young man whom we care
about because of his innocence and underdog status.

The story if rife with villains as well. We meet the eldest son of the widow,
Dmitri (Adrien Brody) who is intent on having the painting for his own. I was
pleased with the coloring of Dmitri. He is a vile man and we get a bit of his
backstory as the scorned son of Madame D.

Dmitri enlists the aid of a diabolical and evil henchman named Jopling
(Willem Dafoe) who has steel teeth and wears rings that double as brass
knuckles. While we don't get a lot of backstory on Jopling, he demonstrates
his villainy with the many killings and maiming of characters in the story.

The two main villains are a detestable pair for different reasons - Dmitri for his loathsome greed and Jopling for his psychopathic brutality. The movie doesn't delve into the details of these two villains' histories or life stories. These bad guys exist mainly to provide a grave challenge to Gustave and Zero.

It's interesting how movies often pack their villains with a familiar one-two punch. The main villain is often the mastermind of the operation, and the secondary villain(s) are usually the muscle who carry out the physical dirty work. This split-structure of villainy represents a departure from the more unified structure of the hero, who in order to succeed must possess both brains and brawn.

Scott, I enjoyed myself at *The Grand Budapest Hotel* and could find myself going back for a second visit. The characters were colorful and unique. While it was a bit slow in places, the film held my interest for most of the time. I give *Budapest* 4 out of 5 Reels.

The heroes in this story were likable, even affable. I enjoyed watching M. Gustave's growing fondness for Zero and Zero's growth under Gustave's tutelage. I give the hero-pair 4 out of 5 Heroes.

The villains were more complete in this film compared to others we've reviewed so far this year. However that isn't saying much. Still, they were stereotypes of villains gone by as the estranged son and his henchman. I give these evil-doers just 3 out of 5 Villains.

Movie: 　Heroes: 　Villains:

 The Grand Budapest Hotel isn't a great movie but it has an endearing and quirky charm that gives it lasting appeal. I give Wes Anderson lots of credit here. After all, "strange" doesn't always mean memorable, but here it does because of Gustave's unique combination of charm, courage, and quirkiness, and also because the film tosses out a look and feel that I've never seen before. Like you, I'll award *The Grand Budapest Hotel* 4 Reels out of 5.

As I've mentioned the hero duo of Gustave and Zero doesn't break much new ground, but I have to admire the transformation of Zero, who learns many life lessons from Gustave, not the least of which is loyalty. This is the trait that inspires Zero to hang onto the hotel decades after any rational person might do so. This hero pair earns a solid 3 Heroes out of 5.

In keeping with the rest of the movie, the villains were an odd pair that movie audiences love to hate. This mastermind-muscle pairing was effective although their characters were not as developed as they could have been. For the same reasons as you, Greg, I give them 3 Villains out of 5.

Movie: Heroes:  Villains:

Guardians of the Galaxy

Starring	Chris Pratt, Vin Diesel, Bradley Cooper
Director	James Gunn
Screenplay	James Gunn, Nicole Perlman
Genre	Action/Adventure/Science-Fiction
Rated	PG-13
Running Time	121 minutes
Release Date	August 1, 2014
Guardians Protagonist	Ensemble, Negative to Positive Moral (Redeemed Episodic Military Heroes)
Quill Antagonist	Single, Untransformed Negative Moral (Untransformed Mastermind Villain)

(Greg Smith, Founder of Agile Writers of Richmond, VA)

Guardians of the Galaxy is Marvel's next big franchise.

(Dr. Scott Allison, Professor of Psychology, University of Richmond)

Seems like it's an ever-expanding Marvel-ous universe. Let's recap.

We're introduced to Peter Quill (Chris Pratt) (who likes to call himself Star Lord). He's an outer space pirate aligned with the Ravagers. He's stolen an orb and wants to sell it on the black market. He no sooner escapes with his treasure when he is accosted by green-skinned Gamora (Zoe Saldana) who is aligned with the evil Ronan. But bounty hunters Rocket (a genetically engineered racoon voiced by Bradley Cooper) and Groot (a tree-like humanoid voiced by Vin Diesel) interfere with Gamora as they try to capture Quill. The lot of them are thrown into prison when the Nova Corps (the intergalactic police) get involved. It is in prison that they meet the very literal Drax (Dave Bautista) and our team of misfit *guardians* is complete.

 The Guardians are charged with the task of preventing the orb from falling into the hands of the evil Ronin, who will no doubt use the orb's powers to conquer the galaxy. Ronin eventually attacks the Guardians and steals the orb. When he unlocks the sphere, we see that it contains a beautiful infinity stone. Ronin absorbs the stone into his warhammer thereby acquiring the powers to destroy the galaxy. The remainder of the movie shows us how the Guardians are able to work together to re-acquire the infinity stone, thus saving the galaxy from destruction.

This was a fun addition to the Marvel universe. The opening scene was a little too reminiscent of *Raiders of the Lost Ark* for me. Quill makes his way into a cave to steal an orb which is immediately stolen by other thieves. Quill even makes an off-handed remark about Indiana Jones later on. The alien characters all seemed to be mere humanoids differentiated by their brightly colored skins. The beautiful Karen Gillan shaved her long red trusses for this film. She looked good as a blue-skinned gal, but sadly she really showed off her lack of acting chops.

As a hero group, I classify this merry band as a military ensemble lead by Quill. Quill has a lot of the qualities we see in hero characters. He's an orphan in a strange world. He has to prove his abilities to those who follow him. His team-mates are solid hero fare as well. Each has an edge to them, but they are all out to do the right thing. And they're funny, which adds a great twist to a hero's journey. The light air of this film really sets it apart from some of the other Marvel films we've seen. There's always a sense of urgency, but Quill and friends make everything look funny.

 Greg, my admiration for Marvel keeps growing. *Guardians of the Galaxy* is the fourth, count'em, *fourth* Marvel feature film released in 2014. We've seen *The Amazing Spider-Man 2*, *Captain America: The Winter Soldier*, *X-Men: Days of Future Past*, and now this quirky ensemble of galaxy-saving guardians. Despite the possibility that *Guardians* may be the weakest of the four Marvel entries this year, it's still an impressive achievement on several levels.

First, I found the always-strong CGI effects to be particularly extraordinary. The sets, production values, costuming, and character visuals are off-the-charts stunning. Second, this film's character development has Marvel's more than capable fingerprints all over it. For the most part, these characters are impressively constructed and also quite *memorable*, from Rocket the rambunctious Raccoon to Groot the shapeshifting tree. One complaint I have is that Peter Quill, our main hero, lacks the kind of charisma and magnetism that I would want to see in a lead character. Still, *Guardians* is a fun and, at times, thrilling roller coaster ride of a movie.

Yes, the CGI was great and nobody builds a universe the way Marvel does. Which does remind me of one problem I had with the film. It seemed to me that too many pains were taken to merge the universes of Thor, the Avengers, and Guardians together. The bit about the evil overlord Thanos and the infinity stones is a plot line that I think they are trying to weave into all the movies.

And speaking of villains, the villains in this story were really lacking. Thanos is the mastermind controlling his minions and having them do his dirty work - there's no real dimension there. Ronan as the henchman was painted equally evil without much character. Gillan's Nebula was Ronan's daughter with an attitude who hated her siblings for reasons we don't know. Of all the Marvel films we saw this year, *Guardians* had the weakest villains for our heroes to play against.

I completely agree with your assessment of the villains here, Greg. Marvel movies usually go to great lengths to craft villains of depth and nuance, but Thanos and Ronan are flat, uni-dimensional brutes. There were silly attempts to call many of the dark features of this movie "Necro" this or "Thanos" that, as if these death-related prefixes would somehow magnify the menacing factor. They didn't.

Still, I managed to enjoy the movie because even Marvel operating at three-fourths its usual effectiveness is better than most films. As you pointed out, Greg, there is plenty of joy and humor throughout the *Guardians*, as when it pokes fun of John Stamos or Kevin Bacon, or when it pulls out a clever pun worthy of evoking a good groan or two. Strangely, there is considerable violence in *Guardians*, more than it needed to retain its sense of danger and adventure. Still, I left the theater fairly satisfied.

Guardians of the Galaxy is a worthy addition to the Marvel tableau of superhero movies. I was thoroughly entertained by the origin story and the through-line of the infinity stone. The CGI mixed with real-world effect made for a visual feast that was worth the price of admission. Despite the fact that there were a lot of characters in this story, everyone got ample screen time. *Guardians* was a lot of fun. I give it 4 out of 5 Reels.

The heroes were pretty standard fare. I was happy to see Gamora played out as very tough and independent, and no-one's love interest. Quill has no superpowers to speak of (yet) so we identify with him as a human character we can all aspire to be. Rocket Raccoon was something I've never seen before in a picture, at least I've never seen a raccoon as an action figure. And who would have thought a tree with regenerating limbs could be a superhero? It was an unlikely ensemble, to be sure. I'm struggling with this score, but I'm afraid I have to give them just 3 out of 5 Heroes.

And as we discussed, contrary to villains in other Marvel films, the villains in *Guardians* are broadly painted with little dimension. And in some cases, given little in the way of villainy to actually carry out. I give them just 2 out of 5 Villains.

Movie: Villains:  Heroes:

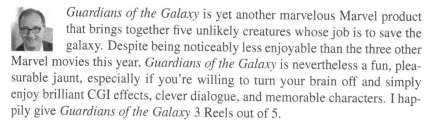

Guardians of the Galaxy is yet another marvelous Marvel product that brings together five unlikely creatures whose job is to save the galaxy. Despite being noticeably less enjoyable than the three other Marvel movies this year, *Guardians of the Galaxy* is nevertheless a fun, pleasurable jaunt, especially if you're willing to turn your brain off and simply enjoy brilliant CGI effects, clever dialogue, and memorable characters. I happily give *Guardians of the Galaxy* 3 Reels out of 5.

The primary strength of the movie is the military-like ensemble of five Guardians. These characters are a diverse collection of misfits who formed a whole greater than the sum of their parts. Drax, Groot, and Rocket are memorable characters whereas Peter Quill, our main hero, is a disappointment. As a group, these Fab Five follow the classic hero's journey and emerge forever transformed by their experiences. Overall, I'll generously award them 4 Heroes out of 5.

The villains are a sad collection of monolithically evil megalomaniacs who are as forgettable as a slice of Wonder Bread. Marvel must have decided that this film didn't deserve an interesting villain, which is a shame because the depth of the villains is a notable strength in every other Marvel offering this year. I can only give a rating of 1 Villain out of 5 here.

Movie: ⬤⬤⬤ Villains: 🤠 Heroes: ◇◇◇◇

Heaven Is For Real

Starring	Greg Kinnear, Kelly Reilly, Thomas Haden Church
Director	Randall Wallace
Screenplay	Randall Wallace, Chris Parker
Genre	Drama
Rated	PG
Running Time	99 minutes
Release Date	April 16, 2014
Burpo Protagonist	Single, Positive to More Positive Moral (Classic Lone Hero)
Board Antagonist	System, Positive to Negative Moral (Organization Fallen Villain)

(Greg Smith, Founder of Agile Writers of Richmond, VA)

Scott, I'm in seventh heaven over this week's film.

(Dr. Scott Allison, Professor of Psychology, University of Richmond)

Heaven can wait, Greg. Let's get on with the review.

Our story opens on Pastor Todd Burpo (Greg Kinnear) who is working odd jobs trying to make enough income to take care of his family. His income as the pastor to a small flock in Imperial, Nebraska is not covering their expenses. He lives a simple life filled with softball games, friends, and his family consisting of his wife Sonja (Kelly Reilly) and two small children including four-year-old Colton (Connor Corum). Things are going pretty well when something dreadful happens. It's any parent's worst nightmare.

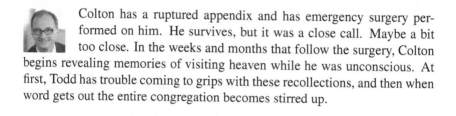

Colton has a ruptured appendix and has emergency surgery performed on him. He survives, but it was a close call. Maybe a bit too close. In the weeks and months that follow the surgery, Colton begins revealing memories of visiting heaven while he was unconscious. At first, Todd has trouble coming to grips with these recollections, and then when word gets out the entire congregation becomes stirred up.

The young man who plays Colton is just adorable as the four-year-old who reflects the innocence of youth. There is a scene where Colton is visiting a sick man in the hospital and Colton sees a child suffering from chemotherapy treatments. He walks over to the child and holds her hand and reassures her that nobody's going to hurt her.

Scott, this movie is based upon the real events documented in the book by the same name. The subtitle of the book is *A Little Boy's Astounding Story of His Trip to Heaven and Back*. The fact, however, is that this is the story of Todd Burpo's experiences and trials after revealing his son's visions to the world. This makes Burpo the hero of the story. Greg Kinnear does a good job of making Burpo look like an everyman with the world on his shoulders.

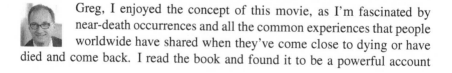

Greg, I enjoyed the concept of this movie, as I'm fascinated by near-death occurrences and all the common experiences that people worldwide have shared when they've come close to dying or have died and come back. I read the book and found it to be a powerful account of a young boy's claim that he visited heaven. I say 'powerful' because if you believe the father's account, there are three compelling pieces of evidence supporting the boy's story: (1) the boy's knowledge of his unborn sister, (2) the boy's knowledge of the grandfather he never met, and (3) the boy's confirmation of the image of Jesus as portrayed by a Lithuanian girl who also had a near-death experience.

But the movie-makers decided that this story alone wasn't powerful enough to carry the movie. So they decided to make the father the hero and to manufacture a good deal of anguish in the poor man. He's depicted as a hothead who kicks furniture and who struggles with the idea that his son has met Jesus. None of this happens in the book, and for good reason - it's a silly notion for the father, a Christian pastor, to disbelieve his son's story that heaven exists. The movie also fabricates a terrible crisis in the church over the veracity and meaning of the boy's story. These embellishments rang false for me.

I didn't read the book and you've pretty much summed up my problems with the story. It wasn't about the boy, it was about the father. 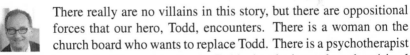 This tack follows a typical Christian pattern wherein the hero of the story (Pastor Burpo) reveals his belief in miracles and the faithful (despite their beliefs) reject him. This creates a martyr of the pastor and he must face ridicule and the wrath of his followers. But through his own faith and tenacity he convinces the un-faithful to follow and believe. It is a story that seems familiar to me from reading the Bible.

There really are no villains in this story, but there are oppositional forces that our hero, Todd, encounters. There is a woman on the church board who wants to replace Todd. There is a psychotherapist who preaches a scientific explanation to Todd when he instead needs spiritual guidance. There are also his own inner demons and difficult circumstances, including dire family finances and numerous personal health setbacks.

Again, many of the struggles that Todd faces do not appear in the book, which wisely centers on the sheer power of Colton's story rather than on reactions to the story. So we have a movie that tells a powerful story of a visit to heaven but strangely focuses on everyone getting wigged out by the story.

I'd have to differ with you there, Scott. The congregation of
Burpo's church are the villains. Or should I say "opposition". There
is no evil intent here. But they create the hardship that Burpo must
work against. Truly, if there were no oppositional force in the movie, there
would be little story.

I think we've seen this story before. Do you remember the classic film *Oh,
God*? In that film John Denver plays a man who talks to God and the entire
world including family and friends turn against him. It's only his faith that
sees him through the challenge.

There are a couple of classic Christian film tropes in store for the viewer.
Burpo makes a trip to a college professor who is an expert in out of body
experiences. She is a non-believer and has recently lost her husband to cancer
and is bitter and hates God for it. We saw this same character played to the
extreme in *God's Not Dead*.

 Heaven is For Real is an unconventional movie that puts all its emotional eggs in a single spiritual basket, namely, the "afterlife" experience of a young boy that seems to defy belief. The movie makes
the unfortunate decision to showcase the father's turbulent journey rather than
the child's, and the result is a film that doesn't ring true to me. There are
good performances by the entire cast, and as you note, Greg, Connor Corum
is adorable as the young Colton. But I cannot give this movie more than 2
Reels out of 5.

Greg Kinnear does a fine job in his role as Todd, but the hero journey lacks
both heft and believability. I found Todd to be one of the least spiritual people
I've seen in the movies, and yet he is a Christian pastor. Toward the end, he
and his wife finally see the light, but why it takes 90 minutes to see such a
bright light is beyond me. I can only give Todd 2 Heroes out of 5.

While I wouldn't call any of the characters villains per se, there were oppositional forces that force Todd to squirm, to suffer, and to change. One could
argue that this movie is a nice story of a family that prevails over serious financial, health, and spiritual setbacks. Still, some of these obstacles, such as
the congregation that freaks out, seem forced and fabricated. For that reason,
I can only give this film 2 Villains out of 5.

Movie: Hero:  Villain:

Scott, you pretty much read my mind. *Heaven is for Real* is a movie that preaches to the choir. If you're a believer you'll believe. If you're a doubting Thomas, you won't be convinced. I give the film 2 out of 5 Reels.

The hero is a simple confection of a good man in a difficult situation. Other films have dealt with this topic in a more convincing fashion with a more humble and sympathetic hero. I give Burpo just 2 out of 5 Heroes.

And the congregation as the villains were predictable and flat. They rate just 2 Villains out of 5. *Heaven is for Real* won't get many revisits.

Movie: 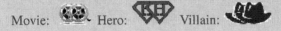 Hero: Villain:

The Hobbit: The Battle of the Five Armies

Starring	Ian McKellen, Martin Freeman, Richard Armitage
Director	Peter Jackson
Screenplay	Fran Walsh, Philippa Boyens, Peter Jackson, Guillermo del Toro
Genre	Fantasy
Rated	PG
Running Time	144 minutes
Release Date	December 17, 2014
Baggins Protagonist	Single, Positive to More Positive Emotional (Classic Lone Hero)
Sauren Antagonist	Single, Untransformed Negative (Untransformed Pure Evil Villain)
Orcs Antagonist	System, Untransformed Negative (Untransformed Military Villain)

(Dr. Scott Allison, Professor of Psychology, University of Richmond)

Greg, it looks like we finally made it to the final installment of *The Hobbit*.

(Greg Smith, Founder of Agile Writers of Richmond, VA)

It looks like we'll finally break the habit of watching *The Hobbit*.

The film opens with the tiny hamlet of Laketown being devastated by Smaug, the oversized, fire-breathing dragon. Tauriel (Evangeline Lilly) is helping many of the towns' citizens evacuate the ravaged city, and meanwhile Bard (Luke Evans) climbs a tower and manages to slay the smug Smaug using the black arrow. Bard leads the townspeople to safe refuge at the ruins of Dale, not too far from Mount Gundabad.

Meanwhile back at the mountain, King Thorin is affected with the dragon's fever and will not give up any of his gold. Meanwhile, the Orcs are planning an all-out assault on the mountain. Meanwhile, Gandalf is being rescued from a far-away place by the queen of the elves. There's a lot going on in this final installment of Peter Jackson's *The Hobbit*.

 Greg, *The Hobbit: The Battle of the Five Armies* is a worthy conclusion to the Hobbit trilogy (which wasn't a trilogy). We've been dazzled by the CGI virtuoso of modern movies before, but this film somehow manages to exceed the highest standards set in previous filmmaking. Seeing the *Battle of the Five Armies* in 3D did enrich the experience; I was blown away by the magnificent realism of every scene, especially scenes involving hand-to-hand combat. It seemed like I could discern every speck of dust and drop of blood. It's a truly an astonishing and mesmerizing experience.

More important, of course, is the story. As you mention, there is no shortage of characters here, nor is there a shortage of armies. Five is a lot of armies. Yet I didn't feel lost or overwhelmed. What I did feel was *fragmented*. By that I mean that the decision to break up the Hobbit into pieces, and then to deliver each piece a year apart, leaves me unsatisfied from the standpoint of coherent storytelling. This film gives us the final third of a single story, and it felt limited in that way because it *is* limited. I did enjoy *Five Armies* but the piecemeal delivery of the storyline has been less than fulfilling.

You're right about the high quality of this movie. The images were
filmed with stereo 5K cameras at 48 frames per second. That technology provides a level of crispness that was heretofore impossible
for film. The result is an image that resembles live action. At first I found
it distracting. But soon I was drawn into the story and the realism enhanced
what I was watching. It was a revolutionary experience.

We have quite a collection of heroes in this story. The main hero is Bilbo
Baggins. He undergoes a transformation from a quiet Hobbit happy to live in
the shire to a true adventurer. We like our heroes to transform and Bilbo covers
the gamut. The dwarf king, Thorin, is especially interesting as he traverses the
range of heroism to villain back to hero again. King Thorin is on a quest to
reclaim his lost kingdom and treasure. But once he regains his gold, he gets
dragon fever and becomes obsessively greedy, not willing to share a coin even
with those who helped him. But once Bilbo gives him a good talking to, he
returns to being a noble king, willing to share the wealth with those who are
deserving. We like to call this kind of hero the "round tripper" as they go from
heroic, to villainous, and then return as a redeemed hero.

No question there are plenty of heroes and villains to discuss here.
I enjoyed witnessing Bilbo grow in his courage with the help of
Gandalf as his mentor. His transformation is underscored by his
return trip home to Bag End. Nearly all of his belongings have been auctioned
off in an estate sale, signalling the shedding of his old self and the celebration
of his new persona. As befitting a classic epic tale, there are other heroes, of
course. But Bilbo deservedly takes center stage here.

This film features a formidable array of villainous characters, too. Foremost
are the Orcs, who embody a pure, relentless evil. The other intelligent races
that populate this movie have a richness and diversity within them, but not the
Orcs. They are all interchangeably evil. One scene near the end of this film
truly disappointed me. It was the *Fatal Attraction* demise of the head Orc,
who appears to be dead underwater until his eyes pop open and he bursts up
to fight one last fight before being vanquished (again). When, oh when, is this
gimmick going to be put to bed for good?

I enjoyed *The Hobbit* but found that three films really milked the story. The action was often slow and lumbering. The final fight scene was pretty impressive. Again, the technology was at the fore delivering amazing effects. However, I was disappointed that, yet again, the giant eagles flew in to save the day. I give *The Hobbit: The Battle of the Five Armies* 4 out of 5 Reels.

Bilbo and King Thorin make for great mythical heroes. Bilbo starts out as naive and grows into a courageous and moral hero. King Thorin starts out as a great leader then falls into the depths of villainy when he is overcome by dragon fever. But he is redeemed in the end. This is a great example of the redemptive hero. I give them 5 out of 5 Heroes.

The Orcs and Sauron are clearly pure evil villains. We don't get much insight into why they're so bad. Although with the introduction of Sauron we see that the Orcs and their leader Bolg create a hierarchy of evil. I give the Orcs 3 out of 5 Villains.

Movie: Villain: Hero:

 From a technical standpoint, *The Hobbit: The Battle of the Five Armies* is an outrageously successful film. Never before has CGI realism achieved such a majestic level of excellence. The story itself was the final third of a novel that was not intended to be partitioned into three units, and so I was left with a sense of incompleteness. Still, there is much to celebrate about richness of the Tolkien universe and the heroism of the characters, especially Bilbo Baggins. I'm therefore happy to award this movie 4 Reels out of 5.

I will grant you that Bilbo follows the classic hero's journey, but this film only shows us the final leg of the journey. Consequently, I didn't see him change or evolve much in this particular movie. I agree with you, Greg, that Thorin is a *round tripper* hero who moves from hero to villain and then back to hero again. We saw this earlier this year in *Maleficent*. But what triggers these changes in Thorin? Dragon sickness is apparently the answer. But why don't the other dwarves catch this disease? And how do a few words from Bilbo snap him out of it? Earlier speeches from others didn't do the trick. So I'm going to curmudgeonly give this movie 3 Heroes out of 5.

The villains were monolithically evil and not terribly interesting. One could say that Thorin's dragon sickness was a "Man versus Nature" villain, but that's a stretch. There are interesting glimpses of villainy among the Laketown residents, elves, and dwarves. These character types were fun to watch and added depth to a fragment of the story that truly needed some depth. Overall, I'll give a rating here of 4 Villains out of 5.

Movie: Villain:  Hero:

The Hundred Foot Journey

Starring	Helen Mirren, Om Puri, Manish Dayal
Director	Lasse Hallström
Screenplay	Steven Knight
Genre	Drama/Romance
Rated	PG
Running Time	122 minutes
Release Date	August 8, 2014
Hassan Protagonist	Single, Positive to More Positive Emotional (Classic Lone Hero)
Madam Mallory Antagonist	Single, Negative to Positive Moral (Enlightened Lone Anti-Villain)

(Dr. Scott Allison, Professor of Psychology, University of Richmond)

Greg, I do believe that a hundred feet would emit a terrible odor.

(Greg Smith, Founder of Agile Writers of Richmond, VA)

Not if it was at the Maison Mumbai where wonderful spices are used. Let's recap...

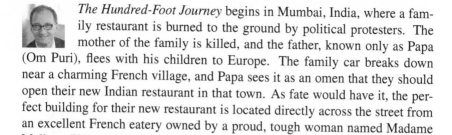

The Hundred-Foot Journey begins in Mumbai, India, where a family restaurant is burned to the ground by political protesters. The mother of the family is killed, and the father, known only as Papa (Om Puri), flees with his children to Europe. The family car breaks down near a charming French village, and Papa sees it as an omen that they should open their new Indian restaurant in that town. As fate would have it, the perfect building for their new restaurant is located directly across the street from an excellent French eatery owned by a proud, tough woman named Madame Mallory (Helen Mirren).

It turns out that Papa's young son Hassan(Manish Dayal) is a natural chef and learned to use spices at his mother's feet. Papa and Hassan go to the local food market to buy ingredients for their opening night when they learn that Madame Mallory has bought up all their goods. And now the war is on. Meanwhile, Hassan has taken an interest in Madame Mallory's sues chef Marguerite (Charlotte Le Bon). She hesitantly shares the secrets of French cuisine with Hassan who takes to learning these details like a duck to water. And now the stage is set with a competition for the tastebuds of the town and a budding romance.

Greg, *The Hundred-Foot Journey* is the perfect movie for people who are obsessed with food. Yes, there are two key relationships that unfold in the story, but they unfold around food, for food, and because of food. I will admit, of course, that this movie is far more than a food movie. Steven Spielberg and Oprah Winfrey have joined forces to produce a moral tale about ethnic differences and how they can inflame hostilities but also how these hostilities can be overcome.

The Hundred-Foot Journey isn't a great movie. Events unfold in a slightly too predictable way, and things wrap up just a tad too nicely at the end. Madame Mallory's sudden change of heart about her Indian rivals also stretches the bounds of believability. But having said all that, this is a film well worth watching. The performances are all first-rate, and we're introduced to characters we grow to care about.

You summed it up pretty well, Scott. I had some problems placing this movie in time. The village the story is set in looks like it fell out of the 1940s. It's not until Hassan makes the big time and moves to Paris that we get the sense that we're in modern times.

The movie's message seems to be that bad things happen when cultures clash, but good things happen when we learn to appreciate our common bonds - especially, in this case, a love of food.

The hero of the story is young Hassan who starts out naive and grows to become more adult and worldly. And he plays the part well. He is naive not only in the ways of fine dining, but also in the ways of love. He innocently plays on the affections of the young lady and gains insights into becoming the chef in Madame Mallory's kitchen.

Madame Mallory is both the villain and the mentor in this story. She starts out as an adversary to both Papa and Hassan. After her main cook sets the Maison Mumbai to fire, she has a change of heart and realizes that she has taken things too far. It's a different villain pattern than we've seen so far this year - that of the villain turned mentor.

 You're exactly right, and that's probably why the good Madame's character defies believability. I suppose I should shed my cynicism and just accept her huge change of heart in the middle of the movie. Although unlikely, this transformation from evil to good is something we all dream about seeing in difficult people. If we keep our focus on the true hero of story, Hassan, we recognize in him a nice coming-of-age tale of a young man who grows personally, professionally, and romantically. Hassan is a bit too perfect of a character, showing virtue and competence at every turn, but he does grow as an individual as he's thrown into the fire, so to speak.

As you point out, Greg, the villains do shift around during the course of the story. At first, Madame Mallory is the villain, but then the obstacles our heroes face begin to shift. Standing in Hassan's way is the cutthroat competition of the restaurant business. We learn that the grooming of a top chef requires more blood, sweat, and tears than the U.S. Navy Seal training program. So we first have a "Man vs. Man" theme (or should I say "Man vs. Woman") that evolves into a "Man vs. Nature" villainesque structure.

I enjoyed *The Hundred-Foot Journey* but I won't be sending back for seconds. It was a sweet, albeit a bit slow, story. You're right, Scott, it was a bit predictable. But I found it satisfied me rather than coming off as trite. The performances were delightful and I liked everyone in the story. I can recommend this movie, especially to my foodie friends. I give *The Hundred-Foot Journey* 3 out of 5 Reels.

The hero of the story is a bit of a Mary-Sue. Nothing he does is evil. Mostly he acts out of naivete more than animus. In that sense, he lacks dimension and I can only give him 3 out of 5 Heroes.

The villain, Madame Mallory, is more dimensional than the hero. She displays pride, envy, even racism. She plots to destroy her competition. But ultimately, she comes to realize that she is a better person than she has been and has a change of heart. This is a nice villain's journey. It's one of the few characters who we have reviewed over the last year that starts out as a villain and turns into some sort of hero. I give her 3 out of 5 Villains.

Movie: 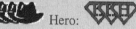 Villains: Hero:

 The Hundred-Foot Journey is a fine meal that is memorable for its color and its texture, but alas, you'll discover that it is a light supper or heavy snack only. I recommend this film for anyone who loves the process of preparing fine food, or who adores French countryside scenery, or who relishes sappy endings to stories about inter-family conflict. Like you, Greg, I award this movie 3 Reels out of 5.

Out of an ensemble hero cast, we see Hassan emerge as the main hero who represents the best of humanity. He is the catalyst for peace between the two families and then boldly pursues a challenging career as a top French chef. It's a fairly strong hero's journey, as we see Hassan navigate his way through cultural barriers, encounter a love interest, and receive mentoring from an unlikely source. I'll give Hassan 4 out of 5 Heroes here.

Madame Mallory proves to be an interesting and touching villain-turned-hero, even if I found her transformation to stretch the bounds of credibility. After her change of heart, there are plenty of social, cultural, and personal obstacles standing in Hassan's way of success. This film's villain structure is complex and shows us that humans are usually their own worst enemies. I'll agree with you, Greg, that the villains here deserve a rating of 3 out of 5.

Movie: Villains: Hero:

The Hunger Games: The Mockingjay - Part 1

Starring	Jennifer Lawrence, Josh Hutcherson, Liam Hemsworth
Director	Francis Lawrence
Screenplay	Peter Craig, Danny Strong, Suzanne Collins
Genre	Science Fiction/Adventure
Rated	PG-13
Running Time	123 minutes
Release Date	November 21, 2014
Katniss Protagonist	Single, Positive to More Positive Emotional/Mental (Classic Lone Hero)
The Capitol Antagonist	System, Untransformed Negative (Untransformed Government Villain)

(Greg Smith, Founder of Agile Writers of Richmond, VA)
I was hungry for another dose of Katniss Everdeen and the *Hunger Games*.

(Dr. Scott Allison, Professor of Psychology, University of Richmond)
I was hungry for bread and found me some Peeta. But enough games. Let's recap.

When we last saw Katniss (Jennifer Lawrence), she was being carried away in a hovercraft to District 13. She wakes up in a hospital room and we learn that she's been there for a couple months.
Plutarch (Philip Seymour Hoffman) is trying to convince President Coin (Julianne Moore) that Katniss is the key to the new revolution. That she is the
Mockingjay. Coin is unconvinced. After some failed attempts to get Katniss
to look heroic, Haymitch (Woody Harrelson) suggests they send her into the
field and get her gut reactions. They do and in the process they get footage of
Katniss destroying Capitol bombers and making a rousing speech.

 A rebel demolition team is sent to the Capitol to destroy a dam,
which is the Capitol's sole source of electricity. Meanwhile, Peeta
(Josh Hutcherson) is being held hostage by the central government
and is also being used as a mouthpiece for propaganda. At the end of one
of Peeta's speeches, he blurts out a warning that District 13 is about to be at-
tacked. His warning saves many lives, but also endangers his own life. Katniss
convinces the president to send a rescue team into the Capitol to get Peeta. But
the reunion between the two star-crossed lovers does not turn out as expected.

Scott, I was pretty disappointed in this prelude to the final episode
in the *Hunger Games* series. It represents only half the last novel
and moves really slowly. It's as if the writers and director were
trying to fill up space to make the film stretch out to 120 minutes. Still, it was
true to the source material. The special effects and acting were very good. But
there wasn't much of a story. It was all a set up for the final movie, due out in
November of 2015.

 Actually, Greg, unlike you, I enjoyed *Mockingjay Part 1* more than I
did the first two *Hunger Games* movies. For a change, there were no
hunger games situations involving kids hunting each other. Instead,
we are presented with an intriguing psychological battle between President
Snow and Panem's rebels. We are shown techniques that governments use

to win the hearts and minds of the masses. It's a fascinating chess game, orchestrated by Plutarch on one side and Snow on the other.

Best of all, we finally see Katniss Everdeen undergo a personal transformation. My main complaint about the first two installments of *Hunger Games* has been the absence of growth in the character of Katniss. She's been a heroic figure from the very outset of the first movie, when she takes her sister's place as a participant in the games. But in *Mockingjay - Part 1* we finally see Katniss develop into something new – a leader. She transcends her role as the brave, selfless, resourceful warrior. By the end of this film she has evolved into an admired leader and statesman, er, states*person*. It's a welcome change to see Katniss ascend to a new, higher level of development.

We've disagreed on this before - I've always thought Katniss was a great hero. But yes, she definitely grows into a new role in this latest chapter. Like a classic hero, she is given the call to adventure but she refuses the call. She doesn't want to be the Mockingjay. But once she realizes Peeta is alive and captive in the Capitol, she takes up the mantle of the hero and becomes the Mockingjay so that she can save Peeta.

President Snow (Donald Sutherland) is exposed to be a villainous lout who rose to his position of power by poisoning his opponents. He represents the classic "mastermind" villain - one who controls others and rarely gets his hands duty. Like a puppet master, he coerces Peeta to record propaganda that tells the people of the districts that Katniss was the evildoer and that they should not follow her.

 On the one hand, you could say that the villain here is a dull and simple mastermind. But in a sense, this movie tells a villain story like no other. Peeta, one of the main heroic figures in the first two movies, has now evolved into an oppositional character. Yes, it is true that Peeta's been brainwashed, but his call for Panem to cease hostilities conflicts with Katniss's plans to reform this dystopian, dysfunctional Capitol government. So you could argue that this film gives us a glimpse of a Stockholm-syndrome-like process of villain development.

I was glad to get another episode of *The Hunger Games* and another dose of a great female hero. We're really getting quite a few of them now (witness *Divergent* and *Lucy*). While I was disappointed that I'll have to wait another year before the final chapter will be played out, I liked this movie enough to give it 4 out of 5 Reels.

Katniss grows more in this film than in previous films. The filmmakers are not dressing our hero in flowing gowns and showing off her "attributes." She's dressed in battle gear. She's a tough, strong leader. I love seeing this growth not only in Katniss, but in the types of female role models that are emerging for our young women. I give Katniss 5 out of 5 Heroes.

The villains are not as pronounced in this segment as they were in previous ones. We're given a little more information about President Snow and his backstory. We are definitely treated to a look inside Snow's mind and how he manipulates not only physically, but also psychologically. I'm hoping we'll see more of that development in the final installment. I give President Snow 3 out of 5 Villains.

Movie: Villains: Hero:

 For me, *Hunger Games: Mockingjay Part 1* is arguably the strongest of the three *Hunger Games* movies. The film has less action but is more psychologically compelling in its portrayal of social movements, leadership development, and brainwashing techniques. Our hero Katniss has stepped up significantly to become much more than a young woman who can survive a deadly game. She is now a heroic leader of the Panem people. I give this movie 4 Reels out of 5.

As mentioned, this is the strongest hero story of the three *Hunger Games* movies. Katniss is thrown into the world of political leadership and, as such, she is required to grow in an unfamiliar world that stretches her personally. She is not only transformed as a person, but she also transforms an entire society. I award her 5 Heroes out of 5.

President Snow is a fairly formulaic mastermind villain, but Peeta's surprising role as an oppositional force to Katniss's leadership turns out to be the main focus of the film. Without Peeta's brainwashed adversarial presence and without his murderous attack on Katniss, this movie would earn a rating of 1 Villain out of 5. But Peeta's unique oppositional role bumps my rating up to 3 Villains out of 5.

Movie: Villains: Hero:

The Identical

Starring	Blake Rayne, Ray Liotta, Ashley Judd
Director	Dustin Marcellino
Screenplay	Howard Klausner
Genre	Drama/Music
Rated	PG
Running Time	105 minutes
Release Date	September 5, 2014
Ryan Protagonist	Single, Positive to More Positive Moral/Emotional (Classic Lone Hero)

(Greg Smith, Founder of Agile Writers of Richmond, VA)

Scott, we just saw *The Identical*. It wasn't Elvis, but an amazing simulation.

(Dr. Scott Allison, Professor of Psychology, University of Richmond)

I had the identical reaction, Greg. Let's recap.

It's the Great Depression and William and Helen Hemsley (Brian Geraghty, Amanda Crew) can't afford to keep their newly born identical twin boys. They decide to give one of them to Reverend Wade and his wife (Ray Liotta and Ashley Judd). The boys are never to know their origins. Dexter Hemsley, the son that stayed, goes on to be a big rock-n-roll star. Meanwhile, Ryan Wade (Blake Rayne) is growing up as a preacher's son - but he has the gift of music. While the Reverend Wade wants Ryan to follow in his father's footsteps, Ryan has other ideas.

 Ryan eventually tells his dad that his true calling is a career as a musician, not as a minister. Reverend Wade does not take the news very well at all. Ryan finds success imitating his twin brother's hit songs on stage, but soon he grows tired of the gig and wants to produce his own original music. One day Ryan discovers that he is actually Dexter's twin brother. He reconciles with his father and has a tearful reunion with his biological dad.

Scott, I have read that Elvis was a twin and his brother died at birth. Elvis spent his life guilt-ridden wondering if he had so much power because he had stolen it from his twin. This movie appears to try to answer the question: "What if Elvis' brother had lived?"

If that is the case then the filmmakers went out of their way to do so without specifically saying so. They hired Blake Rayne (who is himself an Elvis impersonator) who looks so much like Elvis that sometimes you're left wondering if Rayne isn't himself a twin of the King of Rock-n-Roll. The music is patterned after the rockabilly themes of the 1950s but never comes close to really doing justice to the same. And the story itself seems like a retread of movies gone by where a preacher's son just isn't cut out for the cloth and wants to pursue a life of forbidden music (or dance, or acting, or fill-in-the-blank).

Greg, *The Identical* is a simple, sweet movie that's a throwback to 1970s made-for-television films. Today you'd see this type of movie on Hallmark cable television. There's nothing specifically wrong with this movie. The acting, directing, and production are all fine. The problem is that there is nothing distinctive or distinguishing about the film. No new ground is broken, and in fact we've seen tales of this type a thousand times before.

If you are going to take us, the audience, down a well-worn path, you'd better include some especially dazzling scenery along the way. We don't have that here. Even the music is pedestrian. Blake Rayne is impressively Elvis-esque but my feet weren't a-tappin' like they were during *Jersey Boys* earlier this year. I found myself rooting for the characters and hoping that something interesting would happen. Alas, it never did.

As a hero, Ryan Wade does all right. He's a good, honest guy with lots of charisma and boy-like charm. But as you point out about the film itself, Ryan doesn't really have anything interesting to set him apart from other heroes we've seen this year or last. He just goes through the paces and sings some really forgettable songs.

There aren't any real villains in this story. The preacher / father character pushes Ryan down a path like the one he followed. And when Ryan finally diverges from the path, the father delivers contradictory messages by lauding the fact that the boy made an adult decision, then tells him he is breaking his father's heart. It's pretty tame stuff.

 I agree that Ryan is hardly the most interesting character we've seen on the big screen. But I do have to give him credit for undergoing a significant transformation as a hero. He starts out with an overeagerness to please his father, a type of over-selflessness that limits him both professionally and spiritually. His missing inner-quality is his backbone, which he finally develops when he courageously stands up to his father. He summons this same courage later when he defies his business manager. *The*

Identical shows us how we can never fulfill our full potential until we become true to ourselves.

You're right, Greg, that there are no bad people in this story, only some challenging circumstances encountered by a man who is struggling to discover himself. I'm leaning toward calling this a "Man vs. Self" struggle in which the "villain" to overcome (if you could call it that) is one's own inner limitations. Ray Liotta deserves some praise for his portrayal of a good man and a good preacher who smothers his son's potential yet later redeems himself. Reverend Wade could have succumbed to a trite stereotype of the evil, backward southern minister, but to this film's credit, he doesn't.

The Identical won't be winning any awards this year. It was a plodding, uninteresting, conflict-free, two hours of uninspiring music, dialog, and plot. There were some nice performances by veteran actors Ray Liotta and Ashley Judd. Newcomer Blake Rayne has a nice future of playing Elvis, but little else. I give *The Identical* just 2 out of 5 Reels.

Ryan Wade is about as dull a hero as we've ever seen on the big screen. There are no hard decisions or climactic surprises. I give him just 1 Hero out of 5.

And whether you think the opposition is Ryan himself, or the preacher daddy, or Ryan's awkward situation, there aren't any real villains to speak of. And the conflicting forces were pretty weak. I give *The Identical* just 1 out of 5 Villains.

Movie: Villains: Heroes: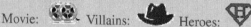

 The Identical might win an award, Greg, but it would be a Razzi Award. To be honest, this film isn't that bad, it's just outdated. Audiences from the 1950s would be impressed by *The Identical* but today's audiences demand greater sophistication in the plot, the characters, and the overarching themes of the story. There is a charming sweetness to the story but it can't carry the plain oversimplicity of everything we see here. I agree that this film merits a score of only 2 Reels out of 5.

As I noted earlier, there is a fairly decent hero story in *The Identical*. Ryan Wade may be a rather simple man but he is forced to grow and develop some cajones to escape the oppressive influence of his father. It's not a particularly inspiring hero's journey but several key elements of the journey are in place here. A more sophisticated, updated version of the hero story might garner a higher rating but I can only muster 2 Heroes out of 5 here.

Ryan Wade encounters no villains other than himself in this movie, and so the villain rating in this film depends entirely on how we witness Ryan overcome the weaknesses that are holding him back as a character. Unfortunately, there isn't much meat on this bone, just some flabby gristle that left me largely unsatisfied as a consumer. The paucity of interesting characters is this film's main deficit, especially in the realm of villainy. Like you, Greg, I can only give a villain score of 1 out of 5.

Movie:  Villains: Heroes:

The Imitation Game

Starring	Benedict Cumberbatch, Keira Knightley, Matthew Goode
Director	Morten Tyldum
Screenplay	Andrew Hodges, Graham Moore
Genre	Biography/Drama/Thriller
Rated	PG-13
Running Time	114 minutes
Release Date	December 25, 2014
Turing Protagonist	Single, Untransformed Positive Mental (Untransformed Lone Hero)
Nazis Antagonist	System, Untransformed Negative Moral (Untransformed Government Villain)

(Dr. Scott Allison, Professor of Psychology, University of Richmond)

We just watched another World War II flick, Greg. This one is quite educational.

(Greg Smith, Founder of Agile Writers of Richmond, VA)

Benedict Cumberbatch does a good *imitation* of Alan Turing. Let's recap:

We meet young Alan Turing (Benedict Cumberbatch), a brilliant mathematician, logician, and cryptologist. Turing is a socially awkward man who is fascinated with communication codes. He is applying for a position in the British military to help the Allied forces crack the coding system used by Nazi Germany. Turing is placed in charge of a small group of other brilliant minds who are assigned the task of deciphering the Nazi's "Enigma" codes.

Things are not that easy for Turing. The commanding officer expects the code breakers to decipher messages in 24 hours. But the cipher codes change each day. Turing believes that he must build a machine that will determine the Enigma settings automatically. This effectively breaks the Enigma code permanently.

But Turing needs help. He creates a math puzzle that is published in the British newspapers to attract mathematically inclined minds. One of the contestants turns out to be a bright young woman named Joan Clark (Keira Knightley). Turing hires her, but she isn't allowed to work with the other men - because she's a woman. So Turing surreptitiously feeds her secret documents so she can help with the code breaking. And now the race is on to crack Enigma before the Germans overtake Great Britain.

 The Imitation Game is one of the better movies of 2014. Like *A Beautiful Mind* and *The Theory of Everything*, this movie tells the story of a male genius scientist who is socially challenged and requires the help of a healthy, stable woman for his genius to be realized. Benedict Cumberbatch is terrific in this role and deserves Oscar consideration.

The hero story here is constructed with care. Turing is sent into an unfamiliar world in which his vast creativity is put to the ultimate test. His abrasive honesty wins him few friends and attracts several enemies within the British military and intelligence unit. His only ally is his woman friend Joan whom we think is a love interest until Turing's homosexuality is revealed. Joan proves to be a loyal friend and mentor whose steadfast companionship, not to mention her own genius, proves essential for Turing to triumph.

You're right that the story is constructed with care, Scott. Sadly, it bears little resemblance to the historical facts. Certain elements are true to life: Nazis, Germany, Britain, Enigma, Joan Clark, Turing, were all there at the same time. But the competition between Turing and the lead general, Commander Denniston, (Charles Dance) was fabricated. Turing's abrasive (borderline Asperger's) personality was exaggerated. The objections of the military to creating a machine to crack the code was a complete fiction. Apparently the truth of history wasn't enough to make a compelling story.

What was true was Turing's homosexuality and his doomed relationship with Joan. This is where the tragedy of *The Imitation Game* hits home. After having literally saved the world from the Nazi onslaught, Turing is discovered in 1950 to be gay and is subjected to chemical castration (or face imprisonment). Turing was unable to live under those conditions and ultimately committed suicide. It wasn't until 2013 that Queen Elizabeth pardoned him. Unlike the other movies you mention, Scott, this one doesn't have such a happy ending for our hero.

 You've pointed out the irony within the tragedy of this story. The very society that Turing saves ends up turning against him. Turing defeats the Nazis but he cannot defeat the English society that is intolerant of his sexual orientation. There aren't many hero stories in which the hero saves the people who kill him. It's truly a sad, embarrassing, and appalling treatment of a man who should have been revered.

That's another of my beefs with this movie, Scott. They had to concoct a villain for Turing to fight against. So they created the "Representative" villain in the form of the Commander Denniston. He represents all the conventional thinking in the military and in British society at large. The unseen enemy is the oncoming German army. The writers also create an enemy in the form of time itself. Since the Enigma code is changed daily, the code breakers have to decipher the messages before midnight each night. So, we get a nice countdown to 12:00 every day which creates a nice sense of tension.

Overall, *The Imitation Game* is two hours well spent, all the historical inaccuracies notwithstanding. Alan Turing is known as the Father of modern computer science and artificial intelligence, and this film gives us some insight into the challenges he faced in developing one of the world's first computers. Turing's heroism may have done more to defeat the Nazis than that of any other single individual. This movie tells a great story and features outstanding performances from the entire cast. As a result, I'm happy to award this film 4 Reels out of 5.

Turing's hero story is a stirring one. The man has many demons to overcome and makes many enemies. Does his character become transformed the way a good hero should? Perhaps not. Ironically, his refusal to change may be the key to his heroism. Maybe this is a tale about a British society that refuses to transform as much as it is a tale about a hero who shouldn't need to. I give Turing's heroism 4 Heroes out of 5.

Turing is surrounded by villains, including his own people whom he saves. The villains here are two institutions: (1) the Nazis with which Britain is at war, and (2) the antiquated moral codes of the English society that ultimately slay Turing. The manufactured human obstacles within the British military are throwaway characters who are caricatures or tropes of typical obstructionist characters in police and military movies. I'll be generous and give this entire diverse array of villains a rating of 3 Villains out of 5.

Movie: Villain: Hero:

Scott, I'm a computer scientist and Turing is one of my personal heroes. He laid the foundation for formal computing theory (the Turing Machine). I am thrilled that a movie that celebrates his genius was given a proper Hollywood treatment and didn't shy away from Turing's homosexuality. However, I can't reconcile the historical inaccuracies that pepper this film. It's a complete fiction that merely borrows the essence of the truth. I would normally agree with your score of 4 Reels, but I'm knocking one off because I think the true story would have made an equally viable movie. I give *The Imitation Game* just 3 out of 5 Reels.

Turing is a tragic hero in that he saves the world from the Nazi scourge, only to be destroyed by the very people he saved. Benedict Cumberbatch delivers a wonderful performance and I agree that he should be nominated for an Oscar. There isn't much transformation here. There is a scene where Joan Clark lectures Turing on playing nice with his fellow mathematicians. After which Turing appears to make friends by sharing apples with his co-workers. But he overcomes obstacles that allow him to rise to the level of a true hero. I give this presentation of Turing 4 out of 5 Heroes.

As you point out, the villains here are pretty generic. Nazis are a pretty safe bet as a villain in any story. And Denniston gives Turing a ripping hard time. I can't summon more than 2 out of 5 Villains for this film.

Movie: Villain: Hero:

Interstellar

Starring	Matthew McConaughey, Anne Hathaway, Jessica Chastain
Director	Christopher Nolan
Screenplay	Jonathan Nolan, Christopher Nolan
Genre	Adventure/Science-Fiction
Rated	R
Running Time	169 minutes
Release Date	November 7, 2014
Cooper Protagonist	Single, Positive to More Positive Emotional/Spiritual (Classic Lone Hero)
Time Antagonist	System, Untransformed Negative (Time Villain)

(Dr. Scott Allison, Professor of Psychology, University of Richmond)

Greg, it's just as I thought – Matthew McConaughey is a space cadet.

(Greg Smith, Founder of Agile Writers of Richmond, VA)

This could have been called *2001: The Year We Make Contact*. Let's recap:

We meet a man named Cooper (Matthew McConaughey) who lives on earth in the not too distant future. The Earth at this point is a dying planet. Dust storms and blight are ravaging a dwindling human population that relies on a weakening agrarian economy. Cooper has a teenage son and a 10-year-old daughter named Murphy (Mackenzie Foy), whose bedroom is the scene of odd occurrences. Books fall off her shelves and dust arranges itself in strange patterns. Cooper figures out that the dust contains coordinates to a location nearby. When he and Murphy drive there, they discover a huge, secret NASA base.

Because the Earth is dying, the only way out is towards the stars. By some miracle a wormhole has emerged near Saturn (why so far away?) and NASA has sent 12 men and women out to find planets on the other side of the wormhole (near other stars) that could sustain the survivors of Earth. But there is a "Plan B" - they've in vitro-fertilized enough eggs to start a new colony of humans on a habitable planet in the event that it takes too long to find a safe world. Take too long, you say? Well, because of the relativistic effects of space travel and flying near black holes and through wormholes, what seems like a few years to our heroes could be a century back on Earth. So, NASA has asked Cooper (a former astronaut) to man the final mission and find the habitable planet. But, he will have to leave behind his young daughter. Will he return in time to save her? Or will he be marooned in space leaving behind the last of his kind?

Interstellar is a complex, ambitious, space epic. It's a long movie, covering almost three hours, and its topic and detailed story are so complex that if it were a television show it could be a long-running mini-series. As a movie, it could have easily been carved into a trilogy. But the decision was made to condense this sweeping arc into a single 170-minute long film. The result is a movie that is breathtaking in scope but a bit too densely packed to give its grand cosmological theme the room it needed to breathe.

Still, I was impressed. *Interstellar* is no lightweight escapist science fiction story. There is a lot to sink our teeth into here, and some of it is pretty heavy emotional material. The earth is in its death throes, the close bonds between fathers and daughters are being shattered, and heroic astronauts are dying in space while trying to save humanity from extinction. We learn that John Lennon was prescient when he sang "love is the answer" more than 40 years ago, as love is interwoven with physics during the film's many attempts to explain the workings of the universe.

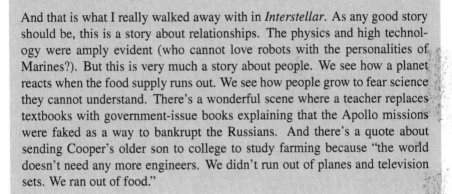

When you look at *Interstellar* you cannot help but compare it to classic science fiction movies gone by. It has the trippy look and feel of *2001: A Space Odyssey*. But it is far more coherent than Kubrick's masterpiece. And, like *Contact*, the relationships and bonds between father and daughter are at the core of this story.

And that is what I really walked away with in *Interstellar*. As any good story should be, this is a story about relationships. The physics and high technology were amply evident (who cannot love robots with the personalities of Marines?). But this is very much a story about people. We see how a planet reacts when the food supply runs out. We see how people grow to fear science they cannot understand. There's a wonderful scene where a teacher replaces textbooks with government-issue books explaining that the Apollo missions were faked as a way to bankrupt the Russians. And there's a quote about sending Cooper's older son to college to study farming because "the world doesn't need any more engineers. We didn't run out of planes and television sets. We ran out of food."

As hero stories go, you can't do much better than *Interstellar*. Cooper follows the classic hero journey almost to the letter. He is sent out into space (the unfamiliar world) and he is charged with saving the world. All heroes are missing some quality, and in Cooper's case he is missing an understanding of what binds the universe together. The answer is not unlike what Dorothy discovers in *The Wizard of Oz* – the answer is love, home, and gravity.

Ironically, Cooper mentors himself, or more specifically (using wormhole time-travel magic) Cooper's older self serves as the mentor to his younger self. Professor Brand (Michael Caine) and an older version of Murphy also assist Cooper on his journey. At the end, Cooper is a transformed individual, having gained an understanding of his place in the universe. Overall, it's a textbook hero story.

I think you're giving short-shrift to the message here. While Cooper already understands how to love - he has an undying love for his daughter. But he doesn't see love as a binding force in the universe - as much as we see time or the three dimensions. He has an argument with co-astronaut Brand (Anne Hathaway) who wants to let her heart be her guide. She posits that finding her lost love (one of the astronauts who went before them) is just as valid as calculating orbits and fuel ratios.

And this is the lesson that our hero ultimately learns. It is his love for his daughter that finally drives him to make a connection with her in the past. He manipulates time and space to send her a message that will save her and what is left of humanity. In the end, the lesson learned is that love binds the universe just as much as any other dimension. That's pretty heady stuff for a geek movie.

If you want to look for villains, we see a different take on villainy here. Professor Brand makes the decision for all mankind that trying to escape Earth and transplant the existing humans on another planet is fruitless. He has decided that Plan B is the ultimate solution. So, he's lied to his daughter as well as everyone else on the mission. Plan A was never the goal. This villainy is different from most that we've seen. This is the villainy of a lack of hope. The Professor gave up hope for all of mankind and reasoned that the only hope was to start over.

One of the castaway astronauts was Dr. Mann (Matt Damon in a surprise appearance). He knew about Plan B. But the planet he found was not appropriate for human colonization. He purposely sent back a glowing report so that someone would come and rescue him. He has the villainous attribute of self-centeredness. This is also the point where the movie talks about preservation of the species and preservation of the individual. The conclusion is that the species can never overcome the selfish aspects of self-preservation.

There is a good reason why *Interstellar* is a November release rather than a summer popcorn release. This movie makes us think, not just feel. We are treated to fabulous CGI effects, of course, but more importantly we are compelled to ponder deeply about our place in the universe and what lengths we would go to save our planet. The integration of love and gravity as the glue that binds us all together is an inspiring take-home message. I give this movie 4 Reels out of 5.

As I noted, the hero story would make Joseph Campbell proud. Most of the central elements of the hero's journey from classic myth and legend shine through in their fullest form. Cooper possesses just about all eight of the Great Eight characteristics of heroes: he is strong, smart, resilient, charismatic, reliable, caring, selfless, and inspirational. There is even a reverse form of "atonement of the father". I give him 5 Heroes out of 5.

The villainy in this movie is difficult to categorize, and you're correct, Greg, that it defies convention in some ways. Professor Brand and Dr. Mann are possible villains, yes, but Cooper's main opponent is Nature. He is in a constant race against time and other laws of physics. *Interstellar* is not a movie about a hero defeating a villain. It's about a hero solving problems of the heart and problems of nature. For this reason, my villain rating is a mere 2 out of 5.

Movie:  Villains: Heroes:

I agree, Scott. *Interstellar* was clearly released in November as an Oscar contender. It has high-caliber stars (McConaughey, Hathaway, Caine, Damon, Chastain) and high-value CGI. But that wasn't enough for *Gravity* last year. We'll have to see what Meryl Streep is up to this year. Still, I was totally engrossed for the full 170 minutes. And I *am* the target demographic for this movie (Baby Boomer Geeks). I give *Interstellar* 5 out of 5 Reels.

McConaughey really delivered in this film (although there were a few truck driving scenes that seemed to echo his recent "Lincoln" commercials). As a hero Cooper has everything we look for. He is so selfless that he gives up a lifetime with his daughter to save the human race. That's a lot of self sacrifice. I give Cooper 5 out of 5 Heroes.

And I hate to agree with you three times in a row, Scott, but it's true: Time is the villain in this story. It is warped and twisted in ways like no other villain we have studied this year. Still, you need a human character to have an argument with, or to be betrayed by. Professor Brand and Dr. Mann weren't the strongest of villains, but they exposed two different parts of the villain's psyche (lack of hope and self-preservation) that we haven't seen before. I give them 3 out of 5 Villains.

Movie: Villains: Heroes:

Jack Ryan: Shadow Recruit

Starring	Chris Pine, Kevin Costner, Keira Knightley
Director	Kenneth Branagh
Screenplay	Adam Cozad, David Koepp
Genre	Action/Mystery/Thriller
Rated	PG-13
Running Time	105 minutes
Release Date	January 17, 2014
Jack Ryan Protagonist	Single, Positive to More Positive Moral (Classic Lone Hero)
Cherevin Antagonist	Single, Untransformed Negative Moral (Face [of Russia] Villain)

(Greg Smith, Founder of Agile Writers of Richmond, VA)

Scott, it's time for a look at the latest Jack Ryan movie.

(Dr. Scott Allison, Professor of Psychology, University of Richmond)

Indeed. Amazing that Captain Kirk has time to work for the CIA.

Jack Ryan (Chris Pine) is a boy-scout-looking young man who
graduated from college with a degree in finance and joined the
Marines about the time of the 2011 World Trade Center bombings.
He is working on his PhD while serving in Afghanistan when his helicopter is
shot out of the sky by a Rocket Propelled Grenade. While in the hospital re-
covering from a crushed vertebrae, he meets Cathy Muller (Keira Knightley),
a young medical student who takes a liking to Jack. Enter a shadowy figure
(Thomas Harper played by Kevin Costner) who comes knocking and entices
Jack to join the CIA as a financial analyst to try and prevent a future 9/11.

 Ryan agrees to serve as a CIA agent while working as a financial
analyst on Wall Street. He soon discovers that Russia has firewalled
away large piles of cash and he suspects the Russians of propping
up the dollar and engineering an American economic collapse from which
Russia will benefit. The only way Ryan can find out for sure is to travel to
Moscow to meet with the Russians. An attempt is made on Ryan's life as
soon as he arrives and, even worse, his fiancee Cathy (who doesn't know of
his CIA status) surprises him by showing up at his Russian hotel room.

Scott, this is the first Jack Ryan movie since Tom Clancy died.
The others (*The Hunt for Red October, Patriot Games, Clear and
Present Danger, & The Sum of All Fears*) were set during the cold
war era. This new incarnation attempts to bring Jack Ryan up-to-date and
place him in the current terrorist era. However, the attempts to make financial
analysis look as sexy as submarine warfare fall flat. *Jack Ryan: Shadow Recruit* is dull and plodding as it tries to make an attack on the USA's financial
infrastructure seem scary. It doesn't and *Jack Ryan* suffers for the attempt.

 Greg, I enjoyed this movie on its own terms. What does that mean?
Well, for me it was a summer popcorn movie intended to allow the
audience a chance to turn its brain off for two hours while people
are chasing and shooting at each other. Kevin Costner does a nice job serving

as a mentor to Ryan, and Chris Pine is well-cast as a young hot-shot financial guru who displays amazing brains as well as brawn. If this movie does one thing well, it sets up the origin stories of both the hero, Ryan, and the villain, Viktor Cherevin (Kenneth Branagh). Both are fairly effective in these roles.

Right on all accounts, Scott. I'm mystified as to how the writers could have missed with such a great cast and a proven hero in Jack Ryan. Ryan hits all the marks of a great hero. He's loyal to his country. He is honest and trustworthy. He's athletic despite his injuries. Harper is a great mentor, arriving at the right time to lay down the Call to Adventure. The wife, Cathy, is smart and eventually is in need of being saved. Great Damsel in Distress material and sidekick as well. The villain leaves a bit to be desired, but is played well by Branagh.

Still, the plot is lacking. It's hard to get my head around the concept that all this money-business is world-threatening. It's easier when you can see a bomb that is ticking down to destruction. THEN you have a sense of impending doom. And, in fact, this is how the plot resolves itself. But selling off bonds on the New York Stock Exchange isn't heady business. To make that sexy, you'd have to take a look at what Martin Scorsese did with *The Wolf of Wall Street*.

This movie shows us glimpses of what differentiates a hero from a villain, Greg. Ryan and Cherevin are both scarred by their war experiences in Afghanistan. Ryan was a gung-ho volunteer whose near-death experience rendered him timid and a bit shell-shocked. Cherevin's injuries kindled a deep bitterness toward America, whom he believed supplied the weaponry that wounded him and his countrymen. Ryan wants no part of further violence whereas Cherevin seeks it. Ryan overcomes his weaknesses en route toward becoming heroic, whereas Cherevin's weaknesses – vodka and women – end up being his undoing.

That's an interesting comparison. It seems that there really aren't many differences between villains and heroes. But is it just a matter of point of view? From the point of view of the Russians, Cherevin is a hero - about to take down their greatest foe. If he is successful, he will be praised as a great Russian.

From our perspective as an American audience, Ryan appears to be the hero. He's protecting us against an aggressor. Could that be the difference between a hero and a villain, then? The hero is protecting against a villain who is poised to attack without cause. We see that too, in *Lone Survivor* where our American Navy Seals are out to kill an Afghan Taliban leader who is responsible for several Marine deaths. The Seals are heroes because they are reacting to a tangible threat. Were the roles reversed, it might be harder to perceive the Seals (or Ryan) as the hero.

 There's no doubt that heroism and villainy are in the eye of the beholder, Greg. We've heard it said that one man's hero is another man's terrorist, and that the winners, not the vanquished, get to write the history books and establish who the heroes and villains are. I also agree with you that heroes take the moral high road, and certainly protecting against an aggressor is more heroic than being the aggressor. But aggression is also in the eye of the beholder, as the aggressor usually justifies the aggression by arguing that it is in self-defense.

These are all slippery slopes and make distinguishing heroes from villains a tricky business. For me, then, the best way to separate heroes from villains is to ask: Who makes the selfless choice? Who is the most non-violent? Who is caring, kind, and willing to make self-sacrifices to save others? In this movie, Jack Ryan is that individual. And the man who embodies the opposite qualities is Viktor Cherevin.

I was disappointed in *Jack Ryan: Shadow Recruit*. It was slow and lackluster and ultimately relied on old-school danger / action plots to resolve the ending. It is possible to make high-finance look interesting and this movie failed in that regard. I look to such films as *Moneyball*

and to a certain degree *The Fifth Estate* to turn such thought-based plots into an exciting event. I give *Jack Ryan* just 2 out of 5 Reels.

Cherevin as the villain is given a lot of backstory here and I appreciated that. So often villain characters are painted as pure evil with no reason behind it. But his hatred for the United States is based on his experiences in the Afghanistan war with Russia. He's also given some personal vices that not only color his personality, but also become his ultimate demise. However, we don't see much of his core intelligence in the film. It isn't clear that he's a compelling rival for Ryan. I give Cherevin just 3 Villains out of 5.

Jake Ryan does pretty well as a hero in my estimation. He hits all the important elements of a classic hero. When you rate him on your list of the Great Eight characteristics of a hero, he comes out on top. But when you look at his flaws, there are few to be found. He doesn't appear to have a missing inner quality or great pain to correct. In that sense he really doesn't develop much in this film. I give Jack Ryan 3 out of 5 Heroes.

Movie: Villain: Hero:

I enjoyed this movie a bit more than you did, Greg. It's certainly no classic and won't win any awards, but for two hours it offered a nice escape from reality. I had a fun ride and have no problem giving this film 3 Reels out of 5. Jack Ryan was a good hero for a number of reasons: We are given a nice backstory that permits us to see Ryan evolve from a quiet financial analyst to a brave, resourceful, and physically gifted CIA operant. His hero journey features an effective mentor, a few key allies, an appealing love interest, and a ruthless villain. I give Ryan 4 Heroes out of 5.

The villain Cherevin is also fairly effective for many of the same reasons: A backstory, a love interest (who happens to also be Ryan's love interest), a henchman or two, and a stereotypical higher-up who of course is even more ruthless than Cherevin. And therein lies the problem. Because the story, understandably, focuses more on the hero Ryan than on the villains, we are left with cardboard villains who fill typical Russian stereotypes, right down to the vodka addiction and cold war rhetoric. So like you, Greg, the best I can do is award 3 Villains out of 5.

Movie: Villain: Hero:

Jersey Boys

Starring	John Lloyd Young, Erich Bergen, Michael Lomenda
Director	Clint Eastwood
Screenplay	Marshall Brickman, Rick Elice
Genre	Biography/Musical/Drama
Rated	R
Running Time	134 minutes
Release Date	June 20, 2014
Franki Valli Protagonist	Single, Positive to More Positive Emotional (Classic Lone Hero)
DeVito Antagonist	Single, Untransformed Negative Moral (Untransformed Lone Villain)
Crewe Antagonist	Single, Untransformed Negative Moral (Untransformed Lone Villain)

(Greg Smith, Founder of Agile Writers of Richmond, VA)

Relax. Frankie goes to Hollywood!

(Dr. Scott Allison, Professor of Psychology, University of Richmond)

Turns out that Frankie experiences some peaks and *vallies*. Let's recap.

It's the 1950's and young Frankie Castelluccio (John Lloyd Young) is a teen living in New Jersey. He's a good boy with a gift for singing. We learn that there are only three ways to get out of Jersey: join the army, get "mobbed up" or get famous. Frankie appears to be doing two out of the three as he's best buds with mobster Gyp DeCarlo (Christopher Walken) who is grooming Frankie to be a great singer.

 Tommy DeVito (Vincent Piazza) has a band and takes an interest in Frankie's unique vocal talents. Tommy also involves Frankie in some of his crime sprees, but Frankie straightens out and is eventually invited to join Tommy's band. An established songwriter, Bob Gaudio (Erich Bergen) joins the group, and then Frankie falls in love with a beautiful woman named Mary (Renee Marino). The band appears headed on a promising trajectory but Tommy's criminal involvement with the mob spells deep trouble for the band.

Scott, I am usually skeptical of biopics, especially those about musicians and pop music stars, but I was very happy with *Jersey Boys*. I have also never really enjoyed the music of the Four Seasons, but this movie added such dimension and color that the story of these four young men from Jersey really hit home with me. I had a very good time at director Clint Eastwood's latest offering.

 I found *Jersey Boys* to be a highly enjoyable romp through the world of early rock'n roll. The music is fun and fresh, and the casting in the movie is spot-on. Frankie Valli's physical and musical uniqueness had to be a considerable casting challenge but John Lloyd Young rises to the occasion. He does a phenomenal job portraying Valli.

As a biopic, we're witness to the complete hero journey, from Valli as a raw 16-year-old to Valli as a grizzled geezer. Valli's entire professional life is challenged by several factors, not the least of which is the corrupting influence of Tommy DeVito. We can see that Valli is more talented and more scrupulous than DeVito, yet has trouble extricating himself from DeVito's control.

It's a wonderful true-life hero's journey after all. There is a scene where all the Four Seasons are assembled in Gyp's house and a loan shark want's money from Tommy. Frankie could feed him to the sharks, but he steps up and takes on Tommy's debt. This is a huge moment where we see that Frankie is no longer a young kid living in Tommy's shadow. He is a full-grown adult taking responsibility for himself and his friend.

There aren't a lot of villains in this story. Gyp DeCarlo is soft-sold as a mafioso with a heart of gold. The record companies are given a pass as they took advantage of the boys. Frankie's wife is portrayed as an alcoholic wife-from-hell who doesn't appreciate him and constantly complains about his absence from home. These don't really raise to the level of villains. So we're left with a nice story of a singer's rise to fame and fall from grace. Still, a very enjoyable ride.

 You're right, Greg, there are several oppositional forces at work, serving as obstacles in the way of Frankie Valli's success. In addition to Tommy DeVito, there is Bob Crewe, the producer who relegates the band to singing back-up vocals for over a year. Another oppositional force is the rough neighborhood in which Valli grew up. He had to overcome a challenging environment and some difficult people.

And let's not overlook the sidekick in the story – Bob Gaudio, whose songwriting ability meshes beautifully with Valli's unusually soaring vocal style. Valli's breakout into the big-time of rock'n roll depended entirely on his collaboration with Gaudio, who is portrayed as both savvy and virtuous. Overall, the developmental arc of Valli's self-confidence and leadership ability in the band is a joy to watch. It's a nice hero's journey.

I fully enjoyed this trip into Rock-n-Roll history. *Jersey Boys* illustrates the genesis of what could be considered the first boy band. It's a story of friendship and loyalty as well as the growing pains of stardom. I give *Jersey Boys* 4 out of 5 Reels.

The hero in this story is Frankie Valli and he goes through all the phases of the hero's journey. Sadly, with little opposition he doesn't rise to the level of heroic action that I'd like to see. I can give Frankie only 3 Heroes out of 5.

The villains in this story were not very clear. Frankie has some obstacles to overcome, but no one in the story was really trying to keep Frankie and the boys down. I give *Jersey Boys* only 2 out of 5 Villains.

Movie: Villain:  Hero:

 Jersey Boys is a must-see for any fans of the early days of rock'n roll. Director Clint Eastwood continues to turn out quality movies, and amusingly he sneaks in a brief clip of his role in an early spaghetti western. *Jersey Boys* oozes energy, pop, and pizzazz. I'm happy to also award this film 4 Reels out of 5.

Nothing disturbs me more than agreeing with you, Greg. As you point out, the hero's journey is quite good here. But it doesn't rise to the level of outstanding because our hero is simply a musician who overcomes obstacles to star in the music industry. There is no great moral achievement, which is the ultimate goal of a quality hero story. This shortcoming reduces my rating of Frankie Valli's heroism to a mere 3 out of 5 Heroes.

The villains are fairly interesting here, especially Tommy DeVito, who is such a classless douche-bag that we're left wondering why Frankie Valli didn't part with him years before DeVito dragged everyone down into a financial abyss. We're witness to DeVito's full backstory and his inability to rise above his mobster mentality. Once again, we see this inability to transcend personal weaknesses as a defining characteristic of villains. So I'm going to give De-Vito and the two other oppositional characters (Crewe and Mary) a hefty 4 Villains out of 5.

Movie: Villain:  Hero:

The Judge

Starring	Robert Downey Jr., Robert Duvall, Vera Farmiga
Director	David Dobkin
Screenplay	Nick Schenk, Bill Dubuque
Genre	Drama
Rated	R
Running Time	141 minutes
Release Date	October 10, 2014
Hank & the Judge Protagonist	Duo, Positive to More Positive Moral/Emotional (Classic Buddy Heroes)
The Judge Antagonist	Single, Negative to Positive Moral/Emotional (Enlightened Lone Villain)

(Greg Smith, Founder of Agile Writers of Richmond, VA)
Scott, it looks like we're about to judge the merits of *The Judge*.

(Dr. Scott Allison, Professor of Psychology, University of Richmond)
All rise, the court is now in session. Greg, you may begin the opening argument.

We meet Hank Palmer (Robert Downey Jr.) who is a highly-paid Chicago lawyer - the kind who defends guilty people who have a lot of money. He's doing pretty well in this capacity when he gets a phone call - his mother has died and now he must return home to Indiana to bury his mother and support his older brother Glen (Vincent D'Onofrio) who runs a used car dealership and his younger brother Dale (Jeremy Strong) who is an autistic savant with a penchant for 8mm film. He must also face his father: Judge Joseph Palmer (Robert Duvall). The problem is, the Judge doesn't think much of his son Hank, so the two have a frosty reunion.

 Hank and the Judge have a long embattled history, and so there are tense moments between the two men during the few days that Hank is in Indiana. Just before leaving to return home to Chicago, Hank notices that the right-front bumper of the Judge's car is dented. Thinking nothing of it, Hank goes to the airport but then receives an alarming message from his brother: The Judge has been accused of killing a man in a hit-and-run crime and the victim's blood has been found on the Judge's car. Hank returns and becomes his dad's legal counsel, and juicy revelations abound during the legal proceedings.

The Judge is a by-the-numbers Hollywood drama. We meet our hero (Hank) in his ordinary world when "something happens" (his mother dies) he transitions into his special world (his dad's accident) where he has a problem to solve (saving his father) and learns a lesson (love people as they are). There's an old girlfriend to rekindle a relationship with. There's a mildly retarded brother to ask the naive questions. There's the nemesis in the form of a prosecuting attorney who is out for blood. With few exceptions, there are no surprises.

 There may be no surprises, Greg, but *The Judge* offers a workman-like buddy story about two men who start out despising each other, mostly because they don't *know* each other. Naturally, the story requires them to spend time together, allowing them to see each other's humanity and depth. The healing of father-son rifts is a common theme in the movies. If Hollywood is right, there aren't too many of us men out there who like our fathers. But movies like this give us hope of atonement.

The story is all quite formulaic, but for me *The Judge* works on the strength of the performances of two heavyweight actors of our time, Robert Duvall and Robert Downey, Jr. These two mega-talents are a treat to watch. There is emotional chemistry and interactive sizzle in every one of their scenes together. Downey, Jr., in particular, dives into every one of his movie roles with a relentless intensity. His Type A personality serves him very well here in his role as a brilliant, workaholic attorney. Duvall's performance is more subdued but he has us riveted to his every word. Not many star-studded pairings work in the movies, but this one, for me, is a grand slam.

Hank is a flawed hero. He is egotistical and has a hidden internal pain: he has an unknown history with his father. It's clear that the two men have an unspoken anger that is exposed only bit-by-bit through the story. It's this mystery that makes the story interesting. As Hank tries to defend his father, we see him slowly grow closer to Judge and we begin to understand why the Judge is so hard on Hank. The growth that Hank undergoes as he comes to grips with his past is what makes this a memorable movie.

You're right, Greg. In any good buddy hero story, we should see each buddy become transformed. Hank grows in his appreciation for his father, not just at a personal level but also at a professional level. We see the softening of Hank's heart along with an awakening of his larger call in life to follow in his dad's footsteps by serving as a Judge himself. As for the Judge, we catch his transformation in mid-stream. The Judge has been battling a life-threatening cancer that has heightened his sensitivity to his legacy. There is a humbling here, wrought by age and disease, that is touching to watch.

The villains in *The Judge* are interesting and varied. Hank's opponent in the courtroom is prosecuting attorney Dwight Dickham (Billy Bob Thornton), who isn't a bad man but he is a skilled professional intent on bringing down the Judge. Another oppositional force is the town's law enforcement personnel that pressures, interrogates, and arrests the Judge. Again, they aren't so much villainous as they are providing the impetus for Hank and the Judge to grow closer together. Also, Greg, you alluded to Hank's inner demons that he must overcome to grow and prevail in this movie. One could say that *The Judge* has the themes of both *Men versus Men* and *Men versus Selves*.

I think you're right, Dickham is the obvious villain character. He has been beaten by Hank in the courtroom and he wants to win this case to get back at Hank. The Judge isn't quite a villain, but he is an oppositional character. He doesn't want Hank's help and nearly gets the chair because he didn't allow Hank to lead the case. This makes the Judge an oppositional character - he is getting in the way of Hank's main goal - to free his father.

The supporting characters in this film are so classic that a parody of Oscar winning film trailers could have been made from *The Judge*. There's the older brother, naive mentally challenged younger brother, old flame from high school, and adorable daughter. There's some decent backstory there but it all comes from the same palette of movies gone by.

The Judge takes us on a journey of healing between a father and a son. The story may be formulaic but we grow to like and admire these characters, even with their many flaws. Moreover, the superb performances in this film carry the day and remind us why Robert Downey, Jr., is the highest paid Hollywood actor today. His counterpart, Robert Duvall, does more than hold his own against the dynamic Downey, Jr. Duvall exudes a quiet strength and depth of wisdom, delivering exactly what his role requires. *The Judge* is a fine film well worth watching. I'm happy to award it 4 Reels out of 5.

Our two buddy heroes, Hank and the Judge, are a terrific pairing that traverse their way from embittered enemies to admiration and even love. Their chemistry together has ample snap, crackle, and pop. Most importantly, Hank and the Judge undergo two personal transformations that involve a growing humility, compassion, and understanding. The performances here are dynamic and memorable. I give these two heroes 4 Heroes out of 5.

The villains are not terribly important in this film other than to serve as the mechanism for our two buddy heroes to work and grow together. I'm not disappointed with the villain characters in this movie, but I also won't walk away from this film with any improved understanding or appreciation for these characters. They do what they do and that's all this film requires of them. Consequently, I can only give a villain rating of 2 out of 5 here.

Movie: Villains: Heroes:

The Judge is a nice film which offers no new territory to traverse. It's a classic story of atonement with the father. On the plus side everyone in the cast delivered a good performance and I left the theater feeling that I got my money's worth. Still, I don't see it winning any awards. I give *The Judge* 3 out of 5 Reels.

The hero is cut from a familiar cloth and played well by Robert Downey, Jr. He starts out as a pretty lousy human being with little to endear himself to us. But as we learn more about him and the reasons he left his home town we begin to realize that there is more to the story than we were at first given. I give Hank 3 out of 5 Heroes.

I have to agree with you, Scott, on the villains. There aren't a lot of oppositional characters. For the most part, the Judge himself is the biggest oppositional character as he tries to handle his own case and gets in Hank's way. While he was superbly played by Robert Duvall, I can only give him 3 out of 5 Villains.

Movie: Villains: Heroes:

Labor Day

Starring	Josh Brolin, Kate Winslet
Director	Jason Reitman
Screenplay	Jason Reitman
Genre	Drama
Rated	PG-13
Running Time	111 minutes
Release Date	January 31, 2014
Frank Protagonist	Single, Negative to Positive Emotional (Redeemed Lone Hero)
Cops Antagonist	System, Untransformed Positive Moral (Hidden Police Anti-Villain)

(Greg Smith, Founder of Agile Writers of Richmond, VA)

Scott, it's not quite summer but it is time to review *Labor Day*.

(Dr. Scott Allison, Professor of Psychology, University of Richmond)

It's never any labor to do a review with you, Greg!

It's 1987 and we're introduced to young Henry (Gattlin Griffith)
who is about 12 years old. His father has left him and his mother
Adele (Kate Winslet) for a younger woman. Adele is a recluse as
she suffers from depression. She is afraid to go out in public wanting instead
to stay home and avoid contact with the outside world. But occasionally she
must venture out to do such things as buying new clothes for Henry as school
starts in just a few days.

While at the local store, Henry is approached by a strange man named Frank
(Josh Brolin) who firmly insists that he get a ride with Henry and Adele back
to their house.

 Adele and Henry bring Frank to their home, but they are clearly
afraid of him and then discover that Frank is an escaped convicted
murderer. But it soon becomes clear that Frank poses no threat to
them and in fact cares for their well-being. He ties up Adele but only briefly
so that she can truthfully tell authorities that she helped Frank against her will.
Then Frank does all he can to do to help out with chores around the house and
yard. Meanwhile, law enforcement personnel searching for Frank begin to
close in on him.

Scott, *Labor Day* is the worst kind of nonsense that we find in trashy
romance novels. It shows a hunky dangerous convict with a heart of
gold. We assume that he was unjustly convicted and the story bears
this out through flashbacks. Frank appears to be a bad man, running from the
law, but gently ties his victim to a chair and feeds her chili - so he can't be
all bad, right? The heroine in the story is helpless not only in her day-to-day
goings on, but also to the dark charms of our hero-villain. This is the sort of
drek that sets modern feminism back 50 years.

Not only that, but the plot tries to tie-in a coming of age story for young
Henry. This sub-plot receives very little attention but is a welcome distraction
from the unbelievable love story. The whole movie is slow and plodding and
I couldn't wait for it to be over.

Greg, I do agree that the premise of *Labor Day* is a weak one, relying on the formulaic tale of a man wrongly imprisoned who escapes and must prove his romantic worthiness. Women who love to reform a bad-boy will love this film. The performances by Josh Brolin and Kate Winslet are excellent; the only problem is that even their immense talent can't spin screenplay straw into gold.

The character of Frank is just a tad too perfect. He fixes things around the house, cleans the dust bunnies under the furniture, repairs the car engine, cooks like an award-winning chef, and is a tender loving caretaker to a child with cerebral palsy. Apparently, the makers of this movie got together and asked, how can we make a convicted murderer and the female lead, Adele, fall in love in only a few days? The answer they came up with was to make him perfect in every way. It just doesn't ring true.

Scott, Frank is a confusing character. On the one hand he is a violent criminal on the run from the law. In most movies that makes him the villain. But on the other hand, he is a hero - acting as a father image to young Henry. He teaches Henry to play ball, and to bake a perfect pie. I've coined a new word for this type of character - the anti-villain. Just as we have anti-heroes (like Bonnie and Clyde) who start out good and turn to evil, the anti-villain starts out as a villain but shows the character traits of a hero.

 I don't see the character of Frank as confusing. He's cut from the same mold as Harrison Ford's character in *The Fugitive* the innocent man victimized by a corrupt and incompetent legal system. We see in flashbacks that Frank had no intention of harming his wife and is in fact a sympathetic character who has suffered more than enough for any wrongdoing he may have done.

I do like your characterization of Frank as an anti-villain, as he is a good man who is on the lamb. The problem with Frank as a character is that his perfection is so neatly intact from start to finish that there is no room for growth or transformation. You could argue that Adele shares the hero role with Frank – she learns to trust and to open her heart again, but as you point out, this reduces her to a tiresome cliche straight from the pages of a cheap romance novel.

I didn't see much growth in Adele. After Frank is taken away, she
still is reclusive and is barely able to function. I don't think every
woman in films has to be strong and independent. But I don't care
for a hero character who is fully reliant on a man to take care of her and make
her happy. That's not heroic and that was no kind of transformation. The way
this movie was made I felt we were watching something that came out of the
1950's rather than 1987.

Young Henry is taken away from Adele and goes to live with his father. He
grows into a fine young man and ultimately returns to Adele's home for his
final semester in high school. Aside from growing up, there wasn't much
growth for him either. Overall, there wasn't much of a heroic story in this
movie.

 Labor Day is a sweet story of love but suffers from unrealistic characters caught in a contrived and cliched plot. If you like the idea of
idealized romance without the messiness of reality to soil it, then
this movie is for you. I admit I'm a sucker for love stories, even poorly told
ones, and I also admire the talents of Josh Brolin and Kate Winslet. For these
reasons, despite its obvious flaws, I'm willing to give *Labor Day* 2 Reels out
of 5.

The hero story here is pretty much non-existent. The hero (or anti-villain, as
you aptly describe him, Greg) is a hollow stereotype with no room for growth.
His story also lacks many of the classic social elements of the hero's journey,
such as the presence of mentors, sidekicks, and father figures. Adele is a
sympathetic figure but is hardly heroic herself. Her role is simply to observe
Frank's greatness and be affected by it. Sadly, I give Frank, and even Adele, a
mere 1 Hero out of 5.

The villains are an inconsequential element of the story in *Labor Day*. The
cops looking for Frank are hardly villains, and they exist merely as props to
bring the romance between Frank and Adele to life. For this reason, I can only
award 1 Villain out of 5.

Movie: Villain: Hero:

Scott, we have vastly different views of this film and yet come away with similar scores. Brolin and Winslet do a great job of acting in this film. Jason Reitman's directing is very good. It's just that I really hated the story. I can't get behind a convicted murderer abducting a woman and her son who is really a good guy at heart. A good guy would never have taken hostages - regardless of how well he treated them. What Adele really underwent was Stockholm's syndrome - where the hostage begins to side with the kidnapper. If it weren't for the excellent craftsmanship of this film I'd have awarded it just 1 Reel. But for good performances and good direction, I give *Labor Day* 2 out of 5 Reels.

Frank comes off as heroic and we pity him his situation. But as far as heroes go, I don't think he measures up. As I just said, no true hero would take hostages. But when you score him on your Great Eight Characteristics, he does pretty well. I give Frank 1 Hero out of 5.

And Frank is also the villain, but because he is the romantic interest and father image he doesn't provide any opposition. I give Frank his anti-villain score of 1 Villain out of 5.

Movie: 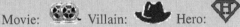   Villain: Hero:

Lucy

Starring	Scarlett Johansson, Morgan Freeman, Min-sik Choi
Director	Luc Besson
Screenplay	Luc Besson
Genre	Science-Fiction/Action/Adventure
Rated	R
Running Time	89 minutes
Release Date	July 25, 2014
Lucy Protagonist	Single, Positive to More Positive Mental (Classic Long Hero)
Choi Antagonist	Single, Untransformed Negative Moral (Untransformed Mastermind Villain)

(Dr. Scott Allison, Professor of Psychology, University of Richmond)

Greg, as a kid I probably watched every episode of *I Love Lucy*.

(Greg Smith, Founder of Agile Writers of Richmond, VA)

Well, there wasn't much to love about *Lucy* - I thought it was *Loucy*.

Ouch! Let's recap. We meet a young woman named Lucy (Scarlett Johansson), who unknowingly delivers a briefcase containing large quantities of a dangerous drug to a Korean mob boss (Min-sik Choi). The drug is CPH4, a powerful hyperactive stimulant. Lucy and three other people have bags of CPH4 surgically implanted into their abdomens. Forced into drug muledom, they are flown to several major European cities.

Lucy is held captive in a Taipei cell and beaten and kicked which causes the bag of CPH4 to rupture. She receives a mega-dose of the drug which then starts to open her mind. Meanwhile, Professor Norman (Morgan Freeman) is in Paris lecturing on the potential of the human brain. He proffers that humans use only 10% of their brain. If we used 20% then we'd have the ability to do amazing things - things he can't even imagine. Lucy uses her newly found powers to escape her cell and is now on a quest to find the man who performed the awful operation on her and exact her revenge.

Lucy is a preposterous yet fun look at what would happen if a human being could maximize her cerebral potential. The movie features a curious mix of scientifically accurate facts about the brain with scientifically spurious fluff. As a psychologist, I probably should have been offended by the movie's bogus premise that human beings use only 10% of their brain capacity. But truth be told, almost every movie we see requires some suspension of disbelief. I just turned off my 10% (sic) and enjoyed the ride.

Despite frequent lapses in veracity, this movie is slick and competently pieced together. Dramatically, we have an interesting hero story featuring Lucy who undergoes about as great of a dramatic a transformation as a hero can possibly endure. It's fascinating to see CPH4 mutate Lucy's mind and body in unimaginable ways. Unfortunately, witnessing her hero transformation is not the most satisfying adventure to witness because, after all, Lucy doesn't voluntarily choose to change. The changes are biologically driven.

Wow. You are so incredibly generous to this complete waste of film.
I don't have your superhuman knowledge of the inner workings of
the brain and yet I was completely offended by the techno-babble
spewing from Morgan Freeman's mouth.

The whole movie was one amazing tele-something super capability after another. Lucy is locked in a cell? At 20% of brain power she has amazing
strength and knows kung-fu. Lucy needs to speak Chinese? At 40% she
learns a language in under an hour. Lucy needs to talk to the Professor? At
60% she controls all functions of the entire internet and can flash lights on
and off from across the globe. This was one implausable event after another.
Whenever she needed something to get out of a jam, another 10% of brain
power conjures the solution. I can't even call this movie science fiction as
there was absolutely no science involved.

Other than that it was fine.

I'm also deeply disturbed by what this film thinks a super-smart female looks
like. When Scarlett Johansson wants to appear intelligent she stares blankly
ahead and twitches her head from side to side. I guess that's her idea of what
smart people do. She loses all emotion and kills people for the slightest in-
discretion - like not knowing how to speak English. She is completely motivated by revenge. Her elevated IQ doesn't give her any insight into the heart
of mankind - only the ability to kill efficiently. There is no internal character
scrutiny here - it is all mindless mayhem at the will of a beautiful black widow
[pun intended].

 For some reason I was able to overlook all the silliness you mention,
Greg. I enjoyed witnessing Lucy's powers evolve over time, not
just quantitatively but also qualitatively. For a while, I felt like I was
watching the origin story of a great female superhero. Like many superheroes,
she is accidentally exposed to a strange chemical which gifts her with special
abilities. Unlike you, Greg, I didn't see her misuse her powers; I only saw her
using her abilities to survive. At the film's end, she gives humanity the gift of
her vast knowledge, a fitting end to any hero's journey.

Sadly, there is plenty of contrived tension featuring bad guys who are closing in on Lucy when it's obvious that she has the power to squelch them effortlessly. One of my complaints - and I do seem to have a bunch of them - is that the villains are ruthless but not terribly well fleshed out. We've seen this too many times: Shallow villains with a foreign look and a foreign accent are a dime a dozen in Hollywood.

I have to disagree with you again, Scott. At least the villain in this story gets his hands dirty. In other villain patterns we see the "boss" or "mastermind" sitting at the top of the food chain giving orders while henchmen do the dirty work. Mr. Jang has no problem carving, shooting, or slashing anything that gets in his way. You're right, the villains were way over the top - quite in line with the absurdity of an all-powerful hero.

Lucy aims high in its ambition to create an intelligent movie with action-adventure thrills. Instead, we get a mindless stream of psychobabble and half-science that even Morgan Freeman with his velvety gift for explanation can't deliver. This is a bad retread of the same premise from 2011's *Limitless* (featuring the beautiful Bradley Cooper) which at least knew its "limits." I give Lucy a mere 1 out of 5 Reels.

The hero is such a blank in every way. Scarlett Johansson gives Lucy no real personality and certainly no heart. The smarter she gets, the less human she becomes. I'd like to think we don't need to fear the superintelligent. This movie delivers a message to young girls that becoming super smart makes you scary to men. But on the bright side, it also means you can become a badass. I give Lucy just 1 Hero out of 5.

Unlike you, I found something to like in the villains in this story. True, they are pure evil with little to ingratiate themselves to the audience. But the main guy at least has the decency to carry out his own acts of barbarism. I give him 2 out of 5 Villains.

Movie: Villain: Hero: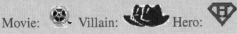

If you're willing to turn a high percentage of your brain off for 90 minutes, *Lucy* is a fun look at what might happen if human beings were able to fulfill their maximum cognitive potential. There are missteps in the making of this film but Lucy manages to make us ponder where the human race is headed evolutionarily. *Lucy* won't win any awards but takes us on an entertaining, multi-continent adventurous ride. I'll generously award Lucy 3 Reels out of 5.

The hero's story is problematic in that Lucy's journey isn't one that any one of us is likely to face. She doesn't naturally overcome any missing quality to prevail, and her ability to overcome obstacles is derived from a biological accident. Still, we do find ourselves pulling for her and she does give back to humanity in a big way at the end. I'll give Lucy 2 Heroes out of 5.

The villains aren't anything special here and merely exist to get in Lucy into trouble and then scramble to thwart her later. Greg, you're right that the main villain actually gets his hands dirty for a change. Alas, this departure from the norm doesn't make him any more interesting than other razor-thin villains we've seen this year, and so the best I can do is award Lucy's foes a mere 2 Villains out of 5.

Movie:  Villain: Hero:

Maleficent

Starring	Angelina Jolie, Elle Fanning, Sharlto Copley
Director	Robert Stromberg
Screenplay	Linda Woolverton, Charles Perrault
Genre	Action/Adventure/Family
Rated	PG
Running Time	97 minutes
Release Date	May 30, 2014
Maleficent Protagonist	Single, Positive to Negative to Positive Moral (Redeemed Lone Hero)
Stefan Antagonist	Single, Negative to more Negative Moral (Untransformed Lone Villain)

(Greg Smith, Founder of Agile Writers of Richmond, VA)

Scott, it looks like Angelina Jolie is back with a Tomb Raider sequel.

(Dr. Scott Allison, Professor of Psychology, University of Richmond)

I'd say she's sprouted her wings and gone beyond Lara Croft. Let's recap.

We're introduced to a very young faerie named Maleficent (Angelina Jolie) who lives in the Moors. The faerie world doesn't get along with the human world so it's quite a big deal when the young man Stefan (Sharlto Copley) appears to her. They strike up a friendship and eventually fall in love. The problem, though is that Stefan has ambitions to become a higher-up in the king's court. This causes Stefan to abandon his new love. Over the years Stefan does grow in the king's graces and he needs to impress the king and be named successor.

To gain the king's favor, Stefan returns to the Moors and wins Maleficent's heart again. One night he moves to stab her in her sleep, but he cannot bring himself to do it. Instead, he cuts off her wings and brings them to the king as proof of her death. Maleficent's disfigurement turns her into a bitter, vengeful witch-like figure. When she discovers that the new King Stefan and his queen have given birth to a daughter named Aurora (Elle Fanning), Maleficent inflicts a curse upon the baby such that Aurora will fall into an endless sleep and can only be revived by a true love's kiss.

Scott, this is a prequel to the classic Sleeping Beauty story. *Maleficent* does for Sleeping Beauty what *Wicked* did for *The Wizard of* *Oz*. The story focuses on the evil queen and how she came to be who she is. The production values are amazing. The world of the Moors is colorful and full of interesting creatures.

I found the story to be captivating and moved along at a nice pace. I rarely felt bored as we were carried from scene to scene as the story twisted along this Villain's Journey. We start out with a young, happy, vibrant Maleficent. Then she is betrayed by her lover. Then she curses the baby Aurora and the story switches to the growth of Aurora. Maleficent also grows during this period. Disney created a beautiful world full of color and life.

I agree, Greg, that this is a fascinating tale. For me, *Maleficent* is first and foremost a story of a hero who can be misunderstood to be a villain. Beyond its obvious entertainment value, *Maleficent* highlights the fine line that exists between heroes and villains. Capitalizing on this ambiguity, and even toying with it, is no doubt one of the main goals of the film.

We're introduced to a sweet young girl, a fairy with impressive wings, who seems by all appearances to be a heroic figure – or at least *potentially* one. After a man physically brutalizes her, she takes on a villainous persona. Bitterness consumes her and leads her to an act of vengeance that she later regrets. Most importantly, she falls in love with the very person who was the target of her vengeance. *This love redeems her.* We witness the healing power of love, as our fairy becomes the sweet person she once was. For me, this is a dramatic and powerful hero's journey.

I was thrilled that we get the full round trip here. Maleficent starts out with all the characteristics a heroic character. She's smart and happy and she does good deeds for those around her. Despite her physical superiority to other faerie people in the Moors, she's their advocate and protector. Then once she is betrayed, she turns dark and starts down a path that appears to have no return. She puts up barriers to the Moors that the humans cannot penetrate. For a generation she steeps in her anger and builds a hatred for the humans. She reaches the pinnacle of her villainy when she lashes out at an innocent child. Aurora is cursed to fall into a deep sleep on the day of her 16th birthday.

Then Maleficent starts on the return path to heroism. She observes the child growing up and as she does she comes to love her. It is this love that touches Maleficent and causes her to return to goodness. Ultimately, Maleficent comes to defend Aurora and it is Aurora who saves Maleficent. It is a wonderful tale of a fall from grace and redemption.

 Totally agree, Gregger. As the film's narrator suggests, Maleficent may be both hero and villain, a combination that is needed to unify the human world with the faerie kingdom. Maleficent's dual role allows us learn many things about the parallel journeys taken by heroes and villains. We learn that both heroes and villains are summoned to an unfamiliar world that challenges them in significant ways. We learn that both heroes and villains acquire a main mission, and they attract allies who help them and foes who oppose them. We learn that both heroes and villains are damaged goods in some way, and that how they handle that damage ultimately comes to define them.

We also learn how villains differ from heroes. Maleficent is a character who illustrates beautifully how heroes find ways to redeem themselves, even when they appear to be irreparably damaged. Heroes never let physical or emotional injury define them, at least not in the long run. Heroes transcend difficult circumstances. Villains succumb to them. Maleficent rises above her pain, thereby cementing her heroic status.

I might argue the Maleficent is the anti-villain. She has to have something to catalyze her to turn from villainy back to heroism. If it weren't for Aurora's beauty and love, Maleficent would have been lost forever. We've seen this catalyst in last weeks' *Million Dollar Arm*. In that movie the lead character was going down a dark path until his girlfriend and the young men from India show him a different way. Both these stories remind us how very close a hero is to a villain.

Maleficent is a colorful, suspenseful, and thoughtful examination of the psychology of villainy. I heartily recommend it both for adults and children. Although, personally, I thought some parts were too dark for younger children. I give *Maleficent* 4 out of 5 Reels.

Maleficent is a great heroic character traveling first from innate heroic qualities, then diving into the depths of villainy due to a painful betrayal and then the return to heroism through the catalyst of love and beauty. Angelina Jolie was just amazing in the role. I give Maleficent 4 out of 5 Heroes. And because we get the full villain's backstory, I give Maleficent 4 out of 5 Villains as well.

Movie: Villains:    Heroes:

Maleficent isn't a great movie but its lead character, Maleficent herself, is one of the most compelling and complex Disney characters ever to appear on the big screen. Angelina Jolie shines in the role and gives Maleficent the depth and nuance needed to portray character's long, painful, yet ultimately redemptive journey. I'm torn between giving the movie 3 versus 4 Reels but because I enjoyed the layers of this character so much I'm going to award *Maleficent* 4 out of 5 Reels.

The ambiguity of the heroic status of Maleficent, and the twists and turns that her character experiences, are great fun to behold. I honestly didn't know whether her turn to darkness was permanent or temporary, and I was delighted to see a character that is redeemed by love. Such a message offers hope to all of humanity. Like you, Greg, I also award Maleficent 4 Heroes out of 5.

The true villain of the story is Stefan, who is slave to his deep desire for power and glory. The only love he knows is the love of conquest and ambition. He's not a particularly deep or interesting villain, as his role is mainly to flesh out the depth of Maleficent's character. Because Maleficent herself shows a villainous side and showcases the fine line between heroism and villainy, I give the pairing of Stefan and Maleficent 4 out of 5 Villains.

Movie: Villains:  Heroes:

Million Dollar Arm

Starring	Jon Hamm, Aasif Mandvi, Alan Arkin
Director	Craig Gillespie
Screenplay	Thomas McCarthy
Genre	Biography/Drama/Sports
Rated	PG
Running Time	124 minutes
Release Date	May 16, 2014
JB Bernstein Protagonist	Single, Negative to Positive Moral (Transformed Enlightened Lone Hero)
JB Bernstein Antagonist	Single, Negative to Positive Moral (Transformed Self Villain)

(Dr. Scott Allison, Professor of Psychology, University of Richmond)

Greg, strangely enough, it looks like Disney has made a movie about the arms race.

(Greg Smith, Founder of Agile Writers of Richmond, VA)
No, it's a new baseball movie about finding new talent in India. Let's recap

We meet JB Bernstein (Jon Hamm), a sports agent who is struggling to attract clients and is on the brink of financial collapse. He concocts an idea to create a reality show that promises to reap fame and fortune. The idea involves going to India to recruit cricket players with the raw skills to become professional baseball pitchers in the United States. J.B. obtains financial backing from businessman Mr. Chang (Tzi Ma), who gives J.B.'s agency only one year to complete the task.

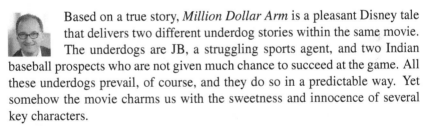

In India JB discovers things don't work as they do in the US. He has to grease the skids with backdoor deals. He meets an enterprising young man in Amit (Pitobash) who loves baseball and offers to work for JB for free. JB scours the countryside looking for players but finds only two: Rinku (Suraj Sharma) and Dinesh (Madhur Mittal). Ironically, neither boy is a cricket fan.

JB brings the boys home to America and convinces the USC pitching coach to train them. JB is focused on the deal and neglects to give the boys the attention they need. Tenant and neighbor Brenda (Lake Bell) urges him to be more sympathetic to the two boys who are far from home and only aim to please.

Based on a true story, *Million Dollar Arm* is a pleasant Disney tale that delivers two different underdog stories within the same movie. The underdogs are JB, a struggling sports agent, and two Indian baseball prospects who are not given much chance to succeed at the game. All these underdogs prevail, of course, and they do so in a predictable way. Yet somehow the movie charms us with the sweetness and innocence of several key characters.

Greg, this movie works because Disney has spent almost a century perfecting the formula for tugging on audience's heartstrings. The two Indian baseball prospects are wonderful young men. Yes, they are naive and jittery, but they wear their generous, innocent hearts on their sleeves. JB is a darker character, self-absorbed to a fault, but lurking behind his careless egocentricity we see hints of inherent goodness. The job of the movie is to develop that goodness into its fullness, which it accomplishes nicely.

I agree, Scott. I'm not a baseball fan, so sports movies occasionally leave me in the dust (witness last spring's *Draft Day*). But this isn't so much a story about sports as it is about overcoming our weaknesses. The young men in the story are honest and eager to please. They see this as an opportunity and also an obligation to reflect positively upon their families back home.

JB is both a hero and a villain in this story. He is the character who is most transformed by the events in the film. But it is his inner demons - those of greed and ambition - that get in the way of seeing the good in people. And it is this missing inner quality that threatens to doom him to failure in his task. Happily, through the intervention of a good woman and the good nature of the young men, JB overcomes his focus on the business of the game and is reminded of what makes baseball fun.

 You're right, Greg. JB doesn't need an outside villain, as he is his own worst enemy here. JB is mentored by two people in this story. Besides the woman you mention, early in the movie JB's contact person in India, Vivek (Darshan Jariwala), plants the seeds of JB's transformation. Vivek tells JB that the two Indian boys represent more than just a great business opportunity; they are first and foremost an important "responsibility." This wisdom reminds me of Stan Lee's oft-quoted line, *With great power comes great responsibility*. It certainly applies to JB, who at first wields his power in selfish and reckless ways before he learns that people come before profit.

I think *Million Dollar Arm* doesn't quite hit a home run with its easy-to-digest sports story. It is predictable and unsurprising in many ways. But it has an honesty and good naturedness that makes it an enjoyable movie to watch. I give the film 3 out of 5 Reels.

JB is definitely a man fighting himself in this story. I was happy to see his slow transformation from all-business jerk to understanding jerk. JB gets 3 out of 5 Heroes from me.

There isn't much of a villain story for us to take home. JB is his own enemy and as such doesn't have much to overcome. I give him just 2 Villains out of 5.

Movie: Villain: Hero: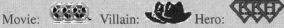

 We're on the same page, Greg. *Million Dollar Arm* is formulaic to a fault yet somehow manages to succeed as a worthwhile film due to its charming cast and fulfilling take-home message. There isn't much new ground covered here, but I enjoyed *Million Dollar Arm* and recommend it for people who are in the mood for a feel-good movie. Like you, Greg, I award it 3 Reels out of 5.

The hero story is interesting and follows the conventional path of sending our hero JB to India, an unfamiliar place where he is a fish out of water. Several key allies assist him on his mission, and while in India he encounters resistance and also cultivates a love interest. Ironically, she is a woman he Skypes as she lives in America. She ultimately helps JB discover his missing inner quality, which is his sense of humanity. Again, it's a bit formulaic for a woman to help a man reform himself, but *Million Dollar Arm* does it in an appealing way. JB deserves 3 solid Heroes out of 5.

The villain, if there is one, is JB himself, or at least it is the dark side of JB's character. We learn in this movie that heroes find ways to overcome their dark sides, whereas villains are either blind to these sides or cannot summon the conscience to overcome the darkness. Greed is a powerful human force and has destroyed many people, and is thus a worthy adversary here. For this reason I'm willing to award the "villain" 3 out of 5 Villains.

Movie: Villain:  Hero:

The Monuments Men

Starring	George Clooney, Matt Damon, Bill Murray
Director	George Clooney
Screenplay	George Clooney, Grant Heslov
Genre	Action/Biography/Drama
Rated	PG-13
Running Time	118 minutes
Release Date	February 7, 2014
Monuments Men Protagonist	Ensemble, Untransformed Positive Moral (Untransformed Military Heroes)
Nazis Antagonist	System, Untransformed Negative Moral (Untransformed Military System Villains)

(Dr. Scott Allison, Professor of Psychology, University of Richmond)

Greg, it's time to review *The Monuments Men* starring George Clooney, who also wrote and directed the film.

(Greg Smith, Founder of Agile Writers of Richmond, VA)

It wasn't a monumental film but I enjoyed myself. Let's recap.

The year is 1944. The second world war is nearing an end as Allied troops close in on Hitler's German forces. As European cities are being reduced to rubble, an American museum curator named Frank Stokes (George Clooney) is concerned about the safety of all the priceless works of art in Europe. These paintings and statues are at risk of being destroyed or stolen by either the Nazis or the Russians.

Stokes needs help and he knows who he wants with him. So, in a scene reminiscent of *The Dirty Dozen* he travels around the art community picking up six old friends (and I do mean old). Richard Campbell (Bill Murray), Walter Garfield (John Goodman), Donald Jeffries (Hugh Bonneville) and Preston Savitz (Bob Balaban) join Stokes along with younger men James Granger (Matt Damon) and Frenchman Jean Claude Clermont (Jean Dujardin).

They are all civilians and so must endure a comical bout of basic training. Once they are on their way, they are met with resistance from men on the front lines. Stokes tries to dissuade allied commanders from bombing priceless buildings only to meet resistance in the face of saving art over saving lives.

 Greg, *The Monuments Men* is a pretty good movie that means well. But it fell far short of what it could have been, especially given that the movie assembled such a luminary cast. In fact, that star-studded cast may have been the albatross that weighed the film down (to mix metaphors). When I see George Clooney, Bill Murray, and John Goodman on the screen, I see those actors rather than the characters they are playing. *The Butler* made the same mistake last year. One or two mega-stars is fine, but having superstar actors in every scene is unnecessary and distracting. Why not find some lesser known quality actors to play a few of these roles?

A second problem the movie suffers from is predictability. There is a scene in *The Monuments Men* where John Goodman gets shot at from a window in an abandoned building. There is tension: who could be this mystery shooter? No one should be surprised that it ends up being a child. And of course we know that the film must conclude with the men finding the prized *Madonna of Bruges* statue. There are other issues, too, but before I go on I want to hear you weigh in here, Greg.

I found *Monuments Men* to be a light (if not light hearted) World
War II era film about a subject that had gone unnoticed until now -
Hitler's obsession with art. As the Germans invaded city after city,
they rounded up all the art (and gold) they could find. The tension in this film
is created by a deadline. With the allies closing in on Berlin, Hitler has given
an order to destroy all the art rather than leave it to the Russians or Americans.

I bought into this story, Scott. I didn't expect a lot of character acting. I was
satisfied to watch the heroes in this story figure out where the stolen art was
being kept and race to find it before the Germans turned it to ash. The lighter
moments of the film were offset by some more dramatic moments. While
there were few very high or very low points, I got the message: people come
and go, but our art tells the story of civilization and it is worth our lives to
protect it.

 To me, that message was communicated somewhat poorly, Greg.
In the middle of the movie, George Clooney's character gives a
rousing speech that says, essentially, that whereas human lives are
temporary, art is forever. That sounds noble, but his speech also implies that
human lives are expendable in the effort to preserve paintings - a not so noble
belief. Bottom line is that characters in this movie willingly die in the service
of preserving artwork, and I can (grudgingly) accept this loss of life because
it was their choice. But one gets the sense that Clooney (and the movie) are
telling us that *any* lives are worth risking to preserve artwork, including the
lives of civilians who certainly aren't freely choosing to risk themselves.

The fourth and final issue I had was that the heroes in the movie don't grow.
Good hero stories show us how heroes become transformed. But these monuments men show a selfless courage from the beginning of the movie to the
very end. I have the same problem with the character of Katniss Everdeen in
the *Hunger Games*, who also shows heroic qualities from beginning to end
and never grows. Yes, the characters in *The Monuments Men* are heroes but
we, the audience, are most satisfied when we see heroes undergo significant
change and evolution. This just doesn't happen in this film.

I didn't get that message from the movie. I don't recall any civilian loss of life in the efforts to save the lost art. The message I got was that these men were so committed to preserving our (combined) heritage that *they* were willing to risk, and in some cases give, their lives. It was both noble and heroic.

And the orders to save this art came from on high. Truman himself signed the orders and that makes him a hero, too. As we've seen before, heroes don't always transform (themselves or others). Sometimes they perform a selfless act and that alone is enough to earn them the badge of honor. In this case, six men who had nothing to gain from their acts risked their lives for an ideal. *Monuments Men* did a good job of selling that ideal to me and I bought it whole.

 The villains in this story are primarily the Germans and the Russians, both of whom want to steal artwork that belongs to others. The Germans especially are cast in an evil light because they prefer to destroy any priceless art that they can't have for themselves. There are countless movies featuring Nazi Germany and Hitler as the villains, and their relentless bloodthirstiness never fails to stir us into hatred for them. But while they are effective villains in this movie, they aren't terribly memorable or noteworthy in any way. *The Monuments Men* is first and foremost a film about the heroism of an ensemble of men who sacrifice themselves to improve and preserve humanity's artistic contributions to the world. The German villains are largely window dressing whose main role is to challenge our heroes.

You're right about that, Scott. Usually when you have an overwhelming enemy like the Nazis the director will pick one character to represent all of the evil-doers. This gives us one person to iden- tify with as the villain. While there was one Nazi curator who ran off with a ton of art, we hardly see him after the first act. Then there was a scene where Stokes confronts a Nazi head of a concentration camp. But that was just a random bad guy. A good hero needs a good villain and *Monuments Men* failed to deliver.

I somewhat enjoyed *The Monuments Men* but was disappointed that it fell short of its potential. As I've noted, the film suffers from too many Hollywood legends in its cast, a tendency to be overly predictable, a somewhat confusing message about sacrificing lives for artwork, and a set of heroes who do not transform themselves during their hero journeys. *The Monuments Men* is a pretty good movie but certainly not a great one, and so I can only award it 3 Reels out of 5.

For reasons stated above, the heroes were clearly heroic but they didn't inspire me with their growth as characters. Because their hero journeys were stunted, I can only give them 2 Heroes out of 5. The villains were certainly villainous – anyone who destroys priceless Picasso paintings merely because they can't have them themselves is indeed dastardly and barbaric. But the individual villain characters are not developed at all and so the best I can do is award 2 Villains out of 5 for them.

Movie: Heroes: Villains:

I think I enjoyed *Monuments Men* more than you did, Scott. Still, I give the film the same score. This was a movie that informed more than inspired and it did that fairly well. I didn't know about Hitler's zeal to keep the world's art to himself. And I didn't know about his desire to put it all into a single museum in the heart of Germany or how close we came to losing it all. I also give *Monuments Men* 3 out of 5 Reels.

I liked the heroes in this film but I agree they weren't as strong as some other hero films we've reviewed. As you point out, there may have been too many stars in this one and not enough story to go around. There is a little bit of a redemption story for Hugh Bonneville's character, but it seemed to be a side dish. And lest we forget the role played by Cate Blanchett as the secretary who kept an itemized list of all the art that went through her museum. The film is full of mini-heroes who just barely add up to 3 out of 5 Heroes.

And the villains: cardboard cutouts of movies gone by. Patently evil and uncaring. Dispicable in the face of their failures. There was no opposition here. I give them a blanket 1 Villain out of 5.

Movie: Heroes:  Villains:

Neighbors

Starring	Seth Rogen, Rose Byrne, Zac Efron
Director	Nicholas Stoller
Screenplay	Andrew J. Cohen, Brendan O'Brien
Genre	Comedy
Rated	R
Running Time	96 minutes
Release Date	May 9, 2014
Mac/Kelly Protagonist	Duo, Positive to Negative to Positive Moral (Redeemed Buddy Heroes)
Teddy/Pete Antagonist	Duo, Negative to Positive Moral (Redeemed Divergent Mastermind/Henchman Villains)

(Greg Smith, Founder of Agile Writers of Richmond, VA)

Scott, we just saw *Neighbors* - is it time we mended some fences?

(Dr. Scott Allison, Professor of Psychology, University of Richmond)

When it comes to legal battles with bad neighbors, the de-fence never rests. Let's recap.

Mac Radner (Seth Rogen) and his wife Kelly (Rose Byrne) are thirty-somethings with a baby girl and a mortgage in suburbia. They are finding out just how hard it can be to be parents and still have a good time. Just as they're figuring it all out, a fraternity moves in next door. They want to be cool so drop by for a visit with an offering of some weed - and an awkward request to "keep the noise down." That night the Delts put on a wild party and wake them. Mac and Kelly walk over to tell their new neighbors to keep it down - when the president of the fraternity, Teddy Sanders (Zac Efron) invites them in. The parental duo live it up and become best buds with the frat boys.

 But all is not well when Mac and Kelly are kept awake nearly every night by the fraternity's non-stop partying. Mac makes what he thinks is an anonymous call to the cops but the cops reveal Mac's identity, putting him on the fraternity's enemy list. The Delts use Mac's car's airbags against him in amusing ways, and they do other things to make the couple miserable. Finally, Mac and Kelly devise a plan to get the fraternity into legal trouble which will lead to its expulsion from the university, but of course the plan does not quite unfold as anticipated.

Scott, *Neighbors* had a great opportunity to be yet another sophomoric gross-out comedy by some of Hollywood's comedy newcomers. But instead we were served up a surprising look at a different kind of coming-of-age story - growing out of the party age and into the responsibilities of parenting. I enjoyed this movie which employed the contrast between young and not-so-old to create a comedic tale of life at the beginning of adulthood.

 Greg, you and I gleaned the same message from this movie. I have a theory about Seth Rogen. The roles and movies he chooses for himself reveal him to be the smartest man in Hollywood. In *Neighbors* he plays a 30-something new husband and father of a newborn baby. Rogen knows exactly what most educated 30-something men are feeling in this situation they want the joys of domestication without losing their old debaucherous college lifestyle. In short, they want it all, and in this movie, Rogen's character and his wife get it all. And then some.

Rogen's genius here lies not only in portraying the dilemma of the post-adolescent young adult male, but also taking that dilemma to absurd and hilarious extremes. His jiggling 30-something body clashes with the six-packed fraternity brothers but Mac raises the ante anyway. He doesn't "use" drugs, he gorges on them to the point of partaking in urination sword-play. Is it a dream come true or a nightmare come true? With a wink to the camera, Rogen tells us it's both.

The heroes here are Mac and Kelly. In our book on movie heroes we identify *Duos* as a major hero category and Mac and Kelly fall into the *Buddy* sub-category. Unlike so many buddy stories Mac and Kelly are aligned in their goals. This is a powerful dynamic. They aren't constantly bickering with each other. Instead, they are united against their more powerful foe. I read an article about Rogen where he talks about how he patterned this buddy pair on his own relationship with his wife. At her urging, he made the Radners a happily married couple. When it comes time to create a plan to fight against the frat boys, this commitment packs a big punch.

 Every hero has a mission, and Mac and Kelly's pre-mid-life crisis clouds their mission. Their domesticated personas want peace and quiet for them and for their baby, but deep down they want to party to just as hard as the fraternity next door. Do they defeat the enemy or make love to the enemy? In this movie they do both, and their confused identity leads to a zig-zagging hero story.

The primary villain is Teddy, head of the Delts next door, but the fraternity itself is the institutional structure that Mac and Kelly are aiming to destroy. Sometimes villains are large organizational bodies with human representatives serving as the proxy. Mac and Kelly are also fighting their own personal issues for example, their lack of full maturity gets in the way of their ability to fulfill their mission.

I think you've nailed it, Scott. Another type of hero we identify in our book is the *Ensemble* and the sub-category is that of the *Fraternity*. Here we see that same pattern but for the villain. The entire Delta Psi fraternity is the villain in this story. But that is a difficult story to write - "the two of use against all of them." So all the attention is poured into Teddy as the leader of the frat.

In other villain patterns we've seen this year, the lead villain as the one who pulls the strings - letting some lesser character do the dirty work. But Teddy is very active in his antics against the Radners. And there is a full transformation for Teddy as well. By the end of the film he realizes that he has to grow beyond his college-age hijinks and become a full adult with goals and responsibilities. It is a nice villain mini-journey.

 On the surface, *Neighbors* is a silly, juvenile movie that is packed with raunchy gags and absurd plot devices. But lurking below the slimy surface is a movie that offers a potent sociological commentary about the challenges young adults face when they form a young family before they are ready to shed their youthful party-animal urges. I enjoyed *Neighbors* far more than I had any right to, for many of the same reasons I enjoyed Rogen's 2013 movie *This is the End*. Both films made my inner-13-year-old boy giggle while making my outer-middle-aged man nod in understanding. I give this movie 3 Reels out of 5.

The two heroes in this film were sent on a journey that most mature adults could handle with little difficulty, but Mac and Kelly's lack of maturity – their missing inner quality – led them to commit one massive mistake after another. Eventually, they "got it", although it's a bit unclear how truly transformed they are by the film's end. I award them 3 Heroes out of 5.

As you point out, Greg, the main villain Teddy is perhaps the one person in this movie who transforms the most. We learn that he isn't a terrible person, just a terribly misguided person. He receives some mentoring from his "villainous" sidekick Pete (Dave Franco) which enables him to outgrow his basest animal house instincts. It's not a very deep villain story but it's a fairly effective one. I award the villains in this movie 3 out of 5 Villains.

Movie: Villains: Heroes:

Neighbors is a fun look back at both college life and life as a new parent. I felt at home with all the characters in this movie as either representatives of my own experiences or people I have known. I was entertained more than I expected and so happily award 3 out of 5 Reels to this film.

The Radners were nice, likable people with a bit of growing to do. Their transformation couldn't come soon enough for me as I never trusted their baby monitor to perform between houses. The initial challenges they experienced as newly-minted parents (never finding a quiet time for lovemaking) gave way to a thorough enjoyment of child-rearing. I also give them 3 out of 5 Heroes.

The *Ensemble/Fraternity* villains represented by leader Teddy was just enough of a challenge for our heroes. In any story the opposition needs to be at least as strong as the hero - and preferably a bit stronger. I enjoyed the transformation for Teddy which gave him the second Villain's Journey this summer. I'll join you in giving Teddy 3 out of 5 Villains.

Movie: Villains: Heroes:

Nightcrawler

Starring	Jake Gyllenhaal, Rene Russo, Bill Paxton
Director	Dan Gilroy
Screenplay	Dan Gilroy
Genre	Crime/Drama/Thriller
Rated	R
Running Time	117 minutes
Release Date	October 31, 2014
Bloom Protagonist	Single, Negative to more Negative Moral (Irredeemable Anti-Hero)
Police Antagonist	System, Untransformed Positive Moral (Untransformed Government Anti-Villain)

(Greg Smith, Founder of Agile Writers of Richmond, VA)
Scott, it's time to crawl out of your hole and write a review with me tonight.

(Dr. Scott Allison, Professor of Psychology, University of Richmond)
I'm out of the hole and at my keyboard. Time to review *Nightcrawler*, starring Jake Gyllenhaal. You first, Gregger.

Louis Bloom (Jake Gyllenhaal) is a disreputable young man who makes ends meet by stealing chain link fence and manhole covers for the money he can negotiate from the smelters. He is scraping the bottom of the barrel when he happens upon an accident where he witnesses some professional videographers who crawl the night looking for stories to film and sell to area newscasts. Louis decides this is an easy way to make money and steals a bicycle which he hocks for a camcorder and police radio receiver.

Lou first films the scene of a fatal accident and takes the clip to a local TV station whose new director, Nina (Rene Russo), welcomes his gory footage. She encourages him to bring her videos of violent accidents and crime scenes with white affluent victims. Lou hires an assistant, Rick (Rick Garcia), and the two men find some success hunting down bloody car collisions and murders to put on film. To obtain better videos, Lou alters some crime scenes and arranges dead bodies to create better images. He even sabotages a competitor's van so that his competitor suffers a gruesome accident for Lou to film. One night he and Rick arrive at the scene of a horrific mass murder before the police have arrived. This sets in motion more graphic violence for Lou to orchestrate (and videotape) with the goal of earning more money from Nina.

Scott, *Nightcrawler* is an intense look behind the scenes of local news. It's not enough to show the events as they happen, but Lou is advised to find events that show the urban world encroaching on the suburban world. Or, to show people of color robbing or killing white people. These are the stories that garner higher ratings. And higher ratings garner more advertising dollars. Lou realizes this and starts to manipulate not only the crime scenes he's supposed to be reporting on, but also the people around him. He convinces his "intern" Rick to work for peanuts and even gets Nina to sleep with him so that he will continue to feed her these high-value videos.

Lou is an unusual hero for a movie. He has many of the characteristics we look for in a hero. He's resourceful as he finds a way to make a living. He is intelligent - he studies the internet and reads up on all things having to do with network news and how it works behind the scenes. In his own way, he is charismatic as he uses his motivational speaker skills (which he learned from the internet) to induce people to do things they really don't want to do. He rises from a position of low social status to running his own business.

But he severely lacks any empathy for how other people feel. He is completely self-absorbed and manipulates people into doing things that are illegal and ultimately even life-threatening. He will do anything to get what he wants, no matter the cost to others. Scott, Lou Bloom is a textbook definition of the anti-hero. He is a villainous person cast in the role of the lead character of the story. Unlike the more likable anti-heroes (like Butch Cassidy and the Sundance Kid, or Bonnie and Clyde), we learn to fear and even despise Lou Bloom.

 For me, *Nightcrawler* is a disturbing look at a disturbed man. Lou is a classic sociopath who lacks a conscience and has no empathy, remorse, or moral core. He uses people and hurts people to obtain his goals. We've seen characters like this in the movies before, of course, but usually they are secondary characters, i.e., the villains who occupy limited screen time. But in *Nightcrawler*, we're subjected to Lou's heinous character for two solid hours. He appears in just about every scene. Although this film was extremely well made, I was uncomfortable being exposed to pure evil for such an extended period of time in the form of Lou's psychopathic personality and escalating malevolent behavior. It was relentless.

As you point out, Greg, we know villains share four of the Great Eight attributes of heroes. Lou is smart, strong, charismatic, and resilient. But Lou is lacking the most telltale signs of a hero: He has no heart. It was repugnant watching him deliberately ignore suffering people, harm others, and even kill them, in order to sell his videos at a higher price to Nina. *Nightcrawler* makes us think about the ethics of paparazzi and ambulance chasers. It even raises ethical issues about television news journalism and where they can and should draw the line between morality and legality.

With Lou already playing such a villainous role, it's hard to identify any villains in *Nightcrawler*. Lou's arc of going from harmless gadfly to devious mastermind is the epitome of the Villain's Journey - which is the mirror image of the Hero's Journey. So, I look for the more heroic characters to offset Lou's villainy.

Nina is already a pretty cut-throat news director. She'll do anything to advance her career - even put clearly illegal source material on the air. She doesn't offer an impediment to Lou's advance. In fact, she aids it. There is a minor character in the form of the station manager, but while he is the voice of morality and reason, he offers little in the way of opposition to Lou.

The rival video company owned by Joe Loder (Bill Paxton) is Lou's only opposition. He's a good guy, plays by the rules. But he's a tough businessman. At one point he see's Lou's abilities and tries to hire him. But instead of taking Joe's offer, Lou tampers with Joe's brake line and causes him to be in an accident that heartless Lou films for the morning news. And that ends any opposition that Lou might have.

Really, the only decent character with any screen time is Rick, who plays the role of the sidekick who repeatedly questions Lou's actions and character. Rick is in such desperate need of money that he looks the other way while Lou engages in awful conduct. Rick's also such a weak character that he is no match against Lou when the two men eventually collide over morals.

If there is an oppositional force at work against Lou, it exists mostly in the form of the ineffectual Los Angeles Police Department, who appear at the scenes of accidents and murders, and who also try to keep Lou from getting in the way of emergency personnel as well as their investigations of what happened at these scenes. The LAPD may be the type of villains that we call *institutional villains* – a large bureaucratic entity that lurks in the background as the main impediment to our main character's goals.

Nightcrawler is more frightening than any horror movie for its vivid portrayal of the realities of mainstream news. The thing that makes it scary is just how real and current the story is. This could be happening now. This is a tale about how we are being fed stories - and how they could potentially being crafted - to titillate and spread fear in the name of news and money. It begs the question - what is news? I give *Nightcrawler* 5 out of 5 Reels for showing us a very scary reality.

Lou Bloom is a terrifying anti-hero cast in the world of network news. He frightens us not for any super powers that he might have, but for how amazingly ordinary he seems to be. He seems in every way an under achiever. He is not handsome, overly intelligent, or even athletic. But he is a cunning villain in the way he manipulates his prey. We are witness to a complete Villain's Journey here. I give Lou Bloom 5 out of 5 Villains.

There are no strong heroes in this story for Lou to combat. You've already pointed out that the LAPD detectives were completely ineffectual against Lou. And rival Joe Loder was no match for Lou. A stronger hero for our anti-hero would have made *Nightcrawler* a completely different movie. I can only give these side-heroes 2 out of 5 Heroes.

Movie: ⬤⬤⬤⬤⬤ Villain: ⬤⬤⬤⬤⬤ Heroes: ⬤

 Nightcrawler is an extremely well made movie but you won't catch me watching it again. The movie is two relentless hours of the devil in human form at work on the streets of Los Angeles. I was disturbed by the main character (notice that I cannot call him a hero) and his wanton disregard for human life, and it was disheartening that no heroic character in the film could even come close to combating him. I don't know what good can come from making such a movie or even watching it, other than the possibility that it can be used as fodder for ethical reform for the ways TV networks solicit film clips for their evening news. I give this movie 4 Reels out of 5 simply out of respect for the filmmaking and for Jake Gyllenhaal's extraordinary performance.

There is no hero in this story, as this is a tale of the triumph of evil. Our main character is the devil running roughshod over everyone in his path. Like a cancer, he just grows and grows in his size and power, and he is shown flourishing in the end. He doesn't change or evolve or transform like a heroic character might. He has no mentors or friends and he eliminates his sidekick when the sidekick outlives his usefulness. Our main character's evil simply gains strength for two disturbing hours. The absence of a hero story here leads me to assign a rating of 0 out of 5 Heroes.

Inasmuch as our main character is a villain, this is a movie about villainy and how it blossoms. *Nightcrawler* shows us how villainy is allowed to prosper when we allow it to prosper, when we condone it, when we cooperate with it, and when we place money ahead of principles. Nina and Rick are probably not terrible people; they simply succumb to greed. As the main character, Lou does encounter some resistance from a rival videographer (whom Lou severely injures), a sidekick Rick (whom Lou eliminates), and the LAPD (whom Lou outsmarts). There aren't many villain stories that are better told than this one, and so I'll give Lou an impressive 4 Villains out of 5.

Movie: Villain:  Heroes: 0

No Good Deed

Starring	Taraji P. Henson, Idris Elba, Leslie Bibb
Director	Sam Miller
Screenplay	Aimee Lagos
Genre	Crime/Thriller
Rated	PG-13
Running Time	84 minutes
Release Date	September 12, 2014
Terri Protagonist	Single, Positive to More Positive Emotional (Classic Lone Hero)
Colin Antagonist	Single, Untransformed Negative Moral (Untransformed Lone Villain)

(Dr. Scott Allison, Professor of Psychology, University of Richmond)

Greg, we just saw a movie about a no-good dude.

(Greg Smith, Founder of Agile Writers of Richmond, VA)

And if no good deed goes unpunished, then indeed, we were punished for watching.

Let's recap. Inmate Colin Evans (Idris Elba) is being transported back to prison from his parole hearing, where he was denied parole. He is serving time for brutally killing several people. During his return trip to prison, Evans manages to shoot the driver and a guard. He then escapes successfully to Atlanta. There he meets up with his former fiance and confronts her about her new lover. After killing her, we see him driving his car in a rainstorm. His car crashes into a tree, and he seeks refuge at the door of a nearby home owned by Terri Henson (Taraji P. Henson) and her baby.

Colin is charismatic and smiles his way into the home and out of the rain by feigning the need to call for a tow truck. When Terri's best friend Meg (Leslie Bibb) arrives, Colin has some fast thinking to do. But Meg is not convinced of Colin's good intentions and confronts him. Meanwhile, Terri realizes that Colin is not so harmless and he begins to chase her through the house. Now it's a battle of wits as Terri must find a way to call for help before Colin can accomplish his dastardly plan.

 Greg, *No Good Deed* is a by-the-numbers story of survival at the hands of a vicious killer. This story has been told countless times before, but what distinguishes *No Good Deed* is that it features a strong African-American female hero who must use both her wits and her strength of character to extricate herself from danger. Taraji Henson does a nice job portraying the role of Terri, and a number of her *Great Eight* characteristics of heroes truly shine through. She is *strong, smart, caring, selfless, resilient*, and *inspiring*.

The first 15 minutes of the movie led me to believe that the villain, Colin Evans, was going to be the hero (or anti-hero) of the story. We, the audience, are provided with more of his backstory than that of Terri. But soon the movie wisely shifts to Terri as the movie's main focus, and we become impressed with her selfless devotion to placing the safety of her two children before her own. As I said, this isn't a great movie by any means, but it does manage to pull us into the drama and leave us wondering how Terri is going to survive.

I have to agree with you, Scott - this is a good movie with a strong female lead. The other thing that distinguishes this movie from others is that Terri fears for her life and the lives of her children, only to discover that Colin's goal has nothing to do with Terri. There's a point in the film (that is shared in the trailer) where Colin chastises Terri by saying, 'I would have thought with all those brains you got, you woulda figured out what game we're playing.' It isn't the standard game of cat and mouse.

Terri is a good hero - she is smarter than the average damsel in distress. And she stands up to her captor. She doesn't just run screaming through the house (although there is a bit of that). She *is* smart and she makes plans to escape.

Colin makes for a good villain, too. He's every bit as smart and determined as our hero. And that is critical for a good villain story. We are given a good deal of his backstory so we know where his anger comes from. Although, he is set up as a "malignant narcissist" by the parole board - we don't get any insight into what created such a person. So I can give points for setting up our villain - and I have to take one away for embedding the fact that Colin is crazy.

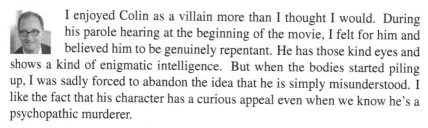

I enjoyed Colin as a villain more than I thought I would. During his parole hearing at the beginning of the movie, I felt for him and believed him to be genuinely repentant. He has those kind eyes and shows a kind of enigmatic intelligence. But when the bodies started piling up, I was sadly forced to abandon the idea that he is simply misunderstood. I like the fact that his character has a curious appeal even when we know he's a psychopathic murderer.

Another virtue of this movie is witnessing the palpable chemistry between Terri and Colin. Her courage in standing up to him is borderline foolhardy but serves her and her children quite well. One unfortunate negative is the number of times that Terri skewers him, crushes his head, shoots him, and maims him, while he does his best Ever-Ready battery impression by still ticking. We also get the standard *Fatal Attraction* miracle revival of the seemingly dead villain. One day I hope the movies finally put this hackneyed gimmick to bed for good.

Yeah, I noticed that too. I liked this movie, but the twist at the end didn't warrant a higher rating. It's a classic thriller with some upgrades. I give *No Good Deed* 3 out of 5 Reels.

Terri is a good hero but still not above average. What I appreciated about her was that she wasn't a typical damsel in distress. She was smart and strong. But I can only give her 3 out of 5 Heroes.

Colin is painted better than the average villain. He has all the great qualities of the hero plus a diabolical tendency toward "malignant narcissism". But he can only garner 3 out of 5 Villains.

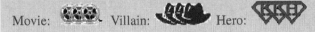

Movie: Villain: Hero:

No Good Deed is a fairly well constructed thriller that gives us a strong woman character who delights us with her brains, her inner strength, and her selflessness. This movie features good tension, good pacing, and good acting. *No Good Deed* is far from great but it provided 90 minutes of solid entertainment. Like you, Greg, I give this film 3 Reels out of 5.

The hero Terri is inspiring to watch. She embodies many of the signature characteristics of a hero, but her Joseph-Campbell-like hero journey is stunted. There is no mentor figure, for example; she's left entirely to her own devices. I'm not convinced that she transforms in any significant way, either. So we're left with a pretty good hero but not a great one, at least not in the classic sense. I'm with you, Greg, that she merits 3 Heroes out of 5.

The villain Colin is a major focus of this movie. He's a complex man with a motive for his mayhem. *No Good Deed* does a good job of portraying the villain's story with greater depth than we see in most movies. His fatal flaw lies in his underestimation of our hero Terri. Colin's intelligence, deceptiveness, magnetism, and complexity make him formidable villain with considerable texture, in my opinion. I'm awarding him 4 Villains out of 5.

Movie: Villain: Hero:

Non-Stop

Starring	Liam Neeson, Julianne Moore, Scoot McNairy
Director	Jaume Collet-Serra
Screenplay	John W. Richardson, Christopher Roach
Genre	Action/Mystery/Thriller
Rated	PG-13
Running Time	106 minutes
Release Date	February 28, 2014
Marks Protagonist	Single, Positive to More Positive Moral (Classic Lone Hero)
Villains Antagonist	Duo, Untransformed Negative Moral (Untransformed Hidden Divergent Villains)

(Dr. Scott Allison, Professor of Psychology, University of Richmond)

Greg, it's time to stop what we're doing to review *Non-Stop*.

(Greg Smith, Founder of Agile Writers of Richmond, VA)

Scott, the action in this movie was non-stop. Let's recap.

Air marshall Bill Marks's (Liam Neeson) personal life is a mess. He's recently divorced and his young daughter just passed away. Now he's an alcoholic, angry at life and very agitated. He boards a flight from New York to London and finds himself sitting beside Jen Summers (Julianne Moore). When the plane is well over the Atlantic, Marks receives a threatening text message on his secure phone line.

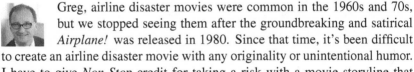

The sender says that someone will die every 20 minutes until his demands are met. That's when Marks goes into action. He consults another Air Marshall who tells Marks his fears are without merit. However Marks discovers the other marshall is carrying a suitcase full of cocaine. When Marks confronts him the two duke it out and Marks is forced to kill him, just at the 20 minute mark.

 Greg, airline disaster movies were common in the 1960s and 70s, but we stopped seeing them after the groundbreaking and satirical *Airplane!* was released in 1980. Since that time, it's been difficult to create an airline disaster movie with any originality or unintentional humor. I have to give *Non-Stop* credit for taking a risk with a movie storyline that shares much of the conventional build-up with those air-disaster movies of yesteryear.

Does this film work? I think it does to some extent. Liam Neeson does a nice job of capturing a tormented father dealing with many personal issues. His character Bill Marks is a classic hero in the sense that he is missing inner peace, self-confidence, and self-respect. The air disaster awaiting him serves as the vehicle of his redemption. This movie is far from perfect, but it did hit all the right notes in terms of following the mythic hero journey.

I have to agree, Scott. *Non-Stop* employs a classic device to make the movie captivating - the countdown timer. Every 20 minutes something has to happen. This creates tension and impending doom. I thought it was a little convenient that Marks killed his colleague just in time for the first countdown, but I was willing to let it slide for the sake of my willing suspension of disbelief.

As a hero Marks does pretty well. He is courageous and a leader when the time comes to act. And, as you point out, has some important personal demons that he has to overcome. He blames himself for not being around when his daughter was dying of cancer. Despite the fact that his job requires him to fly he is afraid of take-offs. And he drinks to excess which is probably not in his job description. I'm not sure that he overcomes any of these imperfections, but he does save the day and that makes him a hero.

 Well, I think we can assume that Marks's drinking was a symptom of his character deficits that his completed hero journey was able to remedy. The man is basically a mess, and just when it looks like everyone on board is about to lynch him, he confesses his sins to the angry mob in an impassioned speech that tugs on every passenger's heartstrings. For me, this was perhaps the only unintentionally humorous scene in the movie, but his brutal honesty does win over the passengers and seems to spur him to take a slew of extraordinary actions that will save everyone's lives.

One nagging question I had throughout much of the movie was why Marks didn't trust the NYPD cop sooner. That oversight made Marks's job tougher than it needed to be. It was also more than a little far-fetched that he happens to be in the right place at the right time to save the life of a little girl who happens to be the same age as his deceased daughter, who of course he couldn't save. Still, despite a few imperfections here and there, I was impressed by Neeson's performance and entertained by the story.

The villain in this story is pretty much invisible until the very end of the movie. This added a certain level of mystery to him and made him a bit ominous. However, when the villain is revealed, we find that he is an Iraq war veteran who is disillusioned with the purpose of the war. He wants to underscore the fact that America is still vulnerable to attack and so hijacked the plane.

I felt this was a lame excuse for a villain's motivation. It was a political statement that should have stayed home. It comes from out of nowhere and has no basis in popular culture. The villain pulled off some pretty impressive feats (like creating a Swiss bank account in Marks's name, bribing an Air Marshall with a massive amount of cocaine, and creating a bomb that eluded detection). I found the villain's story to be clumsy and unbelievable.

 I completely agree with your analysis, Greg. The villains could have been anyone on the plane and were impossible to guess. The backstory of the two (or three) villains did not unfold until the very end, and even then it was a villain origin story that stretched the bounds of believability. Their villainous motives were bizarre and unrealistic, in my opinion. Compared to our hero, Bill Marks, the villains in this movie were a big disappointment.

Non-Stop was a thrilling ride from beginning to the end. Some of the plot points were a bit hard to swallow, but if you hang on during some of the wider turns, you'll enjoy yourself. I give *Non-Stop* 3 out of 5 Reels.

Liam Neeson plays a decent hero with lots of deficits who redeems himself in the end. I enjoyed watching Marks work out the mystery of the hidden villain. I give Marks 3 out of 5 Heroes.

The villain was hidden from us for most of the movie and that amped-up the mystery. But the final reveal was unbelievable and disappointing. I give him just 1 Villain out of 5.

Movie: Heroes: Villains:

 Non-Stop is an entertaining movie that is hardly groundbreaking but still manages to hold our interest with its likeable hero, suspenseful story, and act of redemption. Liam Neeson deserves credit for delivering a terrific performance and for making us feel his pain as well as his satisfying redemption at the end. Like you, Greg, I give this movie a solid 3 Reels out of 5.

The hero story was a strong one, in my opinion. Marks was as emotionally and spiritually beaten up as a man can be, and the dark, dangerous events on the plane allowed him to develop qualities that were the seeds of his transformation. In evolving as a person, he delivers a gift to the people around him by saving their lives. I give Marks 4 Heroes out of 5.

You're absolutely right that this movie's big weak spot was its ridiculous villains whose motives were so absurd that, in my opinion, the actors who played the villains could not even do their jobs well. Quite generously, I award these so-called villains 1 Villain out of 5.

Movie: Heroes:  Villains:

The Other Woman

Starring	Cameron Diaz, Leslie Mann, Kate Upton
Director	Nick Cassavetes
Screenplay	Melissa Stack
Genre	Comedy/Drama
Rated	PG-13
Running Time	109 minutes
Release Date	April 25, 2014
Carly/Kate/Amber Protagonist	Ensemble, Untransformed Positive Moral (Untransformed Sorority Heroes)
Mark Antagonist	Single, Untransformed Negative Moral (Untransformed Lone Villain)

(Greg Smith, Founder of Agile Writers of Richmond, VA)

Scott, it's time to review *The Other Woman*.

(Dr. Scott Allison, Professor of Psychology, University of Richmond)

Just another review about another man's other woman. Let's recap.

We're introduced to high-powered attorney Carly (Cameron Diaz) who has found the perfect man. Mark (Nikolaj Coster-Waldau) is an entrepreneur and drop dead sexy. Carly is so excited about Mark that she has "cleared the bench" and dates no one else. Eight weeks into the relationship Mark cancels a date with Carly because the toilets at his house have overflowed. Carly is not pleased and sends Mark home. Later that night, she regrets her anger and shows up on Mark's front door dressed as a sexy female plumber only to be greeted by Mark's wife Kate (Leslie Mann).

Needless to say, Carly is devastated by Mark's deceit. But her visit to Mark's home arouses suspicion in Kate, who stops by Carly's office and discovers that Mark has been cheating on her. Carly and Kate form an alliance and follow Mark to Florida where they discover that he has a third lover, a buxom blonde named Amber (Kate Upton). The three women conspire to make Mark's life miserable, and in so doing they discover that Mark has some dark financial secrets which they can use against him.

Scott, in our book *Reel Heroes: Volume 1* we categorize heroes into three groupings: Lone Heroes, Duos, and Ensembles. This is an Ensemble hero story. We break Ensembles into The Family, Military & Police, and Fraternity. This movie falls into the last category, only it is more of a Sorority. And on top of that, it's a revenge plot. These women are out for blood.

It's not a complex story. The majority of the rest of the movie is scene after scene of making Mark look bad. And he plays right into the women's plans to make him suffer. Meanwhile, Kate (the wife) is teetering on the verge of forgiving him as he is making their little company grow. But ultimately you know how it has to end, with Mark looking like a big bad schmuck.

Greg, are you ready for another food analogy? Watching *The Other Woman* is like sitting down for a meal and being served popcorn followed by salt water taffy for dessert. It's a disappointment, but this assumes you're expecting a big meal. Most people who go to see *The Other Woman* are probably only expecting a light snack at best, but even with this expectation this film provides only mediocre fare.

A good romantic comedy, such as last year's *About Time,* has some depth to it or at least a take-home message we can chew on for a while. *The Other Woman* delivers only light, puffy jiffy pop. The nicest thing I can say about the movie is that the lead characters are likeable people who are pleasing for men like me to look at. There are no laugh-out-loud moments, only a few smiles here and there. *The Other Woman* isn't a complete waste of time but it is one of the more forgettable movies I've seen.

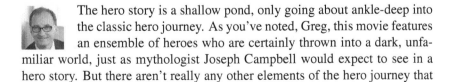

I thought the writers took pains to make Cameron Diaz's character look more heroic than villainous. Since she is *The Other Woman* in this story, she could be played up like a home wrecker. The writers wisely painted Mark and Kate King as a couple without children. Adding kids to the mix would definitely have complicated things and made Carly a villain. The other thing they did was to have Carly exclaim (at least twice) "I'm not a mistress! I didn't know he was married." This tries to remind the audience that she was an unwitting accomplice in the adultery.

Kate King is played in some very odd ways. In one scene she is portrayed as the frumpy housewife where she literally goes to the bathroom in front of her husband as he brushes his teeth. Later, she is portrayed as the brains of the couple's business as she describes her latest internet idea to one of Mark's collaborators. However, in every other scene she is played as ditzy and naive. I found her character to be whatever the writers needed her to be whenever it was convenient.

Finally we have young Amber. As you've pointed out, Ms. Kate Upton is in this film for visual appeal only. While she doesn't embarrass herself on-screen, she is no actor. It takes skill to play the dumb blonde and Ms. Upton isn't up to the challenge. There are several shots of her in bikinis running in slow motion on the beach. So, the men in the audience have something to look at while the real actors in the show carry out the plot.

The hero story is a shallow pond, only going about ankle-deep into the classic hero journey. As you've noted, Greg, this movie features an ensemble of heroes who are certainly thrown into a dark, unfamiliar world, just as mythologist Joseph Campbell would expect to see in a hero story. But there aren't really any other elements of the hero journey that are worth mentioning. To the movie's credit, Kate does undergo a transformation of confidence, becoming an independent woman both personally and professionally.

The less said about Kate Upton's acting, the better. In fact, her character, Amber, has such a limited and impoverished role that you could argue persuasively that this is a buddy hero movie featuring Kate and Carly. Amber would then be a rather minor sidekick or ally to the hero duo.

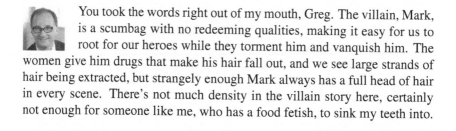

That's an apt observation, Scott. The villain in this story is about as two-dimensional as they come. Mark King is a womanizer and a liar and has no redeeming qualities. We feel no sympathy for him and that makes the bullying and revenge on him seem valid. In the end, the women find that he not only cheated on his wife, but set her up as the patsy in a confidence scheme. That leads to a confrontation scene that seemingly justifies his complete humiliation. It's pretty trite stuff.

You took the words right out of my mouth, Greg. The villain, Mark, is a scumbag with no redeeming qualities, making it easy for us to root for our heroes while they torment him and vanquish him. The women give him drugs that make his hair fall out, and we see large strands of hair being extracted, but strangely enough Mark always has a full head of hair in every scene. There's not much density in the villain story here, certainly not enough for someone like me, who has a food fetish, to sink my teeth into.

The Other Woman is a light comedy that tries nothing new and is a vehicle for its leads to play together on-screen. The girlfriend dynamic between Diaz and Mann is entertaining and they let young Upton play along. The two leads do a good job and deliver decent performances so I give *The Other Woman* 2 out of 5 Reels.

The heroes in this story aren't very strong. Diaz's character is a lawyer, but we don't see much lawyering going on here. Mann's wife character is clueless and a victim for most of the film and we don't much care about her. And Upton is only there for looks. I give them just 2 Heroes out of 5.

And the villain is a cardboard cutout of everything women hate in men. He gets only 1 Villain out of 5 from me.

Movie: Heroes: Villains: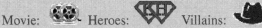

 The Other Woman is a throwaway movie, in that it follows an overused formula of the betrayal of love and typical act of vengeance. Movies that rely on such a common storyline cannot stand out unless they truly excel in other areas, but this film can make no such claim. If you are a Cameron Diaz fanatic, then this movie will appeal to you; otherwise, I recommend staying away. Like you, Greg, I award this film 2 Reels out of 5.

The hero duo was unremarkable and followed the familiar path of two people disliking each other at first and then growing to be best buddies. Leslie Mann's character has some annoying verbal mannerisms that almost made me feel empathy for the villain Mark. Cameron Diaz remains a terrific actress and plays a very smart, likeable character here. Because they break no new ground, I can only award this duo (or trio if you like) 2 Heroes out of 5.

The villain Mark is entirely forgettable. Greg, you are generous by endowing him with 2 dimensions when it is hard to discern any. This movie is an example of a story in which the villain is a mere prop, and the entire film hinges on the success or failure of the rest of the cast and story. So for a lightweight villain, I agree that he only deserves one puny Villain out of 5.

Movie: Heroes: Villains:

Ride Along

Starring	Ice Cube, Kevin Hart, Tika Sumpter
Director	Tim Story
Screenplay	Greg Coolidge, Jason Mantzoukas
Genre	Action/Comedy
Rated	R
Running Time	99 minutes
Release Date	January 17, 2014
Ben & James Protagonist	Duo, Positive to More Positive Mental (Classic Buddy Cop Heroes)
Omar Antagonist	Single, Untransformed Negative Moral (Hidden Mastermind Villain)

(Dr. Scott Allison, Professor of Psychology, University of Richmond)

Greg, it looks like Kevin Hart wants to go along for the ride. Shall we review?

(Greg Smith, Founder of Agile Writers of Richmond, VA)

I don't have the Hart to say no. Let's recap.

We meet Ben Barber (Kevin Hart), who works as a security guard at a local school but aspires to become a member of the Atlanta Police Department. Ben is dating a woman named Angela (Tika Sumpter) who is the sister of a current APD officer named James (Ice Cube). No matter how hard he tries, Ben can't seem to impress James, who doesn't believe that Ben is worthy of dating his sister.

Through a series of awkward events, James challenges Ben to go on a ride along with him in his police car. James offers that if Ben can keep up with him for a full day then he can have his blessing for his sister's hand in marriage. But James stacks the odds against Ben by taking on only the most annoying calls and Ben quickly becomes frustrated.

 Greg, *Ride Along* is a sort-of buddy cop story involving a funny guy, Ben, and a straight man, James. One has to be a Kevin Hart fan to enjoy this movie, and while I don't claim to be his biggest fan, I did appreciate his talent and some of his antics. Hart and Ice Cube are a modern-day Jerry Lewis and Dean Martin; there is nonstop zaniness from Hart followed by scowls of disapproval by James. Both characters are likeable and I found myself rooting for them to achieve detente.

As we've seen with other "buddy" films, the buddies usually start out as adversaries and gradually grow to find a center. This was true of last year's *The Heat* with Sandra Bullock and Melissa McCarthy. In *Ride Along*, we see scene after scene of straight man James introducing Ben to situations he is not able to handle. But, James has a knack for noticing small details that eventually become useful to him.

As the story progresses, we find that James is tracking bad guy "Omar" (Laurence Fishburne) whom no one has seen. This shadowy figure controls the local drug and gun black market. This becomes the main object of the pair's attention.

Indeed. It's a predictable plot and so the appeal of the movie centers on whether you enjoy Kevin Hart's physical comedy and verbally explosive humor. I do give this movie credit for creating two heroes whose characters evolve nicely as a result of their experiences. Ben is given the opportunity to show a crafty courageousness that enables him to win the approval of James. And as for James, he realizes that he has to let his sister live her own life, and he must also swallow his pride by admitting that his negative assessment of Ben was wrong.

As you point out, Greg, this bonding of two cops who initially dislike each other is typical of many buddy cop movies. And so the key here is in the performances and in the execution of the various predictable plot elements. *Ride Along* does a decent job along these lines but it's all pretty standard fare.

You're not kidding when you say this was predictable, Scott. There is the classic ornery boss who wants James not to follow his instincts. There is the go-to snitch on the street. There's the rotten cop on the take. All the elements of the classic buddy-cop movie are here.

The villain was a disappointment. Omar is never seen until the last few scenes of the movie. He is built up as a dastardly dude who controls others from afar. Inexplicably, he shows up at a gun deal and shows how awful he is by killing one of his henchmen, because, you know, he's mean. There is no dimension to this character and zero backstory. He's just a bad, bad, man. Not a very interesting villain.

You're right, Greg. The villain in this story, Omar, is mostly a figurehead who is spoken of ominously throughout the movie. When he does make an appearance at the end, he proves himself to be capably evil but hardly memorable. I was thinking that the only way to salvage my interest in the villain would be to make Kevin Hart, who pretends to be Omar, to turn out to be the actual Omar. But that would have been problematic for other reasons, and so we're largely left with a vacuous villain.

Ride Along is a plodding device for Kevin Hart's humor, like him or not. It borrows from all the buddy-cop movies that came before it and offers nothing new. There was scarcely a joke or giggle for the first 30 minutes and that was a deadly silence to bear. I can only give *Ride Along* 2 Reels out of 5.

Our buddy-heroes were pretty dull - not funny and not interesting. They both did converge into a sense of mutual admiration if not acceptance. I give them 2 Heroes out of 5.

The villain was nearly non-existent and only served to pull a "Snidely Whiplash" and abduct the damsel in distress (James's sister) at the very end of the film. For a lackluster and generically bland villain I give Omar just 1 Villain out of 5.

Movie: Heroes:  Villains:

 As you noted while we walked out of the theater, Greg, I did chuckle twice during this movie. I therefore give *Ride Along* one reel for each chuckle for a total of 2 Reels out of 5. This film avoids receiving the dreaded 1 Reel because Kevin Hart is a good talent, and because Ice Cube deserves credit for handling Hart's goofiness with noble restraint.

Our two heroes do undergo a transformation during the course of events in this movie. The hero story is hardly inspiring but it does contain some rudimentary elements of the hero's journey. For that reason, I'll generously award our dynamic duo a total of 3 Heroes out of 5.

As you point out, the villain was as flimsy as a piece of cardboard. He exists in name only and virtually no effort was made to render him the least bit interesting. So like you, Greg, I can only hand out a measly 1 Villain out of 5.

Movie: Heroes:  Villains:

RoboCop

Starring	Joel Kinnaman, Gary Oldman, Michael Keaton
Director	Jos Padilha
Screenplay	Joshua Zetumer
Genre	Action/Crime/Science-Fiction
Rated	PG-13
Running Time	117 minutes
Release Date	February 12, 2014
Murphy/Robocop Protagonist	Single, Negative to Positive Emotional/Physical (Enlightened Lone Hero)
Sellars Antagonist	Single, Negative to more Negative Moral (Irredeemable Mastermind Villain)

(Greg Smith, Founder of Agile Writers of Richmond, VA)

Scott, it's time for a movie about an Irish policeman: Rob O'Cop.

(Dr. Scott Allison, Professor of Psychology, University of Richmond)

And in the tradition of Madonna and Prince, he became known simply as RoboCop. That's our story and we're sticking to it.

It's the year 2028 and America is in a war with Iran. They clean the streets with Omnicorp's mechanized military. But back in America, such "drones" are illegal. Evil corporate genius Raymond Sellars (Michael Keaton) wants desperately to sell his robot soldier technology to police forces in the US but the Dreyfus Act forbids the use of such tech on the homeland. So, he gets the great idea of putting a live cop inside one of his robots, but finding an appropriately disembodied psychologically ready cop turns out to be harder than he thought.

 A Detroit cop named Alex Murphy (Joel Kinnaman) is horribly maimed by a car bomb outside his home, and Sellars convinces Dr. Norton (Gary Oldman) to fit Alex with a robot exoskeleton. Sellars' hope is that the public will feel more comfortable approving of robots with a human face. At first, Murphy is horrified by his new mechanical appearance, but soon he agrees to fight crime as Detroit's first robocop. He's an instant success, but trouble looms with technological glitches and bad guys lurking all around him.

Scott, this is a remake of the 1987 movie of the same name. And it gets the full treatment. The graphics and animation are impeccable as we witness high speed chases and shootouts with an army of competitor robots. *Robocop* is a well-made action adventure.

Robocop wants to deal with the thorny issue of man versus machine. It offers us Raymond Sellars as a sort of Steve Jobs with no social conscience (he even utters the line, "How does somebody know what they want if they haven't even seen it?" which Jobs is famous for). Sellars doesn't care about the ethical issues surrounding turning the police force over to machines who cannot feel. In fact, he argues, it's better if the robot cannot feel because it increases reaction times. No fear, no hesitation.

 Robocop is derived from a long line of science fiction stories featuring the blending of human flesh with technological implants. We saw it decades ago in *The Six Million Dollar Man* TV show. The *Star Trek* franchise ran with it in their creation of the arch villain Borg, as did the *Total Recall* movies. We see most recently in the *Iron Man* movie franchise, and now we see it here with *Robocop*.

In some ways *Robocop* also reminds me of *Frankenstein. A* "freak" is created from various parts and then is set loose, only to go out of control and eventually become intent on destroying its maker. But *Robocop* separates itself from all the modern incarnations of man-machines by emphasizing the humanity of the hero, a feat seen only in the original *Frankenstein.* Somehow, Murphy's human, soulful essence is able to overcome the technological mutilation of his brain.

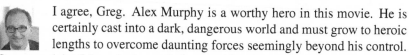

Alex Murphy (aka Robocop) stacks up pretty well as a hero. He starts out as a compassionate and caring father to his son and a good husband to his wife. He's a dedicated cop on the trail of a bad guy named Antoine Vallon who is dealing in illegal drugs and guns. But when he gets too close Vallon has Murphy targeted resulting in the car bombing. This attack on Murphy makes us feel sympathy for him. Once inside the Robocop suit, Murphy wrestles with the fact that he's forever trapped as a part man / part machine. We're given a hero with both a sincere pain and eventually a desire for revenge.

I agree, Greg. Alex Murphy is a worthy hero in this movie. He is certainly cast into a dark, dangerous world and must grow to heroic lengths to overcome daunting forces seemingly beyond his control. One complaint I have is that only by invoking mysterious forces is Murphy able to claw his way out of Dr. Norton's programming. It would have been a more effective hero story if we, the audience, were made explicitly privy to how this transformation takes place. Yes, we can say that his humanity rose above his implants, but this very important part of the story needs some fleshing out (pardon the pun).

As befitting any good hero tale, there are nice supporting allies for Murphy, too. His wife (Abbie Cornish) and child (John Paul Ruttan) are both supportive yet skeptical about Murphy's new role as a Detroit robocop. His police partner Jack (Michael K. Williams) is a supportive sidekick. Then there is

Dr. Norton, who appears to be an ally but we're never really sure until late in the game. Gary Oldman as Norton does a masterful job of straddling the line between hero and villain in this story.

We're dealt a pair of villains in this story. The first is a classic bad guy: Antoine Vallon. He's a very generic dealer in contraband. There isn't much for us to analyze here. He's just a bad guy for Robocop to attempt to bring down.

Only slightly more interesting is Michael Keaton's Sellars character. As I mentioned earlier, he is cut from the same cloth as other corporate geniuses. And like so many other corporate geniuses we see in the movies all he cares about is making a buck. He'll do anything to improve his bottom line. And that includes threatening innocent women and children. Heck, I was expecting him to kick a dog at one point just to show how mean he was. Keaton gives it his best, but Sellars doesn't offer us much to really dislike in this film.

 I thought that Keaton did a terrific job in his role as the main villain of this story, Greg. He pursued his greedy quest in a most cunning and ruthless fashion, and he did it with style and pizzazz. I agree that Vallon was a fairly useless cardboard villain, but Norton, the corrupt cops, and police chief were all effective in their villainous roles. Overall, the main thrust of the story is Murphy's journey as the robocop, and so I was impressed that Sellars' character enjoyed as much development as he did.

Robocop is a pretty good action/adventure with plenty of chases and gun play. I'm sure there will be a video game out soon where we can all live vicariously through Robocop's exploits. For an en- tertaining and well-crafted 2-hour flick I award *Robocop* 3 out of 5 Reels. To get a higher rating I would want more character development for Murphy and supporting characters.

Alex Murphy / Robocop is a fine example of mythical heroes. He starts out as a virtuous man who dies and is resurrected as a more powerful man. We can all feel his loss, pain, and angst. In the end he exacts his revenge and sets things right. I give Murphy 3 Heroes out of 5.

As we've already agreed Vallon is a stock character and doesn't really warrant a score of his own. Sellars was played well by Keaton but I thought he lacked any development. We're just given a typical Hollywood greedy corporate head with ambitions of more wealth. I give him a score of 3 out of 5 Villains.

Movie: Hero: Villain:

I enjoyed *Robocop*, largely because its human elements and story-telling detail allowed it to rise above its appearance as a mindless action flick. In addition, the film raises a philosophical point about the integration of men and machines, as well as the issue of how far we should go to preserve a human life. I agree with you, Greg, that Murphy was a worthy hero but he wasn't a character with a lot of depth. That limits my rating of the movie to 3 Reels out of 5.

Robocop does feature a nicely done hero story. Murphy's journey has many of the classic elements, but as noted above, his character doesn't have the flair or magnetism that I like to see in a hero. For that reason I'll limit my heroes rating to 3 Heroes out of 5.

I was impressed by Keaton's performance here, Greg, probably more than you were. Sellars' obsession with greed and his manipulation of Norton, of public opinion, and of Murphy were a joy to watch. This is a villain that we love to hate. And we never did discuss Samuel L. Jackson as Pat Novak, a sort-of villain whose extreme viewpoints mixed with disingenuous showmanship made me want to vomit. Any villain who is vomit-worthy is worth 4 Villains out of 5.

Movie: Hero: Villain:

Selma

Starring	David Oyelowo, Carmen Ejogo, Tim Roth
Director	Ava DuVernay
Screenplay	Paul Webb
Genre	Biography/Drama/History
Rated	PG-13
Running Time	128 minutes
Release Date	January 9, 2015
King Protagonist	Single, Untransformed Positive Moral (Untransformed Lone Hero)
Racism Antagonist	System, Untransformed Negative Moral (Institutional Villain)

(Dr. Scott Allison, Professor of Psychology, University of Richmond)

Greg, we just saw another movie about the Civil Rights movement.

(Greg Smith, Founder of Agile Writers of Richmond, VA)

Selma was both educational and entertaining. Let's recap:

Selma opens with Martin Luther King, Jr., (David Oyelowo) receiving the Nobel Peace Prize in 1964. He realizes that a lot work remains to be done in achieving racial equality in America. The most pressing issue for him is to abolish restrictions to Black voting in the South. In the 100 years since the Civil War, White-run communities have erected barriers to Black voter registration. King meets with President Lyndon Johnson (Tom Wilkinson) to ask for help, but Johnson tells him that the war on poverty is his top priority.

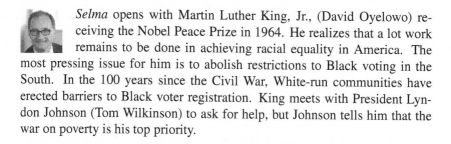

Meanwhile, we're transported to Birmingham, Alabama where the 16th Street Baptist Church is bombed, killing 4 young girls. This is the catalyst that brings Martin Luther King, Jr. to Alabama to begin a movement to change voting laws that prevent Blacks from registering to vote. King understands that voting is the path to true equality because the leaders who look the other way when racist events occur don't fear being voted out of office.

King meets opposition from the SNCC (Student Nonviolent Coordinating Committee) who has already been working on grassroots measures to increase voting rights. King explains to the SNCC leaders that they need a strategy that is non-violent and forces the White leaders to expose their violent nature, thus providing a news-worthy event that wins uninvolved Whites all over the nation to their cause.

Greg, *Selma* should be required viewing for all schoolchildren. For that matter, all adults need to see *Selma*, even those adults who know their Civil Rights Movement history. You and I know from doing years of improvisational work that it is always more powerful *to show* rather than *to tell*. It isn't enough to know that Blacks were once deterred from voting. We need to be shown how, and that's what *Selma* does so well. We see the discriminatory practice and its consequences in vivid, horrid detail.

Selma's greatest strength, in my view, is the way in which it portrays the heroism of Martin Luther King, Jr. We see time and again how King operates at a higher moral plane than everyone else around him. He knows what is right and he knows how to utilize the power of nonviolent demonstration to achieve his noble ends. King is the ultimate mentor figure, and *Selma* is less of a hero story than it is a story about how a heroic mentor wields his influence. King serves as a mentor figure to his friends in the Civil Rights Movement and also as mentor to President Johnson himself. King himself doesn't change but he helps others transform to a higher level of moral understanding.

Selma is, indeed, instructive on so many levels. Unlike other movies about Blacks rising up to take their place as equals in society, *Selma* does not need the benevolent White person to make that change happen. When we look at such movies as *The Blind Side*, or last year's *42* (the Jackie Robinson story), we see that Blacks make their advances thanks to the help of a White benefactor. *Selma* paints the clear picture that King was a true leader and tactical wizard that made the Civil Rights movement work.

Scott, you and I have noted several times over the last couple of years that there are some heroes who don't transform but who transform those around them. As you pointed out, King is just such a hero. I call him a Catalytic Hero because he is the catalyst for change in his followers and in society as a whole.

One thing we do see in King, vividly, is his awareness of the constant danger he is in. We watch him become fearful of what will happen to him and his followers if they make a misstep. At one point he is on the Edmund Pettus Bridge with hundreds of followers marching behind him. The Alabama State Troopers part their blockade for him and the marchers to pass. He takes to his knees and prays for guidance. He makes the decision not to cross the bridge because he fears another disastrous beating as previously occurred. He is increasingly aware of the risks he is taking and their impending consequences.

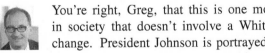

You're right, Greg, that this is one movie about Black progress in society that doesn't involve a White person precipitating the change. President Johnson is portrayed as the White man who is approached for help and for political reasons is reluctant to offer such help. I'm reminded of that great 2012 film *Lincoln* in which a President moves the nation slowly toward legal interracial equality. In contrast to *Lincoln*, which casts President Lincoln in a positive light, *Selma* is less kind toward Johnson, who is seen as unnecessarily slow and plodding in leading the nation toward equality.

The villains in this story are longstanding institutional barriers such as the Jim Crow laws that took advantage of legal loopholes to ensure racial injustice. The two most prominent faces of racial prejudice in *Selma* are the Director of the FBI, J. Edgar Hoover (Dylan Baker), and the Governor of Alabama, George Wallace (Tim Roth). President Johnson is also seen as an obstruction-ist and oppositional character but over time we witness Johnson grow morally and courageously toward Martin Luther King's view of the world. Like nearly all villainous characters, Hoover and Wallace do not budge from their evil ways.

You've covered the villains pretty well here, Scott. We also see that King is facing down his own imperfections. The FBI sends a tape to his wife Coretta Scott King with the sounds of a man and woman in the throes of passion. The voice on the tape threatens to expose King as an adulterer. Coretta confronts King who has to admit his infidelity, but she stays with him. This reminds us that our heroes aren't always perfect. It also points out that Coretta is a heroic character too, as she is the glue that holds King together.

I would like to point out that this film in no way speeds along in its story-telling. It is thoughtful and deliberate. There are many silences in this film. But they are suspenseful. I never felt that the film was lagging. It is a clas-sic example of how negative space is an integral part of the overall picture. Another thing I want to praise *Selma* for is its excellent telling of a true-life event. So often biopic films want to tell everything that happens in the hero's life. Here, we see that the writers focused on one specific event. In telling this one chapter in King's life we are exposed to a number of King's abilities: hu-manity, tactics, leadership, negotiation, not to mention his hopes and dreams and inner turmoil. This is a rich story well told.

Selma is one of the year's best films. In no other movie have I seen a better demonstration of the mechanics and effectiveness of nonviolent demonstration. It could be an ideal instruction manual for those wanting to emulate King's (and Gandhi's) model of bringing about peaceful sociocultural change. The heroic mentorship of Martin Luther King, Jr., is shown in terrific detail here. King was miles ahead of everyone in his moral understanding of the world, and he also had the strength and charisma to move mountains. For it's depiction of a pivotal moment in U.S. history, this movie earns 5 Reels out of 5.

The hero story is unique in that it's less about a hero changing than it is about a hero helping everyone around him change. You call him a catalytic hero, Greg, and that term is as fine as any to describe a mentor. Mentors help other people become heroes. King helped Johnson do the right thing, and in fact he helped an entire nation grow up morally and spiritually. King also possessed all eight of *The Great Eight* attributes of heroes. This powerful heroic mentor story earns 5 Heroes out of 5.

The institutional villainy here is well told, and we are led to despise the faces of racial prejudice and discrimination in the form of George Wallace and J. Edgar Hoover. None of these villainous forces are well-developed but they needn't be in this movie. *Selma* is more about the heroic efforts to overcome the evil of racial hate than it is about the hate itself. So I will give the villains here 3 Villains out of 5.

Movie: Villains: Heroes:

Perhaps the most striking thing about *Selma* is how it echoes the challenges of race relations in America today. We are still seeing voter identification laws passed which limit the ability of the poor and impoverished to cast their votes. We are still wrestling with police violence against people of color - and how the current institutions protect these actions. *Selma* shows us that a lot has been won in efforts to afford equality to all, but it also reminds us that we still have more work to do. I give *Selma* 5 out of 5 Reels.

King leads by example and changes the people around him and people all across the nation. We are witness to his strength and force of character. We are also shown that our heroes are not always perfect. Often, Scott, you and I look for a transformation in the hero, but the transformation King induces in others is second to none. I give Martin Luther King, Jr. 5 out of 5 Heroes.

In our study of villains over the last year we've seen a lot of "mastermind" villains - villains who keep safe in the shadows and have others do their dirty work for them. We definitely see that here. George Wallace as the governor of Alabama has the power to reign in the police and to force the registrars to accept Black applications for voter registration, but he chooses not to. He wants to uphold the institution of racial supremacy. We're witness to the mindless anger and hatred of the crowds in Selma, Alabama. It's a difficult image to watch because it was real. I give the mastermind and institutional villains 4 out of 5 Villains.

Movie: Villains: Heroes:

St. Vincent

Starring	Bill Murray, Melissa McCarthy, Naomi Watts
Director	Theodore Melfi
Screenplay	Theodore Melfi
Genre	Comedy
Rated	PG-13
Running Time	102 minutes
Release Date	October 24, 2014
Vincent & Oliver Protagonist	Duo, Positive to More Positive Moral/Emotional (Classic Buddy Heroes)
Vincent Antagonist	Single, Negative to Positive Moral (Misunderstood Lone Villain)

(Dr. Scott Allison, Professor of Psychology, University of Richmond)

Greg, we just saw a movie about saints, who seem to be very similar to heroes.

(Greg Smith, Founder of Agile Writers of Richmond, VA)

I had the same thought. Let's see how Bill Murray rates against St. Teresa.

We meet a 68-year-old man named Vincent (Bill Murray). Vincent lives alone with his cat, steals apples, and consorts with hookers, racetracks, bars, and loan sharks who want him to pay up. One day, Vincent discovers that a woman named Maggie (Melissa McCarthy) and her son Oliver (Jaeden Lieberher) have moved in next door.

Vincent is down to his last dollar so he makes a deal with Maggie to watch Oliver after school while she eeks out a living as a single mom. Vincent takes little interest in 10-year-old Oliver until he comes home with a bloody nose. Then, Vincent decides to take it upon himself to teach Oliver not only to fight, but what it means to be a man - a role that Oliver's pacifist father has neglected to take on himself.

 Greg, *St. Vincent* surprised me. It surprised me with its sweetness and wisdom in the same way that Bill Murray's *Groundhog Day* did more than two decades ago. You could say that the movie follows the classic sinner-to-saint hero story, but that would be an oversimplification. Like St. Augustine, Vincent is a womanizer and who steals apples. But unlike St. Augustine, Vincent is a complex mix of good and bad his entire life. He was a war hero forty years earlier and now tenderly cares for his wife who suffers from dementia. Yet he is also a jerk all that time, too.

We see plenty of Vincent's dark side. Dishonesty rules his life, and he is surly. But behind the surliness beats a heart of gold. This heart remains hidden until it springs to life thanks to the influence of his new neighbor, the precocious Oliver played brilliantly by Jaeden Lieberher. It's not unusual for movies to show us the wisdom of children. *St. Vincent* is special because the mentoring is bi-directional, and it has heartfelt believability. Vincent and Oliver show each other how to grow up.

I agree, Scott. Vincent is the classic villain-turned-hero. The movie starts out showing us how foul he can be. He seems villainous with his callous disregard for anyone but himself. Even when he agrees to take on the task of babysitting Oliver, it's not for Oliver's sake. It's to take advantage of mom Maggie's situation - and to pay his gambling debts. He lacks the heroic qualities of caring and selflessness - or as Zimbardo would call it - altruism.

When he visits an old lady in a nursing home - we expect it to be just another scam he's running. But he is returning her laundry and taking her dirty clothes. He's actually doing her laundry. Later we see him sitting with her by the dock and we realize this is his wife who suffers from Alzheimers disease. And we realize he isn't uncaring at all. He gives all his money so that his wife can have the best care. And suddenly Vincent the villain becomes Vincent the saint.

 Well, he's not recognized as a saint by anyone until Oliver comes along and sees a side to him that no one else sees (with the exception of the staff at the Alzheimer's facility). Even Oliver is disgusted with Vincent until the boy discovers some discarded photos of Vincent's military service. Oliver is mentored by his teacher Brother Geraghty (Chris O'Dowd), who instructs Oliver about the definition of a saint as a person who sacrifices to better the lives of others. Greg, this is a moving story about hero formation, hero mentoring, and hero recognition.

So *St. Vincent* takes us on a journey of discovery in which two unlikely buddy heroes help each other become better people. I believe this film is Bill Murray's best work since *Groundhog Day* and could almost unfathomably garner him an Oscar nomination. His portrayal of Vincent is not easy to pull off but Murray does it with understated charisma and compassion. We're so transfixed by his character that the ending credits show him lying on a recliner with a hose running – and no one in our theater dared to leave even though we see him doing nothing but squirt water on his feet.

There are a few villains in the story, but not many. The racetrack bookie (played by Terrence Howard) threatens to rough Vincent up. The loan officer at the bank has little sympathy for Vincent. They're all pretty light fare compared to the uncaring head of the nursing home. And Oliver has villains of his own to face down. The schoolyard bully that prompts Vincent to teach Oliver his one fighting maneuver eventually turns into Oliver's best friend. But the villains are all in the background while Vincent is the main attraction.

I enjoyed *St. Vincent* very much. I think Bill Murray has found his rhythm as an actor. Melissa McCarthy also delivered a heartwarming performance of the mother who's just trying to get by - but is a little overwhelmed. There were a lot of comedians in this drama. I've heard it said that comedians make the best dramatic actors because they have a deeper understanding of timing. I'd say that *St. Vincent* definitely demonstrated just that. I give it 4 out of 5 Reels.

Vincent himself undergoes not so much a transformation in this film, but more of a realization. That is, it is the audience to whom Vincent's heroism is revealed. He appears villainous at the beginning, but as we get to know him, we see that he has all the qualities of a saint - and all the qualities of a hero, too. There just doesn't seem to be that much difference. I give Vincent 4 out of 5 Heroes.

Sadly, there are no strong villains in this film. But that's okay because Vincent appears villainous enough for the majority of the film. I give the villains in *St. Vincent* just 2 out of 5 Villains.

Movie: Villains: Hero:

St. Vincent is one of the year's best movies. Bill Murray is at his best when he plays characters with wide moral range. Murray has always been a little mischievous boy inside a man's body, and as he's gotten older this incongruency deepens his complex persona. *St. Vincent* packs a powerful emotional punch toward the end – I found myself shedding a tear or two while Vincent's heroism is being honored by Oliver and others. For a poignant story of an unlikely pairing of people who save each other, I'm giving *St. Vincent* a full 5 Reels out of 5.

This is a buddy hero story that follows the usual pattern of two individuals who start out disliking each other but develop an unshakable bond. As you mention, Greg, the character of Vincent grows in his recognition of his life's accomplishments, but he also develops a softened heart for Maggie, Oliver, and others. Oliver's growth follows the usual coming-of-age storyline, and he ends up mentoring Vincent, his mother, and his entire school about the definition and complexity of sainthood. I give these two memorable heroes a rating of 4 out of 5.

The villains are an interesting assortment in *St. Vincent*. Most conspicuously, the kid who first bullies Oliver at school, a boy named Ocinski (Dario Barosso), undergoes a transformation toward goodness and virtue. One could say that *St. Vincent* is a movie that sends a message about bullies being redeemable, as Vincent could also be considered a redeemed bully. It's both rare and satisfying to see villains undergo a transformation toward redemptive goodness. For that reason, I'll give the villains here a solid score of 3 Villains out of 5.

Movie: ⬤⬤⬤⬤⬤ Villains: 🎩🎩🎩 Hero: 🦸🦸🦸

The Theory of Everything

Starring	Eddie Redmayne, Felicity Jones, Tom Prior
Director	James Marsh
Screenplay	Anthony McCarten, Jane Hawking
Genre	Biography/Drama/Romance
Rated	PG-13
Running Time	123 minutes
Release Date	November 26, 2014
Stephen & Jane Hawking Protagonist	Duo, Positive to More Positive Emotional (Classic Romantic Dievergent Heroes)
ALS Antagonist	System, Untransformed Negative (Disease Villain)

(Greg Smith, Founder of Agile Writers of Richmond, VA)

I thought that *The Theory of Everything* would take forever to tell.

(Dr. Scott Allison, Professor of Psychology, University of Richmond)

Nothing to worry about, Greg. More than a*nything*, it was a theory of *something*. Let's recap.

We're introduced to young Stephen Hawking (Eddie Redmayne), a graduate student at Cambridge University in 1963. He's a gangly young man and socially awkward. He goes to a mixer where he meets young Jane Wilde (Felicity Jones). She's studying the arts. The two seem to have nothing in common. But when they go to the fall gala, Stephen starts talking about the stars. Jane quotes poetry back to him. The two quickly fall in love.

But all is not well with Stephen. He has a clumsy gait and grabs awkwardly at flatware, pens, and chalk. One day he falls flat on his face on a walkway and is sent to a doctor who diagnoses him with ALS, a deadly neurodegenerative disease. Although Stephen is given only two years to live, Jane marries him and the two make the most of the time they have together. Jane volunteers to sing in her church choir and strikes up a friendship with the choir director Jonathan (Charlie Cox). Soon Jonathan helps out with Stephen and Jane's children. But trouble is brewing in the family.

Scott, this movie is problematic as it's not clear who the hero is. It looks like Stephen Hawking may be the lead character because its all about his genius and his battle with ALS. But then they quickly bring in Jane and strangely, the story seems to focus on her. Hawking become a bit of a prop, scooting around in his wheelchair. We get to see him at the chalkboard here or there, or in a lecture. But after the point where Hawking is confined to a wheelchair, this becomes Jane's story.

In our book *Reel Heroes: Volume 1* we break hero patterns down by the number of characters who are in the lead of the story: the lone hero, the duo, and the ensemble. And I think I have to land on this being a duo story, even though Hawking seems to fade into the background in the second half. Further, we break the duo down into the Hero/Sidekick, the Buddy Heroes, and the Divergent Heroes. And I think that last one is where *Theory* falls. This is the story of how two people came together and ultimately fell apart.

I agree that Stephen and Jane are divergent heroes who travel much of the journey together but then go their separate ways. This movie tells a poignant love story of great triumph over significant obstacles - for both characters, not just for Stephen. It also tells a story about the collapse of a family and the loss of love. The film boldly portrays Stephen in a less than positive light in that he shows less loyalty to Jane than she shows him. We're presented with a realistic view of human resilience and human weakness.

While I was impressed with the heartwarming story and with the performances of Eddie Redmayne and Felicity Jones, I was a bit underwhelmed with the movie as a whole. The film ventures perilously close to Hallmark-made-for-TV territory. Moreover, we're not given any more than a fleeting glimpse of the scientific breakthroughs that Hawking is known for. I felt a bit cheated by the constant stream of puns about time that apparently (according to this movie) is the foundation of Hawking's genius. A lot of smart professors in the movie clap and shake his hand, and that's about the only indication of his greatness.

I think you've really struck the nail on the head. This was a love story. I was surprised that the teen-aged ticket taker said that she had seen this movie and it made her cry. Clearly, this movie was more aimed at an audience more interested in the relationship than the story of a man's genius. And since the title is *The Theory of Everything* I think we're right to feel a bit cheated that we didn't get any insights into Hawking's genius, or at least his thinking process.

If there's a villain in this story it's ALS. This is the thing that is stealing Stephen's physical self. It's also the thing that promised to be done with him in two years. By some miracle, he lived and continues to live well into his seventies. And this is the diabolical turn this villain takes. At the beginning of the story we meet two young and idealistic people who are in love. Jane essentially signs up for a two-year stint. But it is the ongoing and debilitating disease that ultimately destroys their relationship. And this is truly heartbreaking.

The Theory of Everything is a commendable story of two people whose love and loyalty carry them through decades of adversity, but alas, not forever. The movie is interesting in its focus on one of the greatest minds of our generation but there is a lack of depth here that left me wanting more. On the strength of the performances of Redmayne and Jones, I can award this film 3 Reels out of 5.

The two divergent heroes travel a remarkable journey, and I was moved and impressed by these characters' strength, loyalty, and resilience. The couple does receive help along the way, and ironically two sources of help (Jonathan and Elaine) end up being the source of the couple's demise. Our two heroes travel a remarkable journey and hence I give them 4 Heroes out of 5.

As you point out, Greg, the villain here is a horrid, destructive force of nature that doctors have labeled ALS. As villains go, this disease is formidable even if it isn't quite as interesting as, say, a human villain might be. As such, I will award ALS a rating of 2 Villains out of 5.

Movie: Villains: Heroes:

The Theory of Everything doesn't deliver on the promise of its title. I kept comparing this movie with a similar story *A Beautiful Mind*. There are strong parallels. John Nash was a brilliant mathematician plagued by schizophrenia and was helped and supported by his wife. But *Mind* succeeded where *Theory* did not because it focused on the struggle of the hero overcoming his obstacles. *Theory* got divided between the struggle with the disease and the loss of the relationship. The goals of the movie were divided and that splits our attention. I give *Theory* just 2 out of 5 Reels.

This is a divergent hero story but unlike other such heroes we've reviewed, the focus starts on one hero and the shifts to the other. The first half of the movie is really about Stephen and the second half is about Jane. It's a weak approach and leaves us wanting more. I give this pair 3 out of 5 Heroes.

Finally the villain is ALS (or time itself) and is not given much screen time. We watch Stephen lose more and more physical ability, but we really don't see much about the disease or how he overcomes it. What we do see is how Jane is increasingly overwhelmed having to take care of not just their three children, but Hawking as well. I give ALS 3 out of 5 Villains.

Movie: Villains:  Heroes:

Transcendence

Starring	Johnny Depp, Rebecca Hall, Morgan Freeman
Director	Wally Pfister
Screenplay	Jack Paglen
Genre	Drama/Mystery/Science-Fiction
Rated	PG-13
Running Time	119 minutes
Release Date	April 18, 2014
Evelyn Protagonist	Single, Positive to More Positive Moral (Classic Lone Hero)
Castor Antagonist	Single, Positive to Negative Moral (Fallen Lone Villain)

(Greg Smith, Founder of Agile Writers of Richmond, VA)
Scott, it's time to rise above it all and review *Transcendence*.

(Dr. Scott Allison, Professor of Psychology, University of Richmond)
Rising is the yeast we can do. Let's recap.

We meet quirky, super-smart computer scientist Dr. Will Caster (Johnny Depp). He has a plan to make super-smart computers that are self-aware. This is a state that Caster calls "Transcendence." No sooner does he unveil his plans than he is shot with a bullet laced with a radioactive substance that gets into his blood. He has a mere matter of weeks to live.

Caster's wife Evelyn (Rebecca Hall) devises a plan to immortalize Caster by uploading his brain and consciousness onto a computer. The plan works, but the same terrorist organization that shot Caster is now intent on thwarting Evelyn's plan. She barely manages to complete the task and she evades the terrorists, but her good friend Max (Paul Bettany) is not convinced that the uploaded version of Caster is actually him. The rest of the movie consists of Caster expanding his powers in big, frightening ways.

Scott, *Transcendence* was a disappointing rehash of a number of science fiction tropes. With Caster becoming "one with the computer" he becomes more powerful than anyone can imagine. And since he is wired into the internet, he can be everywhere at once. We saw this played sweetly in last year's *Her* where Scarlett Johansson voiced a computer operating system that eventually grew self-aware and left Earth for places unknown.

However, in that movie, the super-aware computer didn't become a fearsome monster. It seems that people fear technology growing more powerful than man's ability to control it. You can go all the way back to the original *Godzilla* or even to 1927's *Metropolis* to see examples of this. There was little of interest in this movie and even Morgan Freeman's presence couldn't save it.

I agree, Greg. *Transcendence* fails to transcend; in fact, the movie should be called *Regression*. There's no new ground here, just some recycled ideas from *Star Trek*, such as the idea that (1) consciousness can be imported to a computer, (2) an enhanced race of super-humans can be developed and deified, and (3) a menacing race of villains with a "collective'mind" can threaten earth. And as you mention, we have a re-hash of last year's *Her*, another movie that treats these issues with more originality and style.

What is new is the idea that nano-technology can infiltrate the natural world, affecting clouds, weather, soil, and water. This added menace certainly takes the disturbing abuse of technology a big step further. But the idea isn't developed or pursued at all. One other criticism: the movie is slow-paced. It takes quite a while for the plot to move forward, and so when we finally get to the meat and potatoes, and we are disappointed to see that the meal is the same one we've been served before, although not as tasty as before.

I've noticed a lot of your metaphors deal with food. I should feed you before we write these reviews. The hero in this story appears to be Caster's wife Evelyn. She is the one whom we follow from the beginning to the end of the story. As such, she's a pretty weak hero. She displays a lot of the characteristics of the hero including selflessness and caring. But she just follows Caster's direction without much thinking about the ramifications of the ideas. And she doesn't really have any missing inner qualities to transcend either. She pretty much just sleepwalks through this film.

The Max and Tagger characters (Freeman) are also heroic in their attempts to stop Caster. Max is the only one who transforms in any significant way as he realizes that Caster isn't the man he once was. As Max is quite the secondary character I don't count him as a hero.

 Greg, I think we can agree that the movie starts out as a buddy hero story, with Caster and Evelyn serving as a duo working together to promote positive uses of technology. But as you note, Evelyn emerges as the lone hero while Caster evolves into the villain. The heroes and villains flip-flop half-way through the movie, with Caster turning evil and the terrorists' anti-technology position looking increasingly smart and reasonable.

Johnny Depp seems out of his element here, as he's miscast as a scholarly intellectual. Depp is effective in dark, mysterious, quirky roles but he seems out of place here. I felt badly for Morgan Freeman, who as you say is a good man and good actor trapped in a bad movie. The secondary characters do a pretty good job with their roles but there is so much that is derivative here that my attention was shot to hell half-way through the movie.

You make a good point, Scott. The villains at the beginning of the movie were pretty villainous. They shot and killed a man (Caster) to prevent what they thought was universal armageddon. That's a pretty heinous act. Then about halfway through they emerge as the good guys in the face of Caster's greater villainy. I found it hard to overcome their terrorist acts and see them as heroes.

Caster as a villain really took a while to emerge. As you point out, we have seen this sort of villain even recently. Dr. Zola in last week's *Captain America: The Winter Soldier* was another scientist transferred into a computer system. And Caster was a pretty weak villain at that. One good thing about this villain that we haven't seen up to this point is the fact that we get a backstory to him. We saw that he was a good guy until his consciousness was transferred into the computer. Then the wealth of worldwide computing power corrupted him and he was bent on worldwide control. It's pretty rare for us to get a look at the "Villain's Journey" in a movie.

Transcendence is a derivative story of technology run amok. It's science fiction that would delight and amaze us only if we lived in the 1950s. The film is mildly entertaining in places, and it did make me think, albeit briefly, about the consequences of nano-technology taking over the natural world. But there's precious little new ground broken here, and with Depp miscast as a scholar, I had trouble swallowing much of the story. I can only muster up one single solitary Reel out of 5.

The hero story is interesting insofar as we see our initial hero, Caster, devolve into a villain character. His wife Evelyn then assumes the role of the lone hero, but she's ill-equipped for the task, showing an inability to think critically about her husband's unbridled ambition. She's not much of a hero, and so all I can give her is a puny 2 Heroes out of 5.

Greg, you are absolutely right about the one strong point of the movie being its focus on the step-by-step development of a villain from scratch. We must also ask ourselves whether Caster made bad choices or if his turn to evil was solely a product of his digitization. We know that power corrupts and so the answer may not be clear-cut. Because of this in-depth treatment of villainy, I'm going to give Caster 3 Villains out of 5.

Movie: Heroes: Villains:

There's not much for me to add. This was a pretty terrible movie and I don't see any reason to give it more than one Reel out of 5.

The hero Evelyn was lost and waffling for most of the story. She pretty much does the bidding of the computer/scientist until the very end. It's a pretty dull hero's journey which I can only give 1 out of 5 Heroes.

And finally, looking at Caster as the villain I was going to give him a score of just 1 Villain. But I'm incrementing it to 2 Villains out of 5 because we see a bit of the villain's journey for the first time this year.

Movie: Heroes: Villains:

Transformers: Age of Extinction

Starring	Mark Wahlberg, Nicola Peltz, Jack Reynor
Director	Michael Bay
Screenplay	Ehren Kruger
Genre	Action/Adventure/Science-Fiction
Rated	PG-13
Running Time	165 minutes
Release Date	June 27, 2014
Cade Yeager & Optimus Prime Protagonist	Duo, Untransformed Positive Moral (Untransformed Family Heroes)
Lockdown Antagonist	Single, Untransformed Negative Moral (Untransformed Pure Evil Villain)

(Dr. Scott Allison, Professor of Psychology, University of Richmond)

Well, Greg, we just survived another *Transformers* movie.

(Greg Smith, Founder of Agile Writers of Richmond, VA)

Let's find out if any of the heroes underwent a transformation...

The movie begins with scientists discovering that Transformers killed all life on earth 65 million years ago. We also learn that five years ago, Transformers were narrowly defeated in the 'Battle of Chicago', which left Transformer debris and technology scattered over North America. Then we meet Texas inventor Cade Yeager (Mark Wahlberg), his beautiful teenage daughter Tessa (Nicola Peltz), and his friend Lucas (T.J. Miller). Cade dreams of using abandoned Transformer technology to create inventions that will make his family rich. Meanwhile, his home is being foreclosed, and his daughter is mad at him for being irresponsible and overprotective.

Lucas, unbeknownst to Yeager, has called the Feds because the Transformer they found is Optimus Prime who has a bounty on his head. The CIA is out to destroy all Transformers (both the good Autobots and the evil Decepticons) in favor of a new robotic technology built by the company KSI (assisted by galactic bounty hunter Lockdown). The CIA operatives descend on Yeager's Texas farm and he, his daughter, and her boyfriend Shane (Jack Reynor) are on the run with Optimus Prime and what is left of the Autobots.

Greg, *Age of Extinction* puts the *Stink* in *Extinction*. This is easily among the worst movies of 2014. There are so many problems with the film that I don't even know where to begin. Let's start with the obvious: Director Michael Bay clearly worships at the altar of the "More is Better" philosophy of movie-making. It's the idea that more action, more chase scenes, and longer movies are better. The word that comes to mind to describe this mess rhymes with "cluster-truck". And yes, we see a lot of trucks in the movie, because of course more is better.

For me, watching this movie was an endurance contest, with millions of my brain cells, already damaged by watching past bad movies, fighting for survival. I'm shocked that Mark Wahlberg agreed to participate in this mess – he's proven himself to be a skilled actor capable of attracting far better movie roles. In *Transformers: Age of Extinction*, Wahlberg is reduced to uttering one hackneyed and predictable line after another. For 160 minutes, he's either being chased by Transformers or protecting his daughter from danger. I felt sorry for him.

I feel your pain, Scott.   I was also struggling through-out the nearly 3-hour film to reconcile the multiple plot lines (father/daughter/boyfriend,   CIA/alien/Transformer,   en-trepreneur/inventor, Autobot/alien/Decepticon) with only limited success. If it is any consolation, this is probably the best of the Transformers movies with the addition of Wahlberg over troublesome actor Shia LaBeouf. I've sat through all four of these films and it's clear they appeal to a very specific audience.

The film is too intense for smaller children and a bit too childish for grown adults. It hits its sweet-spot with 13-25 year-old boys and fans of the original Transformers show. It must be a fairly big demographic because over this weekend alone, Transformers brought in about $100 million. It is also on-target to be the first movie to garner $1 Billion in worldwide revenues. There's no doubt that Michael Bay knew what he was doing with this film. Whether you like the film or not, it reaches its audience and in a big way.

The money this movie will make pains me; it is just so undeserv-ing. Never has a major movie relied on so many tiresome set-ups and situations. There is the damsel in distress, shown in full shame-less fashion about 6 dozen times, as poor Tessa needs either her dad or her boyfriend to save her repeatedly. There is the overused idea of government higher-ups conspiring against us all and sticking it to the little guys. There is a little Jar Jar Binks character whose main role is to annoy us even further. There is a 30-second speech that Yeager gives to a bad guy, Joshua Joyce (Stanley Tucci), a speech that miraculously converts Joyce to the good guys' side.

Let's examine the quality of the hero's journey. To me, this film appears to feature a couple of group ensemble heroes: The Yeagers are a family unit and the Transformer team, led by Optimus Prime, is a police/military unit.

You could say that Yeager's character does evolve, as his hatred for Mary's boyfriend eventually turns to admiration. This change, of course, is painfully predictable and hardly convincing. Several basic elements of the hero's journey are here, although they lack depth or interest.

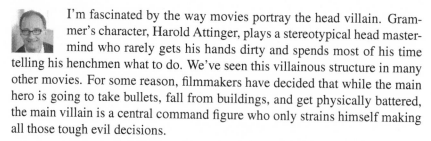

The lead heroes are Yeager and Optimus Prime. Prime is feeling let down by the human race as he came to Earth to save us from the evil Decepticons. Now, he is hunted by humans and he has lost the urge to keep humans safe from their own stupidity. He undergoes a transformation as Yeager pleads with him to help his family and all of mankind. Admittedly, this is a pretty weak story arc. Still it is stronger than what we've been fed in previous incarnations of the Transformers cinematic universe.

The villains aren't much better. We are treated to a good performance by Kelsey Grammer (who, by the way, also appears in *Think Like a Man, Too* released last week). Grammer's character is a typical bad guy government bureaucrat who is running the CIA. Like other villains of this type, we don't get much backstory, only that he is evil. He stereotypically does not get his hands dirty and enlists henchmen to perform his evil-do.

And on the Transformer side of the aisle, there is the evil Lockdown who is an intergalactic bounty hunter. He is also of the pure-evil cast and offers no real counterpoint to Optimus Prime except for an extended robot battle in the climax.

I'm fascinated by the way movies portray the head villain. Grammer's character, Harold Attinger, plays a stereotypical head mastermind who rarely gets his hands dirty and spends most of his time telling his henchmen what to do. We've seen this villainous structure in many other movies. For some reason, filmmakers have decided that while the main hero is going to take bullets, fall from buildings, and get physically battered, the main villain is a central command figure who only strains himself making all those tough evil decisions.

One other word about the Transformers themselves. They are imposing mechanical beasts that serve as yet another example of the movie industry's fetish for size, especially when it comes to villains. How many behemoths have we seen in the movies this past couple of years? I was struck by the shape of these manly, macho mechanical beasts – they sport massive biceps and pecs and teeny, tiny, almost Barbie Doll waists. Do robots really need to show bulging muscles to do their dirty work?

Scott, you called *Transformers* the worst movie of the year. You may have forgotten the travesty and complete waste of time that was *Transcendence*. Or the painfully unfunny *Ride Along*. Or completely misguided *Labor Day*. Still, I have to admit *Transformers: Age of Extinction* certainly does rate down there with them. For an excruciatingly long overdose of robotic chaos I give this film 2 out of 5 Reels.

The heroes are very plain-brown-wrapper and do not stretch our imaginations very far. Wahlberg does a good job of playing the father-who-cares and Optimus Prime "transforms" a bit too. I give them just 2 out of 5 Heroes.

There is no new ground with the villains in this story. The Stanley Tucci character is a Steve Jobs inspired head of corporation who is turned from evil to good. Grammer's character is right out of the evil government playbook. And Lockdown was not even entertaining. I give these poor sketches of characters just 1 out of 5 Villains.

Movie: Villains: Heroes:

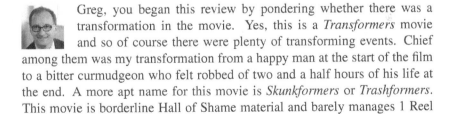

Greg, you began this review by pondering whether there was a transformation in the movie. Yes, this is a *Transformers* movie and so of course there were plenty of transforming events. Chief among them was my transformation from a happy man at the start of the film to a bitter curmudgeon who felt robbed of two and a half hours of his life at the end. A more apt name for this movie is *Skunkformers* or *Trashformers*. This movie is borderline Hall of Shame material and barely manages 1 Reel out of 5.

The heroes were wafer-thin, predictable, and uninteresting. Wait, I take that back. There is one interesting character, Lucas Flannery, but he's killed off early in the film. His quick exit was a portend of things to come. There are elements of the hero journey in this film but they are completely overwhelmed by the relentless onslaught of senseless chase scenes, explosions, and CGI chaos. Your rating of 2 Heroes out of 5 seems about right.

The villains were familiar retreads of villains we've seen a thousand times before. I thought Kelsey Grammer did a nice job in his role, but he and Wahlberg were both good actors trapped in a cinematic mess. I'll agree with you that 1 Villain out of 5 is an accurate rating here.

Movie: Villains: Heroes:

Unbroken

Starring	Jack O'Connell, Takamasa Ishihara, Domhnall Gleeson
Director	Angelina Jolie
Screenplay	Joel Coen, Ethan Coen
Genre	Biography/Drama/Sports
Rated	PG-13
Running Time	137 minutes
Release Date	December 25, 2014
Zamperini Protagonist	Single, Positive to More Positive Emotional (Classic Lone Hero)
The Bird Antagonist	Single, Untransformed Negative Moral (Untransformed Minion Villain)

(Greg Smith, Founder of Agile Writers of Richmond, VA)

Scott, it's time to end our Christmas break and review *Unbroken*.

(Dr. Scott Allison, Professor of Psychology, University of Richmond)

Indeed. Let's take a look at this film adaptation of the best-selling novel by Laura Hillenbrand.

It's World War II and young Louis Zamperini (Jack O'Connell) is
the bombardier of a B-24. He hits his target, but his ship is damaged
and barely makes it's way back to base. This reminds him of his
childhood growing up in the Bronx. He was constantly picked on by the other
boys because of his Italian heritage. He was always getting into fights and
engaging in underage drinking. His brother takes notice and sets him straight.
It's his brother who teaches him "if you can take it, you can make it." This is
a lesson he'll use all through life.

 While on a mission in the South Pacific theater, Zamperini's plane
crashes into the ocean. He and two other men, Phil (Domhnall
Gleeson) and Mac (Finn Wittrock), survive and remain afloat in
a raft for many weeks, barely surviving. Mac dies, but Louis and Phil are
captured by the Japanese military who torture and imprison them on a small
island. Louis is eventually transferred to a POW camp near Tokyo, where he
is brutalized by one particular camp officer nicknamed 'The Bird' (Takamasa
Ishihara).

Unbroken is a longish look at the survival of a man through the trials of torture and abuse in World War II. I thought in many ways it
was a technically fine film, but I don't expect it to win any awards.
One thought that kept going through my mind while watching Zamperini live
through his lost-at-sea adventure, then his torture, and then his POW experiences was - how was his experience any different than any other POW's?
What made him the subject of a book and movie where he was called "Unbroken?" Weren't all POWs in some way unbroken?

 Unbroken is an inspiring and heart-wrenching look at an extraordinary tale of survival. Director Angelina Jolie does a commendable
job of capturing (most of) Zamperini's heroic journey while also
remaining true to Hillenbrand's book. Zamperini was not the only survivor of
the Japanese POW camps but his story is unique and powerful in three ways:

(1) his celebrity status as an Olympic track star; (2) his ordeal on the raft for 47 days prior to imprisonment; and (3) his unfortunate experience with 'The Bird', who singled out Zamperini for especially brutal treatment.

The performances here are all first-rate, although none are exemplary. This story lacks greatness because Jolie omitted what is arguably the most important part of Zamperini's ordeal: His shattered post-war psyche. Hillenbrand's book tells us that Louis suffered from severe PTSD that left him, well, *broken*. The darkest part of Zamperini's life wasn't in the POW camps; it was the alcoholic depression of his post-war life. For *Unbroken* to reach it's full storytelling power, we need to see this nadir and how Louis overcomes it. It's unfortunate that we were deprived of this resolution because we know that redemption is arguably the most central part of any hero story.

I agree with you that the story needed something more to earn the title *Unbroken*. And if the redemption portion of the story that you mention had been told, I might have been more interested. The scenes with Zamperini and friends in the life raft seemed to go on forever. Likewise, his tours in the different encampments seemed to drag on without storytelling purpose. If the intent was to give us all a sense of the pain Zamperini endured, then Jolie succeeded. I was bored several times during the movie.

The main villain in this story is "The Bird" - a Japanese sergeant who ran the camps. We get the sense that he was an underachiever. It seems his parents were aristocrats and that "The Bird" did not live up the their, or the Japanese army's expectations. This made him perhaps more cruel to the prisoners. And even more cruel to Zamperini who was famous as an Olympic athlete. "The Bird" was indeed a sadist and spared no opportunity to make Zamperini miserable.

 I agree, Greg, that Jolie gives us an extraordinary survival story without the all-important hero transformation that any good hero story needs to achieve maximum impact. In some ways, the film is similar to two 2013 films, *Gravity* and *12 Years As A Slave,* which both described remarkable survival tales but also omitted the aftermath of the survival. The aftermath is essential in showcasing the hero's changed state, which ultimately transforms us all.

Attention all movie-makers: Please do not deprive your audience of the aftermath of the hero's survival story. As an audience, we need it to maximize our satisfaction, and as a movie-maker, you need it to maximize your revenue – not to mention your Oscar nominations.

You're right, Greg, that Japan is the *institutional villain* of the story, and "The Bird" is the face of Japan in the movie. We grow to despise The Bird as he senselessly beats Zamperini to a pulp again and again. He is pure evil and has no redeeming qualities other than a pretty face whose boyish qualities belie the sadism taking place.

Angelina Jolie shows she has directorial chops in her adaptation of *Unbroken*. While I thought it was long at 140 minutes and did drag in places, I was glad that I had seen the film. *Unbroken* reminds us of the sacrifices and commitment of the Greatest Generation to overcome evil. This is a fine addition to a spate of WWII movies this year (including *Fury* and *The Imitation Game*). I give *Unbroken* 3 out of 5 Reels.

Zamperini as the hero of the story undergoes an early transformation from a fractious child to a determined adult. Through the mentorship of his older brother, he grows into a man who can withstand the worst that the world can throw at him. However, this early transformation is not where the story lies. As you point out, Scott, it is overcoming the damage done to him that is the true *Unbroken* nature of Zamperini. I give this version of him 3 out of 5 Heroes.

"The Bird" is clearly an evil character who shames and humiliates Zamperini and the other POWs. As the face of the *institutional villain* he was not very well-drawn. I wish there had been more insight into his character, rather than just his vicious acts. I give "The Bird" just 3 out of 5 Villains.

Movie: Villains:  Heroes:

Unbroken is a well-made film that moves us with a harrowing tale of survival, perseverance, resilience, and courage. Angelina Jolie shows us that she can direct movies with the best of them, but she makes a critical error by denying us the redemptive core of Zamperini's story. I love Zamperini's tale, despite the movie not quite living up to the lofty heights of the book. For this reason, I'll award this film 4 Reels out of 5.

The hero story is remarkable in every aspect, although it is unfortunate that Jolie chose not to show us Zamperini's psychological recovery from the trauma of the war. This film needlessly shortchanges his heroism, and thus I can only award his movie character 3 out of 5 Heroes here.

The institutional villain is capably portrayed by a number of fine Japanese actors, with Takamasa Ishihara delivering an especially standout performance as the deceptively boyish face of evil. We aren't given much back-story about The Bird, other than a throwaway line or two, and so I can only grant this evil camp officer 3 Villains out of 5.

Movie: Villains:  Heroes:

Whiplash

Starring	Miles Teller, J.K. Simmons, Melissa Benoist
Director	Damien Chazelle
Screenplay	Damien Chazelle
Genre	Drama/Music
Rated	R
Running Time	107 minutes
Release Date	October 15, 2014
Neiman Protagonist	Single, Positive to More Positive Emotional (Classic Lone Hero)
Fletcher Antagonist	Single, Untransformed Negative Moral (Untransformed Lone Villain)

(Greg Smith, Founder of Agile Writers of Richmond, VA)

Scott, I thought *Whiplash* was a movie about car accidents.

(Dr. Scott Allison, Professor of Psychology, University of Richmond)

Well, there is a bad car accident in this movie. But the story is about much more. Let's recap.

We're introduced to young Andrew Neiman (Miles Teller), a fresh-
man music student who wants nothing more than to be one of the
greatest jazz drummers of all time. He is practicing in the halls
of Shaffer Conservatory when the imposing music director Terence Fletcher
(J.K. Simmons) walks in. He is the conductor of the school's award-winning
jazz ensemble. Fletcher auditions Neiman and allows him in as an alternate
drummer. Fletcher drives all his students with both physical and emotional
abuse. It isn't long before Fletcher starts abusing Neiman by throwing chairs
and slapping him.

 Neiman is obsessed with being the best drummer of all-time. He
practices until his fingers bleed onto his drumset. He breaks up with
his girlfriend so that he can spend every waking moment fulfilling
his dream. Fletcher creates a ruthlessly competitive atmosphere to bring out
the best in his players, and Neiman knows he cannot miss a beat if he wants to
keep his job on the band. One day when Neiman gets into a bad car accident on
the way to a competition, he chooses to arrive at the competition battered and
bloody rather than lose his spot. He attacks Fletcher after Fletcher dismisses
him, and is expelled from Shaffer. But the two men later cross musical paths
one last time.

Whiplash is a battle of wills between a young man who wants to be
the best jazz drummer no matter what the cost to him personally,
and a man who wants to train the best jazz musician no matter the
cost to those he teaches. And this is the difference between a hero and a
villain. According to Joseph Campbell (mythologist and author of *The Hero
With A Thousand Faces*) a hero is someone who *will do anything he can to get
what he wants at his own expense* whereas a villain is someone who *will do
anything he can to get what he wants at someone else's expense*. This sets up
our young Neiman as the hero and Fletcher as his villain.

The movie doesn't waste any time getting to the heart of this. And in some
ways I thought it rushed certain plot points. There is a wonderful scene with
Neiman and his father (Paul Reiser) at dinner with his uncle and community-
college cousins. They're having a battle of opinions over whether it would be

better to live a long happy life or a short and spectacular one. Neiman points out that Charlie Parker was the best jazz musician of all time. The uncle throws in that he lived to be only 35 years old. But Neiman is unrelenting, firing back that while it may be true that Parker lived a short life, he impacted everyone as they are still talking about him around the dining room table.

Whiplash surprised me. It's a low-budget movie without a huge star in it, and yet it is very effective in capturing the most important steps and missteps in life. *Whiplash* pits two men against each other. One is an underdog, an up-and-coming college kid who will do anything to become the best at his craft. The other is an older, established teacher who will do anything to remain at the top of his profession. You would think that the teacher is the helpful mentor figure here, but you would be (mostly) wrong. These are two characters destined to collide. The kid's triumph over his evil mentor is the crux of the hero story, and it is both fun and disturbing to watch.

Although I enjoyed this movie, I'm left somewhat confused by its message. Maybe ambiguity about ambition is the point of the movie. On the one hand, Fletcher's teaching methods inflict emotional damage on his students. On the other hand, we learn that his methods ultimately turn Niemen into the best jazz drummer Fletcher's ever seen. I'm reminded of Tiger Woods, whose father Earl ruthlessly drilled greatness into Tiger but at great personal cost. Is the movie telling us that this is the only roadmap to greatness? I hope not.

I think you've misplaced the role of Fletcher. He *is* a mentor - but a dark mentor, villainous in his approach. He recognizes talent in the young Neiman and while Neiman is trying to impress his mentor, the mentor refuses to acknowledge any talent the young man may have. Fletcher believes that only by challenging the student will the greatness arise. In the end, Neiman is humiliated by Fletcher and Neiman is ready to quit. But at the last minute he turns around and takes control - not just rising to the challenge Fletcher has laid down - but overpowering him with his intense drumming. Finally, the master has found the student he has been seeking and the student has found the teacher he deserves.

I think this movie *is* telling us that one can achieve greatness only at huge personal expense. And it is left to each of us to decide if the price of greatness is worth it. As Neiman points out in his dinner-time argument, if greatness were easy, everyone would do it. It's pretty clear that the moral of the story is that if you want to be great, you have to give it 100% of everything you have. Nobody achieves greatness giving their best 90%.

 J. K. Simmons does an absolutely wonderful job portraying the villainous Fletcher. His performance may even be Oscar-worthy. I think you're right, Greg, that Fletcher is an anti-mentor. Just as we have anti-heroes (e.g., *Nightcrawler*), we also have anti-mentors who send heroes down dark paths that can lead to ruin. It's then up to the hero to overcome the dark mentor. In *Whiplash*, Neiman's dad plays the good mentor role whose unconditional love is there to counteract Fletcher's bad mentoring influence. I don't think we've seen dueling mentors at all in the movies this year, and *Whiplash* shows this battle in full force.

I think this is also dueling father figures, Scott. At the end of the film, Neiman is humiliated and goes running to his father for solace. At the moment he is about to surrender and fall into his fa- ther's arms (going back to the safe and comfortable) he turns instead and fights back against the conflict-ridden father image that Fletcher offers. You're right, Simmons' performance is spot-on. It is forceful without being over the top.

This also reminds me of the coming-of-age stories of a teen who has to beat his father at sports to emerge as an independent adult. Also, this is reminiscent of the samurai movies where the student must endure torture from the master in order to discover the hidden kung-fu master within. Paul Moxnes has a family-oriented hero structure that includes the good mentor and the evil mentor or wizard. Fletcher is offering Neiman the road to greatness, but it is a dark path.

Whiplash is a fascinating coming-of-age tale with a dark edge to it. This movie had my full attention for nearly two hours and I give it credit for emotionally moving me and offering surprises at the end. The performances are rock solid and there are also some damn good musical performances throughout. I'm more than happy to award this film 4 Reels out of 5.

The hero journey follows the classic pattern and throws in a few welcome surprises. Neiman is cast into a dark, dangerous world and doesn't realize how much he's in over his head. Fletcher's mentoring seems destined to hurl Neiman toward destruction, but with love and encouragement from his good mentor, our hero musters up the strength and courage to outwit his evil foe. There is a love interest, a father figure, dueling mentors, and more. I see no missteps here at all, only outstanding performances from the entire cast. I'm giving our hero 5 Heroes out of 5.

As we've noted, the villain character is an anti-mentor whose cruel, self-aggrandizing methods come at the expense of our hero. I'm thrilled that *Whiplash* shows us a rarely-seen brand of villainy. This film teaches us to be wary of how we choose our mentors; not all of them look out for our best interests. Fletcher is a lying, cold-blooded, abuser who doesn't quite get his full comeuppance at the end but is nevertheless defeated. I'm giving him 5 Villains out of 5.

Movie: Villains:  Heroes:

 Whiplash had very little that left me wanting. I thought the love interest was sort of thrown in with little development, so I didn't really feel a sense of loss when Neiman dumps his girlfriend. Also, the father/son/uncle/cousins story was not fully developed - but it was enough to show a contrast between the thinking of someone who wants to be excellent versus the rest of us, content to do "just fine." But these had to be given less time so that the contest between dark mentor and rising star could be investigated to its fullest extent. I give *Whiplash* 4 out of 5 Reels.

I agree with you, Scott, that Neiman represents the classic hero coming of age story. In the classic tradition of "when the student is ready, the master will appear," Fletcher and Neiman come together at a time when each is seeking the other. And Neiman makes the transformation from neophyte to master in 120 minutes. I give Neiman 5 Heroes out of 5.

And what a wonderful gem of a villain/mentor we have in Fletcher. He is driven not to be the best, but to find someone he can mold *into* the best. We get a sense that he is living vicariously through his students, perhaps having given up on his own greatness hoping to live it out through others. This is not a simply evil character, but a textured and even tortured soul. I give Fletcher 5 out of 5 Villains.

Movie: Villains: Heroes:

X-Men: Days of Future Past

Starring	Patrick Stewart, Ian McKellen, Hugh Jackman
Director	Bryan Singer
Screenplay	Simon Kinberg, Jane Goldman
Genre	Action/Adventure/Fantasy
Rated	PG-13
Running Time	131 minutes
Release Date	May 23, 2014
Professor X/Magneto Protagonist	Duo, Positive to Negative Moral (Divergent Buddy Heroes)
X-Men Protagonist	Ensemble, Untransformed Positive Moral (Untransformed Episodic Heroes)
Trask Antagonist	Single, Untransformed Negative Moral (Mastermind Untransformed Villain)

(Greg Smith, Founder of Agile Writers of Richmond, VA)

Well, the days are past when we can see *X-Men: Days of Future Past*.

(Dr. Scott Allison, Professor of Psychology, University of Richmond)

I predict that in the immediate future, we'll review this movie. Let's begin.

Our story begins in the not-too-distant future where robots with amazing morphing capabilities (Sentinels) are hunting the X-Men to extinction. Young Kitty Pryde (Ellen Page) is able to send messages into the past by mind-melding with another X-Man. She is visited by Professor X, Magneto, and Wolverine (Patrick Stewart, Ian McKellen, Hugh Jackman) who want her to send Wolverine's consciousness back in time to 1973 where he must convince young Charles Xavier and Max Eisenhardt (Professor X and Magneto) to team up and change the dystopian future that awaits them if they cannot prevent mutant Mystique (Jennifer Lawrence) from killing the inventor of the Sentinels, Dr. Bolivar Trask (Peter Dinklage).

Wolverine goes back to 1973 and convinces a young, broken Xavier to stop Mystique from killing Trask. Wolverine enlists the aid of Quicksilver (Evan Peters), whose super-speed enables them to free Magneto from a prison cell beneath the Pentagon in Washington. In Paris, where American and Vietnamese representatives are negotiating the end of the war, Mystique attempts to assassinate Trask but her plan is thwarted. Magneto decides that killing Mystique is the only way to foil her plan, complicating Wolverine and Xavier's mission. When President Nixon approves the Sentinel program, all hell breaks loose as the X-Men try to stop Mystique while battling Trask, the Sentinels, and Magneto himself.

Scott, Marvel does it again. This is a story full of action, suspense, and thrills. Nobody creates a complete story the way Marvel studios does. There are at least a dozen stars, although the story centers around Wolverine and the young Charles and Magneto. There isn't a wasted moment both in terms of the plot or in the on-screen action. This is a complete win in terms of both story and special effects.

There are plenty of heroes to choose from here. In the future, all of the remaining X-Men are battling to save their world. In the past, Charles is the one with the most transforming to undergo. And undergo it he does. We see him start out as a beaten man, taking drugs to make his legs work, which also dulls his mental powers. Wolverine is all action and no growth (which is the mold he filled in last year's *The Wolverine*). And we look for growth in Max/Magneto but he falls into his old patterns and devolves into a villain again.

You nailed it, Greg. Marvel is on a roll this summer with yet another rich, dense, and ambitious story of super-heroism and super-villainy. Like *Spider-Man 2*, which we reviewed recently, *X-Men: Days of Future Past* has many characters, but not too many; it has a complicated plot, but not too complicated; and it conveys messages about life and virtue that resonate with us all. Almost without exception, the characters in this movie attract and maintain our interest. They show depth and nuance, and they behave in surprising ways. They also delight us with their quirky, memorable inner qualities and behavior.

We have an ensemble hero cast, with Wolverine and Professor Xavier serving as the main hero duo within the ensemble. In any good story, the hero undergoes a transformation, and as you note, Greg, Wolverine doesn't change much in this movie. But Xavier is radically transformed. During the flashback to 1973, Xavier is a lost soul, bitter about the toll that the Vietnam War has taken on his school and also resentful about having to choose between the loss of his legs or the loss of his mental powers. With help from Wolverine, Xavier grows to see beyond his disability, deciding to sacrifice the use of his legs so that he can access his superior mental abilities which will help defeat Trask and the Sentinels.

There are villains a-plenty here as well. Mystique walks the line as she stalks Trask with murder on her mind. But she's stopped at the last minute. We get to the end of the story and she appears to turn to the side of good, but it is a bit ambiguous where she goes from there.

We see the familiar "brother" pattern that we saw in *Spider-Man 2* - two close friends start out with a common cause but are separated by ideology by the end of the story. Xavier and Magneto work together at first, but Magneto ultimately returns to his diabolical ways. He's certain that the only way forward is a war between mutants and humans, and as a result, he becomes the opposition force in the end. Then there's the overlord villain in the form of Trask. This villain is bent on the destruction of anyone who doesn't fit his idea of "pure" and will do whatever it takes to kill off every mutant. His lack of selflessness and caring make him the typical evil villain.

For me, the primary villain here is Trask. He's an interesting villain in that his motives aren't entirely evil. Trast genuinely wants to protect the world but he overestimates the threat that the mutants pose and cannot entertain the possibility of living in a world where mutants and non-mutants can co-exist. This is a common shortcoming of villains. They see divisions between people, and often exaggerate those divisions, whereas heroes seek cooperative unity between people.

One other note about Trask - he is a dwarf, which in a way is an unfortunate choice as it suggests that villainy and physical deviance are somehow connected. But it's also not uncommon in fables and mythic tales for villains to be physically different from the norm. If nothing else, Marvel makes movies that resonate with ancient storytelling. The Sentinels are a formidable foe, showing an invincibility against the X-Men's powers. Again, this movie invokes a common pattern in storytelling by showing us a main villain, Trask, who enlists the aid of a monolithic herd of henchmen, and in this case they are diabolical, technologically sophisticated instruments of evil.

I thoroughly enjoyed myself at *X-Men: Days of Future Past*. The story was well-told (although a bit thin in places) and there weren't too many plot holes. The special effects were seamless and abun- dant, but always in support of the story. The characters were rich and colorful - literally. I really can't find fault with any aspect of the presentation and so I award the film 5 out of 5 Reels.

The heroes were many and varied. There were the war-weary heroes of the future and the innocent verging on naive heroes of the past. While Wolverine doesn't grow much, it is Charles Xavier who overcomes his inner demons and shows us a transformation worth the price of admission. I give them all 4 out of 5 Heroes.

In classic Marvel fashion, the villains were as potent as the heroes. This gives our heroes something to work against. The powerful Trask and his high-tech Sentinels were an oppressive force to be reckoned with. And Magneto started out as an ally kept true to his wicked self and turned into the villain he needs to be for the X-Men universe to maintain some sense of conflict and tension. I give them 4 out of 5 Villains.

Movie:  Villains:  Heroes:

Once again, Marvel constructs a movie that is deliciously meaty and doesn't insult its audience's intelligence at all. Anyone who enjoys superhero movies should thoroughly enjoy *X-Men: Days of Future Past*. Besides delighting us with great characters and a juicy plot, the movie gives us several thoughtful take-home messages, the main one focusing on the role of adversity in shaping our destiny and character. This wisdom is far from original but it is used effectively to help young Xavier transform himself. This film is a terrific two-hours spent in the theater, and I award it 4 Reels out of 5.

As I've noted, the hero duo of Wolverine and Xavier truly shines, as we not only witness the transformation of Xavier but also the transformation of their friendship. All of these characters are complex, including those of a couple of the X-Men (Magneto and Mystique) who defy simple categorization of good or evil. This ensemble is impressive and the duo within it shines. I'm happy to award them all 4 out of 5 Heroes.

You're right on target about the villains, Greg. Trask, the Sentinels, Magneto, and Mystique are all either fully villainous or show streaks of villainy. Another oppositional force that Xavier must contend with is his own inner demons. The Marvel universe works so well on so many levels, including the interpersonal and intrapersonal levels. The villains here are all great fun and make us think, too, which is great praise for any movie. I give them 4 out of 5 Villains.

Movie: Villains:  Heroes:

Part III.

Best Heroes and Villains of 2014

Best Movies of 2014

(Dr. Scott Allison, Professor of Psychology, University of Richmond)

There was much to admire in the movie industry in 2014. Let's compare our individual top 10 lists.

For me, I listed my favorite films by how badly I wanted to see them again. I also ranked them based on how much I was entertained. Here's my list:

Greg's Top 10

10. Captain America: The Winter Soldier

9. The Hunger Games: The Mockingjay: Part 1

8. The Fault in Our Stars

7. Maleficent

6. Jersey Boys

5. Interstellar

4. Gone Girl

3. Nightcrawler

2. Whiplash

1. Selma

 I based my list on the depth of the story and the quality of the filmmaking. Also factored in, of course, was the juiciness of the heroes and villains in the movie. Here's my list:

Scott's Top 10

10. Boyhood

 9. The Fault in our Stars

 8. American Sniper

 7. The Imitation Game

 6. Unbroken

 5. Whiplash

 4. St. Vincent

 3. Gone Girl

 2. Selma

 1. Birdman

That's a great list. I see a few there that were just outside my top 10. It would take too long to go into detail on all 20, so let's just compare notes on each of our top 5.

You selected *Whiplash* as your #5 pick, which was my #2. I was captivated by the intensity of J.K. Simmons' performance as the perfectionist villain/mentor. It was a complex film all about the strength of the commitment of the lead (Miles Teller) to stand up to the unrelenting bullying of his teacher. I was totally sucked in and would definitely see this film again.

Whiplash is a fascinating coming-of-age tale with a dark edge to it. A beastly mentor figure attempts to hurl our hero toward destruction, but with love and encouragement from his *good* mentor, our hero musters up the strength and courage to outwit his evil foe.

Let's now turn to your #5 pick, *Interstellar*. This movie didn't crack my top 10 list but as a science fiction buff I enjoyed it immensely, Greg. *Interstellar* made me think, not just feel. We are treated to fabulous CGI effects, but more importantly we are compelled to ponder deeply about our place in the universe and what lengths we would go to save our planet. The integration of love and gravity as the glue that binds us all together is an inspiring take-home message.

It's true, Scott, this movie was a technical marvel. And it held itself up to high scientific standards. It was made with the best understanding we have today of what interstellar travel would look like. Plus, it was mind-bending in the ways of time distortion and time travel. But for me the clincher was the bond between father and daughter. As the father of two girls, that hit home for me more than anything else. And that's why *Interstellar* was in my top 5.

Appearing at #4 on my list is *Gone Girl*. This was a surprising film, especially if you went in without having read the novel. It starts out looking very much like something out of the tabloids where the husband is a suspect in the disappearance of his wife. Then at the halfway point, we learn that it was the controlling wife who was framing her husband for her own death. The movie takes a sharp turn and the villain and victim are reversed. That made for a thrilling roller coaster ride.

Gone Girl is #3 on my list of Best Movies of 2014. This film is a stylish portrayal of love, treachery, and murderous revenge. It drags us through the muck of human relationships and the nadir of human conduct. I enjoyed this movie despite the fact that afterward I was left feeling alarmed and ashamed of the human race. The film also features one of Hollywood's most formidable and memorable villains we've seen in years. I believe her level of malevolence rivals that of Hannibal Lecter.

Our next movie is *St. Vincent*, which occupies #4 on my top-10 list. This film packs a powerful emotional punch toward the end I found myself shedding a tear or two while Vincent's heroism is being honored by Oliver and others. It's a poignant tale of an unlikely pairing of people who save each other. *St. Vincent* is also a great buddy hero story, with young Oliver mentoring Vincent, his mother, and his entire school about the definition and complexity of sainthood.

I liked *St. Vincent*, too, but not as much as you did. Bill Murray starts out looking like a slob and ne'er do well. But in the end we peel away the onion skin to reveal a sweet core. As much as I liked this film, I didn't think I'd get anything more from a second look, so it didn't make my top-10.

At the number 3 spot on my list is *Nightcrawler* which fascinated me (much more so than it did you, I think). We're introduced to naive yet unsavory Louis Bloom who wants to get into the video news business. We follow him as he becomes more and more corrupt, staging events so that they become newsworthy - even the death of his partner. It was a wicked anti-hero story that was crafted so well that I want to see it again to watch Louis's descent into villainy and to see how it was accomplished.

Greg, I was just as fascinated as you were by *Nightcrawler*. The film was impeccably made but I could not bear to honor a movie that shows us two relentless hours of the devil in human form at work on the streets of Los Angeles. I was disturbed by the main character – notice that I cannot call him a hero – and his wanton disregard for human life. It was disheartening that no heroic character in the film could even come close to combating him. Our main character is pure evil running roughshod over everyone in his path. Like a cancer, he just grows and grows in his size and power, and he is shown flourishing in the end. The absence of any hero story here motivated me to omit this film from my top 10 list.

 Our next movie is *Selma*, which I ranked as the #2 movie of the year while you gave it top billing. Never have I seen a better demonstration of the need, rationale, and effectiveness of nonviolent demonstration. It could be an ideal instruction manual for those wanting to emulate King's (and Gandhi's) model of bringing about peaceful sociocultural change. The heroic mentorship of Martin Luther King, Jr., is shown in fabulous detail here. King was miles ahead of everyone in his moral understanding of the world, and he also had the strength and charisma to move mountains.

Yes, Scott, all that is true. But the reason I gave *Selma* my #1 spot is because it echoes the problems we still see today. We still have voter obstruction through the imposition of unbalanced voter identification requirements. And we still see the brutal beating and killing of people of color by police - without due process of the perpetrators of that violence. *Selma* reminds us of the battles that have been won and the battles we have yet to fight.

And that brings us to your #1 pick for the year: *Birdman*. It didn't make my list of the ten best because I really didn't want to see it again. It was a skillfully made movie with a lot of subtext and art. But it was a very huge wink to itself and the Hollywood community. It was incredibly self-indulgent and I felt that it wasn't made for me, the average movie viewer, but made for the Hollywood elite. It wasn't even released to the general public until the new year so that "everyman" could see it. Despite its technical achievement, I felt alienated and I won't be going back for seconds.

Greg, my number 1 choice, *Birdman*, reminded me so much of one of my favorite novels, *Song of Solomon* by Toni Morrison. This film is a complex and gripping piece of cinematic art. It is exhilarating, thoughtful, and complex. We are treated to intelligent character exchanges and nimble camera direction. Most notable about Birdman are the extraordinary performances from the cast. Keaton and Norton deserve Oscar nods for their portrayal of two men attempting to overcome powerfully neurotic, loveless lives. These are men who dive into the acting profession because it is a reprieve from the facade of reality. The themes of authenticity and flight to freedom sustain our attention and (for me) encourage a second visit to the theater.

So there you have it. Our top 10 lists overlap somewhat but there are some key differences, too. Overall, I would give the movies of 2014 a rating of 3 and a half Reels out of 5. The quality of films started out poorly but finished fairly strong. I believe 2013 was a slightly better year in the movies; I'd give 2013 a rating of 4 Reels out of 5. You can read our reviews of the films of 2013 in our first book: *Reel Heroes: Volume 1*.

Scott, I think your summation matches the industry assessment as well. The 2013 domestic box office receipts tipped the scales at $10.9 billion. Whereas the 2014 income figures are around $9.8 billion. While we had a crop of good films this year, many of them didn't arrive until Oscar season. The 2014 crowd of summer popcorn films had less staying power than in 2013, as well.

We'll be collecting our reviews of 2014 (plus our insights into what makes a great hero and villain) in our upcoming book *Reel Heroes & Villains* (due out in March). Until then, follow us as we review the movies of 2015 which will focus not only on heroes and villains, but also on supporting characters. And look for our review of the Best Heroes of 2014 and Best Villains of 2014.

Best Heroes of 2014

(Dr. Scott Allison, Professor of Psychology, University of Richmond)

Greg, we've reviewed the Best Movies of 2014. Now it's time to review the Best Heroes of the year, too.

(Greg Smith, Founder of Agile Writers of Richmond, VA)

We saw some great heroes this year, Scott. Let's jump in.

 To evaluate this year's movie heroes, I examined the features of the classic hero journey, especially whether the hero transforms as a result of encounters with allies, mentors, father figures, villains, and love interests. Here's my top 10 heroes list:

Scott's Top 10 Heroes

10. Maleficent (*Maleficent*)
9. Chris Kyle (*American Sniper*)
8. Katniss (*The Hunger Games: The Mockingjay Part I*)
7. Mason (*Boyhood*)
6. Vincent and Oliver (*St. Vincent*)
5. Riggan (*Birdman*)
4. Cooper (*Interstellar*)
3. Hazel (*The Fault in Our Stars*)
2. Triss (*Divergent*)
1. Martin Luther King, Jr. (*Selma*)

I also looked to the hero's journey for guidance as well as transformation - not necessarily for the hero, but transformation in those around the hero.

Greg's Top 10 Heroes

  10. Riggan (*Birdman*)

   9. Cooper (*Interstellar*)

   8. Katniss (*The Hunger Games: The Mockingjay Part I*)

   7. Neiman (*Whiplash*)

   6. Triss (*Divergent*)

   5. Hazel (*The Fault in Our Stars*)

   4. Bilbo (*The Hobbit: The Battle of the Five Armies*)

   3. Maleficent (*Maleficent*)

   2. Alan Turing (*The Imitation Game*)

   1. Martin Luther King, Jr. (*Selma*)

 You've generated a good list, Greg – almost as good as mine! Let's begin with my #5 choice, Riggan, who is the hero of *Birdman*. One of the most memorable characters in the movies in 2014, Riggan is an actor who uses his craft to mask his inner demons. He is obsessed with restoring a heroic image that is forever lost, and he must learn to "fly" in a different direction – literally. Riggan's transformative growth rings true to me and his inspiring flight at the end suggests a magical, triumphant conclusion to his epic journey.

Riggan only made the #10 spot on my list. I liked watching Riggan
work through his issues and struggle with being an absent father.
He was successfully painted as a tortured man, constantly arguing
with his inner Birdman. However, I was troubled with his final resolution to
his problems. He shoots himself in the "beak." I have to wonder if he was
trying to kill himself and failed - and that somehow led to his revelation? I'd
have to watch the film again to decide. Ultimately, he was at peace with who
he was, and that's a heroic transformation.

My #5 pick was Hazel from *The Fault in Our Stars*. she starts out in this film
as being reclusive and afraid to love others. She meets a young man, Gus, who
pulls her out of her shell and gets her to live life while she has it. Tragically,
Gus dies, leaving Hazel to feel lost without her soulmate. But finally, she
realizes that her time with Gus was worth a lifetime of love and emerges full
of life and love.

Hazel is my #3 choice, Greg. I enjoy watching her character become transformed from the influence of Augustus and also of Anne
Frank, whose recorded voice in Amsterdam opens Hazel's heart.
The hero journey evokes painful emotions but somehow manages to be uplifting, too. Hazel is an unforgettable hero, and Gus is her unforgettable mentor,
lover, friend, and symbol of life and hope. The hero and her friends, allies,
and companions are all fully present and are quite moving.

My #4 choice is Cooper from *Interstellar*. When it comes to hero
storytelling, you can't do much better than this film. Cooper follows the classic hero journey almost to the letter. He is sent out
into space (the unfamiliar world) and he is enlisted with the task of saving all
of humanity. All heroes are missing some quality, and in Cooper's case he

is missing an understanding of what binds the universe together. The answer is not unlike what Dorothy discovers in *The Wizard of Oz* the answer is love, home, and gravity.

I picked Cooper as my #9 hero of the year. Cooper has all the qualities you mention, Scott. He has a deep and abiding love for his daughter. So much so that he risks never seeing her again to save her life. Then, when all seems lost, he returns to her through time and space to send her a message that will either save humanity, or doom it to failure. It's a heartbreaking scene and one that any father can relate to.

My #4 pick was Bilbo Baggins of *The Hobbit* trilogy. I have to admit that I cheated a bit on this one, as I was rating Bilbo based on his transformation from the beginning of the trilogy, through the end. He starts out as shy, repressed, even fearful of the great beyond. He goes on his journey and takes on the characteristics of the mentor characters he meets. He returns to the shire a confident, strong master of the two worlds. It's a great Hero's Journey that people return to again and again.

Bilbo didn't make my top-10 list for the reason you mention, Greg. I will grant you that Bilbo's story, in its entirety, follows the classic hero's journey, but this film only shows us the final leg of that journey. Consequently, I didn't see him change or evolve much in this particular movie. But there's no doubt that his character, as a whole, undergoes dramatic growth and is one of the greatest heroes in all of literature.

We already talked about your #3 pick, Scott. So let's look at my #3 - *Maleficent*. This was a great story of a character who has traditionally been a villain in the Disney universe. Maleficent is given a full backstory here. She starts out innocent and good - the queen of the fairies. And then is betrayed by the man she loves. She turns evil and casts a spell on the baby princess - but over time learns to love her. She then returns to goodness at the end of the story when she saves the princess. It's a great "round trip" for our hero, one of the first such stories we've reviewed.

Maleficent was my #10 choice. As you point out, her heroic journey follows some non-traditional twists and turns, and underscores the idea that there exists a fine line between heroism and villainy. You and I have had many long discussions about that blurry line and Maleficent shows us that often the same person can occupy the role of both hero and of villain.

Next we turn to my #2 choice, Triss from *Divergent*. Shailene Woodley is outstanding in her role as Triss, a young woman on a voyage of self-discovery. I found Triss to have far more depth and nuance than Katniss showed in the first two installments of *The Hunger Games*. Triss spends this movie trying to reconcile others' expectations of her with her own quest for self-knowledge and self-growth. *Divergent* has every-thing one would want in a hero journey here. Triss attracts allies among the Dauntless and is mentored by both her mother and a colleague named Four, who also serves as a love interest. Challenges both physical and intellectual in nature are met and resolved in sometimes surprising ways. The hero journey here is packed to delicious satisfaction.

I liked Triss, too, Scott. Unfortunately I thought her character was a bit of a copy of Katniss, and so she didn't rise to my top 5. Also, she was a bit too reliant on the men in her life. I did like her trans-formation from uncertain young girl to a fully realized hero by the end of the story. I'm looking forward to seeing more of her in the coming years.

My #2 slot is occupied by Alan Turing from *The Imitation Game*. I had some trouble reconciling the events in the movie with actual history. But that doesn't change my opinion of Turing and his accomplishment. Breaking the Enigma code was quite possibly the event that won the war for the Allies. The whole world owes a debt to Turing that can never be repaid. Turing is a tragic hero because he ultimately takes his own life when the country he saved turns on him for his homosexual lifestyle. It's a compelling story that I won't soon forget.

 Turing didn't crack my top 10 but I agree that his hero story is a stirring one. The man has many demons to overcome and makes many enemies. Does his character become transformed the way a good hero should? Perhaps not. Ironically, his refusal to change may be the key to his heroism. Maybe this is a tale about a British society that refuses to transform as much as it is a tale about a hero who shouldn't need to.

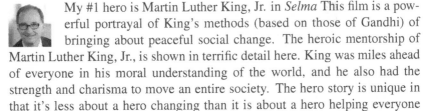 My #1 hero is Martin Luther King, Jr. in *Selma* This film is a powerful portrayal of King's methods (based on those of Gandhi) of bringing about peaceful social change. The heroic mentorship of Martin Luther King, Jr., is shown in terrific detail here. King was miles ahead of everyone in his moral understanding of the world, and he also had the strength and charisma to move an entire society. The hero story is unique in that it's less about a hero changing than it is about a hero helping everyone around him change. King guided an entire nation toward moral and spiritual maturity.

We're in full agreement, here Scott. The thing that impressed me
most about King is what he risked. That is something that separates ordinary people from heroes. Martin Luther King, Jr. risked
everything to create a more equal status for Blacks in a White-ruled America.
He risked his relationship with his wife, time with his children, his standing
in the Black community, and even his own life. *Selma* shows us not only his
strength and determination, but also his fears, concerns, and weaknesses. This
reminds us that Martin Luther King, Jr. was a person like so many of us. And
it was his inability to stand by and watch that made him a hero. And so can
we all be heroes.

Well, Scott, that brings us to the end of 2014's best heroes. I'm
looking forward to presenting our findings on what makes a great
hero in our upcoming book *Reel Heroes & Villains* where we'll also
look at what makes a great villain.

 Stay tuned for our list of the Best Villains in the movies in 2014!

Best Villains of 2014

(Greg Smith, Founder of Agile Writers of Richmond, VA)

We just got through reviewing the Best Heroes of 2014, Scott. Now let's pick the Best Villains of 2014.

(Dr. Scott Allison, Professor of Psychology, University of Richmond)

The phrase "best villains" sounds like an oxymoron, but it is actually a paradoxical truth: The better the villain, the more we love to hate him or her.

I picked my villains for how insidious they could be, or how they transformed from one state to another in the film.

Greg's Top 10 Villains:

10. Time (*Interstellar, Imitation Game, The Fault In Our Stars*)
9. Disease (Cancer in *The Fault In Our Stars* & ALS in *The Theory of Everything*)
8. Koba (*Dawn of the Planet of the Apes*)
7. The Bird (*Unbroken*)
6. Walter Keane (*Big Eyes*)
5. Madame Mallory (*The Hundred Foot Journey*)
4. Racism/George Wallace (*Selma*)
3. Amy Dunne (*Gone Girl*)
2. Terence Fletcher (*Whiplash*)
1. Louis Bloom (*Nightcrawler*)

For me, a villain's strength lies in the character's backstory and depth of development. I love a villain to the extent that we gain an understanding of the origins of his or her villainy. Also, the more complex and realistic the character, the better.

Scott's Top 10 Villains:

10. Madame Mallory (*The Hundred Foot Journey*)

9. Trask and the Sentinels (*X-Men: Days of Future Past*)

8. Alexander Pierce and Brock Rumlow (*Captain America: The Winter Soldier*)

7. Teddy (*The Equalizer*)

6. Louis Bloom (*Nightcrawler*)

5. Koba (*Dawn of the Planet of the Apes*)

4. Max Dillon and Harry Osborne (*The Amazing Spider-Man 2*)

3. Maleficent (*Maleficent*)

2. Terence Fletcher (*Whiplash*)

1. Amy Dunne (*Gone Girl*)

It looks like we have some villains in common. Let's review each of our top five villains, starting with my #5 pick - Madame Mallory from *The Hundred Foot Journey*. When an Indian family moves in across from her French restaurant and opens their own restaurant, she is appalled. The newcomers have invaded her space and have interfered with her goal of raising her 4-star restaurant to 5-stars. She starts to sabotage the new restaurant by buying out all their ingredients at the local farmer's market. The tit-for-tat battle increases until one of her chefs attempts to burn the Indian restaurant down and injures their young chef. This is when Madame Mallory realizes that she has gone too far and has a change of heart. She takes in the young chef and teaches him the ways of fine French cuisine and becomes his mentor. I loved this "redemptive villain" and felt we got a nice look at her backstory as well as a look into her inner self.

 Madame Mallory was my 10th most favorite movie villain in 2014. What I loved about her character was her transformation from villain to hero. The reasons for her original villainy are clearly spelled out; she feels threatened by the new upstart Indian restaurant that has opened across the street. But gradually she reveals her human side and is won over by the good nature of the Indian family. This change of heart struck me as both realistic and inspiring.

My #5 choice was Koba from *Dawn of the Planet of the Apes*. Koba portrays a character that exudes tragic realism. He is an ape who has been abused and tortured by the humans. Koba has lost the ability to trust and carries around a great deal of anger and a need for revenge. As a result, he cannot fathom Caesar's open-mindedness about striking up a positive relationship with a group that once physically and emotionally scarred his fellow apes. Koba's character struck a chord with me, as his experience illustrates a central reason why there is so much inter-group conflict in our world today.

I rated Koba as my #8 villain of 2014. As you point out, we get some of the reasons for Koba's hostility towards humans. Eventually, his hatred turns him against Caesar and he attempts to murder him and sets fire to the village - blaming the humans. We see in Koba very real and human actions and I enjoyed his descent into villainy, treachery, and betrayal.

My #4 pick is the institutional racism from the movie *Selma*. Sometimes it's hard to portray an idea as a character in a movie. To deal with this, *Selma* uses Alabama Governor George Wallace as the face of racism. Wallace refuses to intervene in anything that happens in his state that interferes with Blacks getting the right to vote. Not only that, but he won't reign in the sheriff of Selma, Jim Clark, who uses his posse of men to beat and even kill innocent Blacks. Racism is a blind and mindless villain which *Selma* shined a bright light on.

The racist hatred of Wallace and J. Edgar Hoover is certainly vile, but it didn't make my top-10 list. For me, the movie *Selma* was more about Martin Luther King, Jr.'s heroic and courageous fight against those racist institutional barriers than it was about those barriers themselves. Still, I understand your inclusion of this important and tragic phenomenon in American history (and, sadly, in America today as well).

My #4 pick was a pair of villains in *The Amazing Spider-Man 2*: Max Dillon and Harry Osborne. This villain pairing impressed me because the filmmakers went out of their way to show us the genesis of their evil. Dillon and Osborne both turned to villainy because they were adversely affected by some traumatic event. They didn't start out evil; they allowed their pain to skew their moral judgment and determine their life purpose. In this way they are similar to Koba from *Dawn of the Planet of the Apes*. I don't mean to imply that trauma always leads to villainy – consider the story of Batman, who as a child witnessed his parents' murder. Somehow, heroes use pain to better themselves and the world, whereas villains use pain to avenge the world.

That's a good observation. I agree that these characters (and most characters in the Marvel universe) are given better backstories. I didn't vote these guys in because I felt we had seen this story before in dozens of other superhero movies. There were other villains this year who more capably caught my imagination.

Among them was my #3 pick, Amy Dunne from *Gone Girl*. She starts out the film looking very much like the victim of a murder. Her diary entries all point to her husband Nick as a controlling, narcissistic, and unfaithful husband. Just when you're ready to mentally convict Nick, it's revealed that Amy is alive and well and is framing Nick from afar. It's such a shock, and so skillfully delivered we're blown away. We're then led through Amy's vindictive plot step-by-step until she kills an ex-boyfriend and claims he kidnapped and raped her. Amy returns home to Nick and reveals that she's pregnant with his child (through sperm she froze) and has roped him into a life with her. Amy Dunne is a cold and calculating villain that was as frightening as any since Glenn Close in *Fatal Attraction*.

Amy Dunne from *Gone Girl* was my #1 movie villain of the year. I agree with you, Greg, that she is the ultimate villain, making everyone around her look foolish as they try to keep up with her true motives or her next move. Amy is a force unto herself, literally; there are no henchmen or henchwomen to aid her. She is a true lone villain, perhaps the most formidable force of evil in the movies in 2014. I consider her to be Hollywood's most memorable villain we've seen in years. Her level of malevolence rivals that of Hannibal Lecter. She tops my list because of her magnetism, her backstory, and her ability to surprise us with one chilling act of evil after another.

My #3 pick is the character Maleficent from the movie of the same name. The film is a prequel to *Sleeping Beauty* and it injects some surprising complexity to the so-called evil queen in that classic fairy tale. We see how Maleficent starts out as quite a benevolent presence in the forest and only turns toward darkness when she is betrayed and disfigured by an evil man. We also are treated to Maleficent's restoration to her true good self by the transformative power of love. This theme of love having the ability to change people is also present in movies such as *Interstellar*. Maleficent is a *round tripper* protagonist, having undergone an evolution from hero to villain then back to hero again.

I so heartily agree with you - except that I categorize Maleficent as a hero, not a villain. She starts out good, is betrayed and through this hurt falls into villainy. Then, through the love of a child, she turns good again. We aren't treated to this kind of hero's journey (or is it a villain's journey) often. I would have included her in my Villain's list, too - but she was my #3 hero of 2014.

My #2 pick is Terrence Fletcher from *Whiplash*. Young Andrew Neiman is a first-year music student at Shaffer Conservatory when he meets Fletcher. Fletcher is the conductor of the school's award-winning jazz ensemble. All Neiman wants is to be the greatest jazz drummer of all time. So when Fletcher invites him to take second seat drum, he jumps at the chance. But it isn't long before we realize that Fletcher is an extreme perfectionist. He screams at the students when they make the smallest mistake. He hurls a chair at Neiman's head when he is out of rhythm and slaps him around. By the end of the story, Neiman is demoralized and ready to quit. But he goes back on-stage and drums his heart out - effectively forcing Fletcher to accept him as his drummer. Fletcher is the first villain/mentor I have ever seen, and is a character that will live in my mind for a long, long time.

 Terrence Fletcher from *Whiplash* is my #2 pick, also. Fletcher is an anti-mentor, the type of character who send heroes down dark paths that can lead to ruin. It's then up to the hero to overcome the dark mentor. Fletcher is a true scumbag and his cruel, self-aggrandizing methods come at the expense of our hero. This film teaches us to be wary of how we choose our mentors; not all of them look out for our best interests. Fletcher is a lying, cold-blooded, abuser who doesn't quite get his full comeuppance at the end but is nevertheless defeated.

Finally we come to my #1 pick: Louis Bloom of *Nightcrawler*. Louis starts out as a naive low-level thief of hubcaps and manhole covers. When he stumbles upon a film crew taping late-night accidents, he realizes that he is capable of delivering the same content. Louis then enlists the aid of sidekick intern Rick to work the night. Louis realizes he has to eliminate the competition so cuts the brake line of the van of his nearest foe. Finally, he stages a shooting and films his sidekick getting murdered. Louis Bloom has a chilling villain's journey where he starts out amoral and falls deeper and deeper into depravity. Since he's the main character of the story, I would normally call him the hero. But since he's a villain, I categorize Louis Bloom as the anti-hero.

Louis Bloom of *Nightcrawler* didn't make my top 5 list of villains but there's no doubting the fact that he is Evil with a capital E. Bloom is a classic sociopath who lacks a conscience and has no empathy, remorse, or moral core. He uses people and hurts others to obtain his goals. *Nightcrawler* is a movie about villainy and how it blossoms. The film shows us how villainy is allowed to prosper when we allow it to prosper, when we condone it, when we cooperate with it, and when we place money ahead of basic principles of decency. I considered including Bloom in my top-5 but we are never told how he become such a scumbag, and without any backstory I just couldn't include him in my list.

That brings us to the end of another year of movies, heroes, and villains. Tune in throughout 2015 as we continue to review movies and their heroes. We will keep looking at the villains in the movies, and we will start looking at the supporting characters beside them as well. If you haven't already, check out our Best Movies of 2014 and the Best Heroes of 2014.

Part IV.

Appendix

Reel Heroes Indexes

The following few pages list our movie reviews by the quality of the movie (Reels), the quality of the hero, and the quality of the villain. Use these indexes to find the movies with the best features.

Reels Index

1. 5.0: American Sniper 66
2. 5.0: The Fault In Our Stars 134
3. 5.0: Gone Girl 154
4. 5.0: Selma 277
5. 4.5: The Amazing Spider-Man 2 61
6. 4.5: Interstellar 199
7. 4.5: Nightcrawler 248
8. 4.5: St. Vincent 283
9. 4.5: X-Men: Days of Future Past 314
10. 4.0: Birdman 77
11. 4.0: Boyhood 83
12. 4.0: Captain America: The Winter Soldier 88
13. 4.0: Dawn of the Planet of the Apes 94
14. 4.0: The Grand Budapest Hotel 159
15. 4.0: The Hobbit: The Battle of the Five Armies 174
16. 4.0: The Hunger Games: The Mockingjay - Part 1 184
17. 4.0: Jersey Boys 210
18. 4.0: Maleficent 229
19. 4.0: Whiplash 308
20. 3.5: Big Eyes 72
21. 3.5: Divergent 105
22. 3.5: Edge of Tomorrow 124
23. 3.5: The Equalizer 129
24. 3.5: Get On Up 139
25. 3.5: Guardians of the Galaxy 164

26. 3.5: The Imitation Game 194

27. 3.5: The Judge 214

28. 3.5: Unbroken 303

29. 3.0: 3 Days to Kill 56

30. 3.0: Deliver Us From Evil 100

31. 3.0: Dumb and Dumber To 116

32. 3.0: The Hundred Foot Journey 179

33. 3.0: Million Dollar Arm 234

34. 3.0: The Monuments Men 238

35. 3.0: Neighbors 243

36. 3.0: No Good Deed 254

37. 3.0: Non-Stop 258

38. 3.0: RoboCop 272

39. 2.5: 22 Jump Street 51

40. 2.5: Draft Day 111

41. 2.5: Godzilla 149

42. 2.5: Jack Ryan: Shadow Recruit 205

43. 2.5: The Theory of Everything 288

44. 2.0: Earth to Echo 120

45. 2.0: The Giver 144

46. 2.0: The Identical 189

47. 2.0: Heaven Is For Real 169

48. 2.0: Labor Day 219

49. 2.0: Lucy 224

50. 2.0: The Other Woman 263

51. 2.0: Ride Along 268

52. 1.5: Transformers: Age of Extinction 297

53. 1.0: Transcendence 292

Heroes Index

1. 5.0: American Sniper 66

2. 5.0: Birdman 77

3. 5.0: The Hunger Games: The Mockingjay - Part 1 184

4. 5.0: Interstellar 199

5. 5.0: Selma 277

6. 5.0: Whiplash 308

7. 4.5: The Amazing Spider-Man 2 61

8. 4.5: Boyhood 83

9. 4.5: The Fault In Our Stars 134

10. 4.0: Dawn of the Planet of the Apes 94

11. 4.0: Divergent 105

12. 4.0: Get On Up 139

13. 4.0: The Hobbit: The Battle of the Five Armies 174

14. 4.0: The Imitation Game 194

15. 4.0: Maleficent 229

16. 4.0: St. Vincent 283

17. 4.0: X-Men: Days of Future Past 314

18. 3.5: Big Eyes 72

19. 3.5: Captain America: The Winter Soldier 88

20. 3.5: Edge of Tomorrow 124

21. 3.5: The Equalizer 129

22. 3.5: Gone Girl 154

23. 3.5: The Grand Budapest Hotel 159

24. 3.5: Guardians of the Galaxy 164

25. 3.5: The Hundred Foot Journey 179

26. 3.5: Jack Ryan: Shadow Recruit 205

27. 3.5: The Judge 214

28. 3.5: Non-Stop 258

29. 3.5: The Theory of Everything 288

30. 3.0: 3 Days to Kill 56

31. 3.0: Deliver Us From Evil 100

32. 3.0: Jersey Boys 210

33. 3.0: Million Dollar Arm 234

34. 3.0: Neighbors 243

35. 3.0: No Good Deed 254

36. 3.0: RoboCop 272

37. 3.0: Unbroken 303

38. 2.5: Draft Day 111

39. 2.5: Dumb and Dumber To 116

40. 2.5: The Giver 144

41. 2.5: The Monuments Men 238

42. 2.5: Ride Along 268

43. 2.5: Transcendence 292

44. 2.0: 22 Jump Street 51

45. 2.0: Earth to Echo 120

46. 2.0: Heaven Is For Real 169

47. 2.0: The Other Woman 263

48. 2.0: Transformers: Age of Extinction 297

49. 1.5: Godzilla 149

50. 1.5: The Identical 189

51. 1.5: Lucy 224

52. 1.0: Labor Day 219

53. 1.0: Nightcrawler 248

Villains Index

1. 5.0: Gone Girl 154
2. 5.0: Whiplash 308
3. 4.5: The Amazing Spider-Man 2 61
4. 4.5: Nightcrawler 248
5. 4.0: Birdman 77
6. 4.0: Dawn of the Planet of the Apes 94
7. 4.0: The Equalizer 129
8. 4.0: Maleficent 229
9. 4.0: X-Men: Days of Future Past 314
10. 3.5: Big Eyes 72
11. 3.5: Boyhood 83
12. 3.5: Captain America: The Winter Soldier 88
13. 3.5: The Hobbit: The Battle of the Five Armies 174
14. 3.5: No Good Deed 254
15. 3.5: RoboCop 272
16. 3.5: Selma 277
17. 3.0: American Sniper 66
18. 3.0: The Fault In Our Stars 134
19. 3.0: Get On Up 139
20. 3.0: The Grand Budapest Hotel 159
21. 3.0: The Hundred Foot Journey 179
22. 3.0: The Hunger Games: The Mockingjay - Part 1 184
23. 3.0: Jack Ryan: Shadow Recruit 205
24. 3.0: Jersey Boys 210
25. 3.0: Neighbors 243

26. 3.0: Unbroken 303

27. 2.5: Divergent 105

28. 2.5: Draft Day 111

29. 2.5: Edge of Tomorrow 124

30. 2.5: The Imitation Game 194

31. 2.5: The Judge 214

32. 2.5: Million Dollar Arm 234

33. 2.5: St. Vincent 283

34. 2.5: The Theory of Everything 288

35. 2.0: 3 Days to Kill 56

36. 2.0: Deliver Us From Evil 100

37. 2.0: The Giver 144

38. 2.0: Godzilla 149

39. 2.0: Heaven Is For Real 169

40. 2.0: Interstellar 199

41. 2.0: Lucy 224

42. 1.5: 22 Jump Street 51

43. 1.5: Earth to Echo 120

44. 1.5: Guardians of the Galaxy 164

45. 1.5: The Monuments Men 238

46. 1.5: Transcendence 292

47. 1.0: Dumb and Dumber To 116

48. 1.0: The Identical 189

49. 1.0: Labor Day 219

50. 1.0: Non-Stop 258

51. 1.0: The Other Woman 263

52. 1.0: Ride Along 268

53. 1.0: Transformers: Age of Extinction 297

About the Authors

SCOTT ALLISON is Professor of Psychology at the University of Richmond. He has published over 100 articles and books on social behavior. His work has been featured in media outlets such as National Public Radio, USA Today, the New York Times, the Los Angeles Times, Slate Magazine, MSNBC, CBS, Psychology Today, and the Christian Science Monitor. His HEROES blog (blog.richmond.edu/heroes) has attracted over a half-million visitors. He loves chocolate, golf, all things Star Trek, and ballroom dancing, in roughly that order.

Scott can be reached at sallison@richmond.edu.

GREG SMITH founded the Agile Writer Workshop in 2011 with the mission of finding a new approach to helping beginning writers complete a first-draft novel in 6 months. Greg created "The Agile Writer Method" based upon the writings of experts in mythology, screenwriting, psychology and a little project management.

His seminars on the Agile Writer Method have informed and delighted hundreds of writers, scholars, and university students. Since 2011, Agile Writer authors have completed over 30 first draft novels, 5 published novels, and several members have been nominated for the coveted James River Writer Best Unpublished Novel Contest. Greg loves improv, crab legs, comic book heroes, tango, and computer software.

Greg can by contacted at greg@agilewriters.com.

Together Greg and Scott contribute to their blog at Reel Heroes. They update the site weekly with new movie reviews and hero analysis. In 2015 Greg and Scott are breaking new ground as they further study the secondary characters in movies.

Follow them weekly at http://ReelHeroes.net.

Other Books by Scott Allison and Greg Smith

Allison, S. T., & Goethals, G. R. (2011).
Heroes: What They Do and Why We Need Them.
New York: Oxford University Press.

Allison, S. T., & Goethals, G. R. (2013).
Heroic Leadership: An Influence Taxonomy of 100 Exceptional Individuals.
New York: Routledge.

Goethals, G. R., Allison, S. T., Kramer, R., & Messick, D. (Eds.) (2014).
Conceptions of Leadership: Enduring Ideas and Emerging Insights.
New York: Palgrave Macmillan.

Allison, S. T., Kocher, C. T., & Goethals, G. R. (Eds.) (2016).
Frontiers in Spiritual Leadership: Discovering the Better Angels of Our Nature.
New York: Palgrave Macmillan.

Allison, S. T., Goethals, G. R., & Kramer, R. M. (Eds.) (2017).
Handbook of Heroism and Heroic Leadership.
New York: Routledge.

Smith, G., & Allison, S. T. (2014).
Reel Heroes: Volume 1.
Agile Writer Press.

Smith, G. (2014).
Agile Writer: Method.
Agile Writer Press.

Smith, G., Golinowski, D., Watson, B., et. al. (2007).
Mining the Muse.
Chesterfield Writers Club.

Smith, G. (2013).
Shards.
Agile Writer Press.